COLLEGE IS ONLY THE BEGINNING

A Student Guide to Higher Education

Edited by

John N. Gardner
Associate Vice-President for University Campuses and Continuing Education
Director, University 101 Freshman Seminar Program
Professor of Library and Information Science
University of South Carolina, Columbia

and

A. Jerome Jewler
Codirector, University 101 Freshman Seminar Program
Professor of Journalism
University of South Carolina, Columbia

Wadsworth Publishing Company
Belmont, California
A Division of Wadsworth, Inc.

English Editor
Cedric W. Crocker

Production Editor
Jane Townsend

Managing Designer
Andrew H. Ogus

Designer
Design Office Bruce Kortebein

Copy Editor
Carol Dondrea

Cover
Design Office Bruce Kortebein

Print Buyer
Barbara Britton

Signing Representative
Neil Oatley

Printed in the United States of America

　　5 6 7 8 9 10—89 88 87 86 85

ISBN 0-534-04275-9

Library of Congress Cataloging in Publication Data
Main entry under title:

College is only the beginning.

　　1. College student orientation—Addresses, essays,
lectures.　I. Gardner, John N.　II. Jewler, A. Jerome.
LB2343.3.C65　1984　　378'.198　　84-15369
ISBN 0-534-04275-9

To Vicky Howell, administrative assistant for University 101, the freshman seminar course at USC, who keeps our program, our Freshman-Year Experience conferences, and a myriad of other challenging events from dissolving into utter chaos, and whose assistance in producing the manuscript for this book has been invaluable. To Donna Gardner and Belle Jewler for giving us the time beyond normal working hours to put it all together. To our very special authors for sharing their expertise with us and with our readers. Finally, to freshmen and their instructors everywhere, for what must be one of the most trying, challenging, frustrating, and ultimately rewarding twelve months in the transition from youth to adult. To all of these people, we dedicate this volume.

CONTENTS

iv

PREFACE

Greetings to the classes of the 1980s and 1990s from a graduate of the class of 1965! As I write this, I'm more than twenty years removed from my own freshman year in the fall of 1961 at Marietta College, Marietta, Ohio. That experience proved to be the foundation for much of the rest of my life, just as your freshman year will be a foundation for your life. It began with our college president telling an auditorium filled with scared freshmen to "look to your left and look to your right, and four years from now neither of the people on either side of you will be here when you graduate!"

After that optimistic prediction of our bright futures, I launched into my freshman year with much anxiety. I didn't have the advantage of many of the services described in this book, and there was no freshman orientation course or seminar of the kind in which you may be enrolled and through which you find yourself reading this book. My first semester grades were terrible, below the required C average, and I was placed on academic probation. I was lucky to be taken off probation the second semester!

Why have Jerry and I developed this book? For one thing, we've been working for more than a decade at the University of South Carolina in a unique orientation course, University 101—The Student in the University. University 101 is a three-credit course with goals identical to our goals for this book:

1. To help you obtain a sound and thorough introduction to the concept, meaning, and significance of higher education and to your particular university or college.
2. To improve your attitudes toward the teaching and learning processes and toward the college faculty who will attempt to involve you in that process.
3. To help you get involved in the extracurricular life of the institution.
4. To make you more aware of many of the support service personnel on your campus.
5. To enhance your self-awareness and self-esteem.
6. To provide you with a variety of survival skills that can help you adjust successfully to your freshman year, make better grades, have more satisfying relationships, and increase your probability of successfully graduating.

In our work with freshmen, we discovered that no book existed that provided the kind of information they needed to be successful college students. And, we believed the process of adjusting to higher education to be so complex that no one individual could possibly know all the answers. So, we decided to ask a number of people with various areas of expertise to write about helping freshmen make a successful adjustment to college.

The chapters in this book are not meant to be complete treatises on the subjects they present. They are meant to introduce you to the topics and to stimulate additional discussion and exploration on your part. We hope you'll make an effort to find and use the same kinds of services, resources, and helping individuals that our contributors have described.

You're extremely important to the institution where you've just enrolled, to your families, your country, and especially to yourself. As we tell freshmen at USC, "freshmen are not peas in a pod—they're VIPs, very important people." And just as you're our most important natural resource, college can be an extremely important resource for you. Not only is it the ticket to upward social mobility, but it can also be the key to a more rewarding life. In this book, we hope to show you how to begin enjoying that life more fully.

Should you want to give Jerry or me any feedback or advice on how to revise this book in the future, please fill out the form in the back of the book. We'd love to hear from you. Jerry and I are what you want to become: self-fulfilled former freshmen. If you practice what this book preaches, we can predict with almost 100 percent certainty that you, too, will soon be a successful former freshman.

JOHN N. GARDNER

My father had died the year before, my mother had opened a small retail business to support the rest of us, and I found myself entering college as a somewhat bewildered, anxious, and vaguely disillusioned freshman. It's been more than twenty-five years, but I can still remember the smell of the dank, musty field house where the university president welcomed the freshman class, although I don't remember what he said. I can recall the old, wooden floor creaking under my feet as I shuffled through line after line in the dusty armory, vainly attempting to sign up for the classes I needed at the times I needed them.

That fall I sat through an early morning English class and three or four other courses in which I vaguely knew the instructor and felt he knew me about as well. In the middle of the spring semester, I announced to my family that I was dropping out of college to help Mom with her small shop. I can thank my mother, grandmother, and aunt for talking me out of it. But what saved me, I think, was my introduction to the campus newspaper. I joined the staff in a moment of desperation and, suddenly, college was beautiful. By the time I was ready to graduate, I was also ready to spend another fifteen months earning a master's degree. Without the degree, I probably would never be teaching today, or participating in a freshman seminar program, or writing this book.

Whether you use this volume in a freshman seminar course or read it on your own, I hope it will make you more keenly aware of three things: of yourself and the potential you carry within you, of your college or university and the potential for growth it offers you, and of the value of the friendships you'll make in these years.

Finally, I wish to thank my coeditor and dear friend, John N. Gardner, Director of the University 101 freshman seminar program at the University of South Carolina, for getting me involved with the entire area of freshman studies. It's our pleasure to offer this volume of sage advice to you as you begin one of the most significant periods of your life. College is only the beginning, but it's how you begin that can make what lies ahead so rewarding.

A. JEROME JEWLER

Acknowledgments

The authors are grateful to the following reviewers: David Ammerman, Florida State University; Wallace I. Honeywell, formerly University of Houston; George Lavery, Catonsville Community College; Michael McHargue, Foothill College, and Randi McHargue; James Dickson McLean, University of Tennessee; Alicia Perez, Del Mar College; Robert M. Petty, Santa Clara University; Patricia E. Watt, Duquesne University.

Part One

BEGINNINGS

Making the Transition

A. Jerome Jewler
and John N. Gardner

"You won't want to come into the office today anyway," [a colleague] tells me. "The freshmen are arriving, and it's a mess over here. . . ."

It certainly is a mess. Hundreds of station wagons packed with steaming students, their families, and their endless belongings seek nonexistent parking spots along a few feet of curb. Irritable mothers and fathers bicker about when, where, and whether to park. Campus police do what they can to direct traffic, but they know it is beyond their control; the rules will have to bend a little more than usual today. . . . It *is* the messiest day of the year, no doubt about it. It is also my favorite.

So begins Charlotte J. Patterson's tribute to arriving freshmen. A psychology professor at the University of Virginia, Patterson feels a great deal of empathy with new students—with their hopes, dreams, and fears. What does it mean to be a freshman in a new setting on the first days of a fall semester? Professor Patterson views it as a new beginning:

It makes me think of those slushy days in early spring when the snow is melting and one cannot step down anywhere without splashing. Even when I am cold and wet, I cannot hate those days; they presage too much. Freshman arrival is also a mess, but I cannot hate it either. They appear in town like young green shoots, sprouting up everywhere, looking for light. Their faces hang out the windows of dorms like tiny new buds on an old, old tree. Someone else may worry about the sun and the soil and the possibility of frost; for them, it is enough just to *be.*

Yes, today is the beginning of a new life. One day you're Mama's child, living at home; the next day, you're a freshman and on your own. The end of childhood. Instant adulthood. Or is it? *Freshman!* I like the word. The very label itself suggests the dilemma. Should it be pronounced with emphasis on the *fresh* or on the *man?* It points both ways. It doesn't matter whether you think of adulthood as a journey or as an arrival; today it is clearly a step on the path. Freshman fantasies and freshman fears can be seen on every young face.

Even if you are returning to college after several years' absence or are entering for the first time after working or raising a family, attending college in the 1980s will be an adjustment for you. College is an exciting time, perhaps the most exciting time in your life. But it's also a time of major adjustments and some disappointments. Most fields of study have become quite competitive, and the information explosion has lead to greater demands on those attempting to absorb all that information. There is a growing need for a more structured and formalized introduction to college, and freshman orientation/freshman seminar courses have become popular on campuses from Maine to California.

How college is different

Consider the many differences between high school and college, and you'll understand why so many freshmen feel like lost souls when they first arrive on campus. It's the first time many of you will be paying for your own education, the first time you may have chosen voluntarily to continue with school—a school of your choice. Not only does it cost just to attend classes, it also costs to have textbooks, a place to live, and food to eat, and it costs to pursue the collegiate lifestyle.

But perhaps the most disturbing change you'll find is a new-found sense of freedom. It's probably the first time in your life that you've been entrusted with structuring your own time. As a result, you've been given more of the responsibility for succeeding or failing, and most freshmen find that responsibility extremely awesome.

As a matter of fact, we believe that the single greatest problem college students face is the problem of freedom—too much freedom. As a college freshman you will enjoy an enormous amount of personal freedom, probably more than you have ever had or will ever have again in your life. The problem of freedom and what you make of it and how well you use it will have an impact on all other aspects of your college career. John recalls that as a freshman he read what was for him a very important book, a book that gave him intellectual insight into the problem of "too much freedom." The book was *Escape From Freedom* by Erich Fromm, and in it Fromm argues convincingly that freedom is an enormous problem because it is a burden people don't know how to cope with. The members of some societies, he argues, have even found freedom such a burden that they have voluntarily chosen totalitarian lifestyles and structures that remove their freedom and hence provide an ultimate solution for dealing with it. While this kind of conclusion is certainly extreme for most college freshmen, it is apparent from our studies of American college freshmen that many definitely join groups that add structure to their lives (such as fraternities and sororities), and that in turn make many decisions for them as to how they will use much of their freedom.

Let's consider this further by looking at the flipside of the freedom coin, namely, at the responsibility you now have as a college freshman for making numerous important decisions on a daily basis. Look at all the decisions you have to make suddenly at college because of what, for most of you, is new-found freedom. For example, you may need to decide whether to:

1. Get up in the morning or not
2. Wear traditional clothes or something funky (Would your parents approve?)
3. Eat breakfast or skip it
4. Attend classes or cut them
5. Study each day or just for exams
6. Start a paper two weeks before it is due, or do it the night before
7. Eat properly balanced meals or junk food
8. Drink or not drink (alcoholic beverages)
9. Use marijuana and other contraband substances or not
10. Choose this person or that person for a friend
11. Go through fraternity–sorority rush and then join or not join
12. Exercise or not
13. Get 4, 5, 6, 7, 8, 9, or 10 hours of sleep
14. Keep your room/apartment picked up or not picked up
15. Have premarital sex at all, or have it with this person vs. that person (If so, under what conditions?)
16. Accept responsibility for birth control or leave that to your partner
17. Choose what courses to take this semester and what to take next semester
18. See your advisor
19. See your professor for extra help
20. Drop this course
21. Choose a major
22. Choose a career to pursue
23. Choose whom to marry
24. Choose what to do with the rest of your life

How college orientation can help

Knowing where to go for help when you feel lost, and knowing what your college or university offers beyond a dorm room and classroom instruction can mean the difference between four years of personal growth and four years of haphazard drifting. Perhaps we are exaggerating the difference, but few will disagree that a proper orientation to college life can be a positive factor in how much you derive from your college experience.

The primary goal of a college orientation program is to help you make the transition from high school to college. Using college faculty, staff, and students, the orientation program offers you a rare opportunity to learn all you can about your college before you begin the harried life of a college student. It is an experience that comes only once, and it could be one of the most meaningful experiences of your entire four years. At many colleges, orientation is an optional experience. If it is not mandatory at your college, we strongly urge you to take advantage of it anyway. It could be the determining factor in a successful versus an unsuccessful first semester in college. Even if your college charges an additional fee for orientation, as most colleges do, it's well worth it. Also, most schools permit and encourage participation by parents. We do too! Bring your parents along. They'll gain a better understanding of what's ahead for you, and that means they can give you more support (and maybe even a better allowance, once they see all that college life entails). We believe it is particularly important for your parents to attend your orientation if they did not go to college themselves. In that case you are what educators call a "first-generation college student" and your parents, like you, need help in understanding the college freshman experience.

Many colleges hold formal orientation programs in the summer, or just before the fall semester. During orientation, you will preregister for the first semester of course work, take a tour of the campus, and receive the necessary details on dining services, dormitory living, financial aid, and other pressing matters. In all likelihood, you'll be welcomed by the president of the university, the dean of students, or other representatives of the administration, and will be given a chance to talk with other students about the things a freshman needs to know most.

If you have chosen your major, you will probably be transported to your new college or department, meet the head of that academic unit, or meet your academic advisor, and plan your course work for the coming semester. But since few orientation programs last more than one or two days, you'll return home with a thousand unanswered questions: Will I be able to figure out how to use the college library? How do I become active in student media? What if I'm just plain depressed the first month I'm away from home? Will I be able to understand my professors? What kinds of students will I be meeting and how will they like me?

Orientation is a continuing process

Once you arrive on campus for your first semester, you'll be facing these questions and more. Although freshman orientation is behind you, it is important to remember that you have a lot to learn that will not be covered in the classroom. It is also important to realize that no freshman orientation program can orient you to everything you need to know *before* classes actually begin. Often you won't even know what you need to be oriented *to* until after classes have already started. Many students don't realize that the experience of college is like starting life over. In high school, you may have been the president of your class or some other "big shot." It comes as quite a shock then to suddenly realize that you're a little fish in a big pond! No one knows you, so it's important to get involved and make the campus *your* community.

If you are already living on campus, you may have discovered some of the services and activities we are about to mention. If not, here's a chance to find out in just how many ways your college or university may be able to help you. One suggestion: As you read the following list, use a plus (+) to indicate the services you've already used and a check (√) to indicate those you'd like to find out more about. Not every service listed may be available on your campus, but chances are many of them will be—along with others we haven't covered. Also, many of these services deal with subjects so critical to freshman success that they will be treated in detail elsewhere in this book.

Certainly, you don't want to rush out and join every club that tickles your fancy without first determining how much time you'll have left after you subtract class time and study time and job time, if you have a job. The first thing to remember is that you came to college to get an education. The next thing to remember is that, once you've set aside time for the academic part of college, it's important to work just as hard at structuring the rest of your time.

Most educators agree that learning that takes place outside the classroom is very important to your total educational development. And an important part of personal growth during these years will result from your involvement in college life. Meeting students from different places, understanding and accepting value systems that are different from your own, and becoming involved in developmental services and clubs and in many other activities can help you develop skills that will make you a more rounded individual.

Academic advising centers

Most campuses now maintain special centers where full-time advisors are available to meet with students at any time they need advice and information. Do you have an advisor yet? Are you satisfied with your advisor? Are you getting all the help you need? If not, come look into the advising center on your campus.

Academic skills development center

The academic skills development center teaches reading and study skills to students (note taking, preparing for exams, listening, time management, test taking, and so on). The center typically offers short courses at little or no charge and may provide individual counseling and tutoring. Someone once remarked how ironic it is that we go to school for twelve or more years, yet no one has ever taught us how to go to school! Here is where you will learn how.

Alcohol awareness

Alcohol awareness programs help students make responsible decisions regarding the use of alcoholic beverages. Such programs help you to understand that the decision to drink or not drink is a personal one, and should not be determined by peer pressure. They also make you more aware of the physiology of alcohol use, and of the kinds of food that should be eaten while drinking. Many of the myths of drinking such as "coffee helps you sober up" are discussed. Ask your residence hall advisor or your student affairs office about the availability of such programs.

Anxiety and stress management

Learning the basic principles of relaxation, such as self-hypnosis and biofeedback, can help you become a better scholar as well as a more fulfilled individual. Learning these principles can help you particularly in managing and reducing test taking anxiety and thus help you improve your grades. Many campus counseling centers offer help in this area.

Assertiveness training

Assertiveness training teaches the skills of respectful and responsible interpersonal communications. Knowing how to stand up for your rights without denying the rights of others can be extremely helpful, whether you're interacting with parents, professors, or friends. Such training is particularly helpful for freshmen from small high schools going to large universities. Check your counseling center.

Career planning and placement

Whether you have declared a major or not, but especially if you can't decide on one, your career center may prove invaluable. In addition to its career library, where you may study hundreds of career possibilities, you may also be able to take various career inventories and receive personal one-to-one counseling, which can help you determine what types of work you enjoy most. These services are usually offered at no charge to full-time students.

Chaplains

Chaplains representing major religious denominations provide personal counseling as well as worship services and fellowship for students away from home.

Commuter services

For those of you living off-campus, the office of commuter services normally provides current listings of apartments, houses, and rooms for rent; roommate listings; orientation to the community; maps; information on public transportation; babysitting lists; and other worthwhile data.

Counseling

Most campus counseling centers are staffed by licensed counseling psychologists, who help students with personal and interpersonal concerns ranging from a disagreeable roommate to a prolonged state of depression. Services are usually free, and are always confidential. Many freshman problems are *normal*—needing and receiving counseling does *not* mean you are "sick." Counseling is a growth and learning experience.

Disabled student services

Disabled student services support those of you who are disabled and who need help in overcoming physical, educational, or attitudinal barriers to achieve your full educational potential.

Financial aid and scholarships

The financial aid office coordinates all financial assistance received by students on your campus. It administers major programs of financial aid and receives and authorizes all outside scholarships and grants. If you need financial aid, you should contact this office. They will tell you what is available and how to apply for it.

Greek affairs

Students interested in joining a fraternity or sorority may find information on these groups by contacting the local coordinator of Greek affairs in the student affairs division of the university.

Health centers/infirmaries/hospitals

Many college freshmen are initially unaware of the very adequate health care facilities colleges and universities maintain. Many of these facilities include specialized clinics and medical specialists such as gynecologists, psychiatrists, orthopedic specialists, and so on. Medical personnel not only examine and treat student illnesses but also prescribe medicines, which are available at significantly reduced costs. This may also be the place on your campus to visit if you need birth control advice, information, and/or prescriptions.

Health enrichment

Many campuses offer students guidance in the many areas of personal health, including nutrition, weight control, physical fitness, exercise, and human sexuality. When these programs are offered through a peer advisement center, you may enjoy the counsel of other students who both respect and understand your needs.

Housing office

This office can help you locate on- or off-campus housing and advise you on the advantages and disadvantages of each. Hall advisors or dorm proctors who live in the residence halls can, through personal counseling and educational, cultural, social, and recreational programs, help you become oriented to campus life.

Intramural and recreational sports

The campus intramurals office promotes, organizes, and administers a broad program of competitive and recreational activities in a variety of sports. Dorms, organizations, or colleges may form teams and compete with each other in an organized program, with an emphasis on recreation and fun. So you can be athletic in college even if you aren't on a varsity team!

Law enforcement and safety

With responsibility for parking, vehicle registration, policing, transportation, fire safety, and crime prevention, the law enforcement and safety division assists students through crime awareness programs that help protect your property and person.

Legal services

Your campus may or may not offer legal services to students. If a law school exists on your campus, you might want to check with them to see if upperclassmen are available to you for legal counseling.

Library

Knowing how to use your campus library will make a significant difference in your academic performance during your four years in college. Be certain you receive a proper orientation. If one is not offered in a class, such as freshman English, ask the reference librarian in the main library to help you. College libraries offer more services than you might imagine. Learn as soon as possible what they are and how to use them.

Museum

Many institutions now maintain museums, rare book collections, and other special exhibits, collections, and archives. Familiarization with such facilities can make you more aware of your institution's traditions and heritage and also give you a better feeling about what kind of an institution you have chosen to attend.

Peer counseling programs

Some college freshmen feel reluctant at first to share their problems with adult professional counselors and/or faculty members. If you are like that, you might prefer to talk with a peer counselor, that is, a professionally trained undergraduate student who is willing to lend a sensitive ear to some of your freshman problems. Many college campuses have peer counseling centers where you can find this kind of support.

Physical education center

One of the best ways to reduce stress when you're a student is to become involved in physical sports. The campus PE center may offer such varied facilities as basketball, tennis, racketball, handball, and squash courts; a dance studio; a swimming pool; an archery range; a weight room; and many more indoor and outdoor facilities. Take advantage of them!

Student activities

The student activities department is the center for extracurricular activities on campus, such as clubs, organizations, fraternities and sororities, student media (newspaper, yearbook, magazine, and so on), and intramural and recreational sports. Becoming familiar with your student activities office will help you immensely in planning your activities outside class.

Student employment office

Most colleges maintain an office to help students obtain part-time and/or full-time employment. Such an office will have information on both on-campus and off-campus jobs and they also provide information on various types of student assistant positions within your institution.

Student government

Many of you enjoyed participating in student government in high school, but often freshmen assume that because they are freshmen, there are no such opportunities for them in college. This is often a totally incorrect assumption. Student government associations are often on the outlook for students who are interested enough to become involved. Working in student government can provide excellent training and experience for your life after college.

Student media

Students interested in reporting, copyediting, layout and design, photography, feature writing, advertising sales, news gathering, broadcasting, programming, production, and engineering should find out about student media (newspaper, yearbook, literary magazine, radio and television stations) on campus. Experiences in these areas are beneficial, and you might even earn some money.

Student union

The term *student union* usually refers both to the many student activities offered through this facility and to the building that houses these programs. Student unions offer educational, cultural, and entertainment programs throughout the year. These events are planned by student committees, and membership on one or more assures you of having a voice in the programs offered by the Union. The Union building also may house a movie theatre, dining facilities, meeting rooms, a music center, a newsstand and candy shop, a game room, and other facilities.

University theatre

You don't have to be a theatre major to enjoy the live theatre productions offered on your campus. Most colleges offer first-rate productions at a fraction of the price you would pay downtown. Find out about the college theatre season when you arrive on campus and add to your education in this entertaining manner.

Undeclared majors

If you have not chosen a major, you will probably be assigned to a center for undeclared majors, which provides academic advisement and career planning services. Most schools require that you choose a major in order to graduate. This service will help you make a wise decision.

Volunteer services

Many institutions maintain offices that help you become involved with volunteer service agencies in the community. Often such work enables you to earn academic credit for certain "on the job" courses while at the same time becoming involved in and contributing to the local community. This invaluable experience will look very good on your resumé and will tell potential employers that you have real hands-on experience in your intended field.

Writing/tutorial center

Most colleges maintain a writing and/or tutorial center where you can get free assistance in improving your writing skills; in getting themes, book reviews, and term papers in proper shape, and so on. These centers are run by writing professionals who are full-time employees of the college and may be staffed by graduate and/or undergraduate students who serve as peer tutors under professional supervision.

Beyond orientation: the freshman seminar experience

Imagine a college course designed to help freshmen make the most out of college, a course in which students are free to voice their concerns to an understanding college professor/professional staff member/administrator who may call on representatives from the many offices of the campus to help students learn all they can about the next four years of their lives.

Not too many years ago, such a course was nonexistent, and if you had suggested one to college faculty, they might have considered the suggestion of teaching students how to attend college quite redundant. But, as we mentioned earlier in this chapter, the one thing colleges haven't been teaching students is how to grow—how to mature academically, spiritually, emotionally. As life has become more complex, however, as the world has become more anxiety ridden, certain educators decided to do something about helping college freshmen survive without having to depend exclusively on their own wits and wiles.

No one is certain exactly when and where the idea of a freshman orientation course was born, but we can be fairly certain that it is an idea whose time has come. Today, campuses from Maine to California offer a freshman experience of this sort, and the results indicate that freshmen enrolled in these courses tend to get more out of college than those who don't avail themselves of such a "survival course." We have also learned that students who take such courses are more likely to "survive" the freshman year and return as sophomores. Furthermore, students who participate in freshman seminars are more knowledgable about the helping services and resources of the campus, more likely to use such services, more involved in extracurricular activities, more positive in their attitudes toward faculty and the institution, and more likely to report that they received a good orientation to the college.

What follows is a sample of comments from students who have taken such a course at the University of South Carolina. Better than anything else, these statements reveal the value of a comprehensive orientation to college.

I got to know where everything was and I understand the system here much better. I also found out about many activities.

The speaker on assertive training woke me up as to why you should say "no" sometimes, even to your best friend.

Being able to sit in a group and talk about each other has enabled me to realize who I am and what I am in relation to others. I'm not really sure how to put it, but I feel good about myself as a result.

Class gave me a chance not to be so formal and serious as in all my other classes and I think every student needs to get away from all that seriousness once in a while. Thanks for letting me know that all teachers aren't unconcerned.

The class became quite close knit, like a family. It was a great help in introducing me to the activities and happenings on campus.

I've made a lot of good friends that I feel I really know. I hope that I will continue to see them next semester.

Some people could go here four years and not know about all the things on this campus. This course gave me that information.

Some of the exercises were embarrassing, but it is a way to get to know people. I found out that most people were as unsure as I was, yet we have reached the point where we can be ourselves, be open, and have a good time. It is also the only course where I know everyone's name and something about them.

I would recommend this course to others because it is a great learning experience.

What can be accomplished in an orientation course is limited only by the aims of its teacher and pupils. In a typical semester, such a class might begin with a discussion of the importance of college, swing into conversations about typical freshman fears and how to overcome them, and go from there into a myriad of activities and guest speakers, each designed to make you feel more comfortable about your decision to attend college.

One typical syllabus for a course like this includes the following activities:

- A chain introduction, in which students learn each other's names during the first meeting.
- An assignment in which each student plans his or her coming four years in college, including academic courses, activities, and a statement of goals.
- An orientation to the college library.
- An explanation of university policies.
- An introduction to proper study skills.
- A tour of the physical education center and a discussion on wellness.
- A visit to the career center and a discussion of majors and careers.
- A required interview with a professor.
- A discussion of sexual responsibilities and values, together with presentation of information on birth control techniques.
- An explanation of assertiveness training.
- A discussion of stress management.
- Various exercises in values clarification.
- Readings in a required textbook that deals with the college experience, personal involvement, or some related area.
- Attendance at university theatre presentations and other campus activities.

The only criterion for such topics and activities is that they must relate in some way to student survival. A typical breakdown of this broad criterion includes topics that (1) help students get to know themselves better, (2) help students interact more comfortably with others, and (3) give students a better understanding of what their college or university can do for them.

It is appropriate to conclude this chapter as we began it, with a final excerpt from Professor Patterson's eloquent discussion of a freshman's first day:

This is a day that I mark for myself also. Freshman arrival signifies that it is time to come out of my summer's hibernation; time to use the dreams of a long summer to breathe life into teaching again; time, as they say, to "cultivate young minds" again. I am never as conscious of how much in need of cultivation my own mind still remains. There are always regrets about manuscripts as yet unwritten, books as yet unopened, problems as yet unresolved; but there is no time now for regrets. It is time for new students, new lectures, new discussions, new research. It is time to begin again.

And that is why I like this day. For all its obvious, outward specialness, it is really no different from any other day. We are always ending something, and we are always beginning something else; we are always cherishing hopes and hiding fears, always searching for a new life and a new birth. Freshman arrival is a reminder that we are always, as Gertrude Stein once put it, "beginning again and again"—that, insofar as we are fully human, every day is always fresh. Freshman arrival changes everything and it changes nothing; it makes us stop to look at what was always there for us to see.*

So, take heart. You have many faculty like Professor Patterson and John and me, who have looked forward to your arrival almost as much as you have!

---

*Excerpted by permission from "With Fall, A Fresh Start," by Charlotte J. Patterson, Department of Psychology, University of Virginia, and originally published in *The Washington Post,* September 1, 1980.

Part Two

GETTING COMFORTABLE WITH CAMPUS: SKILLS FOR SUCCESS

2

Discovering Your College Catalog

Ed Ewing, *Advisor*
Center for Undeclared Majors
University of South Carolina

If you'd told me in 1965 when I began college that I would ever work as an academic advisor serving some 3500 students, I would have told you you were crazy. I had planned to become a career army officer, and had chosen my college major, political science, in a very simple manner. After finding out that the army didn't care what major I chose, I thumbed through the college catalog and picked the one that was most interesting to me. That's it! I didn't give it any more thought than that. Then, after four years at The Citadel, an all-male military college, I raised my hand on graduation day and became a second lieutenant. I served in such exotic locations as Fort Benning, Georgia, the Panama jungles, and Vietnam, and then decided that full-time military service was not for me.

When I left the army, I entered the University of South Carolina's graduate program in history. To pay my bills, I accepted a part-time job working in the dean's office helping students choose courses to fulfill their graduation requirements. After earning a master's degree, I was offered a full-time job advising freshmen in a new office called the Center for Undeclared Majors. I was at the "right place at the right time" and my part-time job, rather than the degree I earned, got me the job.

My jobs and duties have changed over the years, but mostly I

19

spend my days talking to students about courses, majors, and jobs after graduation. What I try to do is ease the new students' transition to college by providing them with the best academic advice I can give.

You'll have to make a lot of decisions while you're in college, but there are a lot of people you can go to for advice. Use them— and get to know your college catalog as well. You may not fall into a career as I did, so be smart and use all *the resources available to you.*

As an object of attention, it is far less exciting than football and blander than a carry-out pizza. Any senior will tell you that reading it cover to cover can be dull, at best. So why get a copy of your college catalog? Because the rules and regulations for staying in college, along with other important information, are all there. If you don't have a copy now, get one right away, and don't bury it in the bottom of the desk drawer. Keep it where you can refer to it often. Your college catalog can be one of the best friends you'll ever have.

You may have first stumbled across a catalog in a high school guidance counselor's office, or you may have browsed through one belonging to an older brother or sister. You may have received one when you applied for admission to college. One thing to remember is that college faculty can change degree requirements at almost any moment—and this brings us to our first rule for college students who wish to have the least difficulty satisfying academic requirements:

> RULE ONE: *Never use an old catalog. Instead, have one that is current for the year you begin your college program.*

As a protection to students, most colleges allow you to complete the degree requirements printed in the catalog that existed when you began your freshman year. Should the requirements change while you're enrolled, see your advisor at once to find out if any of the changes apply to your degree program.

Finding your catalog

Many colleges and universities distribute catalogs during orientation programs. Others expect you to pick up your copy from your advisor or dean after the school year begins. Rising printing costs have caused some schools to substitute departmental booklets or sheets of paper that list requirements for a specific degree along with a suggested program of study. Such "curriculum sheets" are helpful, whether or not you have a catalog, because they're easy to read and come in handy when you're discussing your program with your advisor.

Catalogs differ, just as colleges and schools do, but most of them contain information that can be grouped into five major areas: General Information; Admission, Fees, and Financial Aid; Academic Rules and Regulations; Degree Programs, Curriculum Outlines, and Course Descriptions; and Student Activities/Student Services. Although a particular catalog may not use precisely these terms, it should be easy for you to find the following information in almost any college catalog you may run across. As we discuss these topics, you should begin to see how they will enable you to reach your goal: a college degree without loss of time or money.

General information

This section contains two kinds of information, the "nice to know" and the "need to know" types. The former might include a brief history of the school, its geographic location, and a description of the prominent buildings and facilities. You may learn how the school is governed, and who its principal officers are. Titles such as trustee, president, provost, chancellor, dean, department head, and director may appear. Some day you may need to know who your dean is, so remember where you saw this information in your catalog.

The "need to know" items in this section are the accreditation statement, the academic calendar, and the educational philosophy of the school.

Accreditation statement

Accreditation is difficult to explain, but it generally involves an evaluation of a school by a team of professionals. Colleges and universities are evaluated at least every ten years by such teams. One type of accrediting team consists of faculty and administrators from other colleges and universities. These schools belong to an association of colleges representing a particular region of the country. The accrediting team evaluates libraries and other facilities and most academic programs. If the college "passes," the school receives accreditation or has its previous one renewed.

Another type of accrediting team consists of members of a specific profession. The American Bar Association, for example, accredits all law schools. Other organizations that do accreditation represent the fields of health, engineering, and business.

> RULE TWO: *To transfer college courses from one college to another, to gain acceptance to graduate schools (including law or medical schools), you must attend an accredited college or university. Doing so will also enhance your job eligibility when you graduate.*

The academic calendar

Academic calendars tell you when to register for classes, when you have a holiday from school, when you will be taking final exams, and when you may drop or add courses. Calendars provide useful information and, of course, they change annually.

RULE THREE: *Get a copy of the academic calendar each year and keep track of the important dates.*

Keeping track of deadlines is a student's responsibility, and many colleges will not allow you to make changes once a deadline has passed. A great way to keep track of deadlines—and many successful students do this—is to carry a portable calendar with you at all times and note in it your assignment "due dates" and other important obligations. You can buy these in your college bookstore for only a few dollars and carry them in purses, notebooks, briefcases, and so on. Carrying a portable calendar is also a good habit to maintain after college.

Educational philosophy of the school

Why should the philosophy of the school be of any concern to you? My answer comes from my own college experience. I attended an all-male military college where the educational philosophy called for the development of the "whole man." This included keeping haircuts very short, not being allowed to cut any classes at all, wearing a uniform every day, having mandatory evening study periods, attending mandatory chapel, and more of this sort of thing. The literature describing the school encouraged all who wished to consider this institution to visit campus as the guest of a freshman cadet during a spring weekend. In this honest and straightforward way, the school, through its catalog, was telling prospective students that its educational philosophy might not be for everyone. My point in telling you this is to emphasize that you should not apply for (and certainly not enroll in) a school whose educational philosophy radically differs from your own. Check the catalog to find out.

Admission, fees, and financial information

In the catalogs reviewed for this chapter, information on admission, fees, and financial aid was combined in some books but divided into different sections in others. Regardless of how it appears, though, this information is "need to know" when you are applying for college, but parts of it are merely "nice to know" once you have enrolled.

Admission

No rule can explain who is admitted to college and who is not. Each college or university sets its own standards, and these can change very quickly. Some colleges may even admit a student to one type of program but deny him or her entry into another.

RULE FOUR: *Admission to a college or university does not guarantee admission to every program or major offered.*

Different admission rules may apply for new freshmen, transfer students, and readmitted students. Deadlines are stringent, and many schools will not accept or process an application to a dormitory until a student has been accepted for admission.

RULE FIVE: *Be aware of the application dates/deadlines and requirements for admission to your chosen program, and apply early to the college or university of your choice.*

One final warning: Certain degree programs are much more popular than others and, with costs going up, enrollment in these programs may be limited. If you have been denied admission to the program of your choice, and no other program at that school meets your career goals, it may be wise to discuss your goals with a counselor before you make future plans. Although many students think they may be able to switch majors after arriving on campus, there's never a guarantee, and you should select a college with this fact in mind.

Fees

Just as there is no simple way to explain admission, there is no easy way to explain a university's fee policy, except to say that fees are rising. Most catalogs note that fees are subject to change, and you may accept that without question. Fees may include application fees, testing fees, tuition, student activity fees (which often include athletic tickets and use of the infirmary), housing or dormitory fees, and parking decal fees. The catalog will list nearly every fee you will be responsible for. Many catalogs also provide an estimate of the cost of attending for one year. Be aware when you see this estimate that it normally is directed to a full-time student living in a residence hall. It's a good idea for you to prepare a personal estimate, using the catalog estimate as a guide and marking prices up for inflation.

Financial aid

Colleges and universities offer a wide variety of financial aid programs. You should request information on this vital subject when you request an admissions application. Many schools reserve certain scholarships for entering freshmen, who continue to receive the money for four years. Some scholarships come with strings attached. For example, a student may be required to major in the field of study specified by the donor, or live in a certain county.

Most colleges have a financial aid office with personnel who will direct you in your search for appropriate scholarships. In addition, these counselors will discuss the possibility of your obtaining grants, loans, or part-time employment. Remember that the responsibility for meeting deadlines for such financial assistance is yours. Before the federal government will grant financial aid, you may be required to complete a number of forms. And since money is often awarded on a first come, first served basis, you should complete these forms as early as possible.

The federal government, as you may know, is reducing the amount of financial assistance for students in college, but money may still be available for you. The best place to find out is at your financial aid office, where counselors can help you keep abreast of changes in the availability of money, as well as determine your eligibility. Keep in touch with them.

Academic rules and regulations

As an academic advisor, I have seen more students lose time, money, and even the opportunity to complete a degree program of their choice because they never bothered to read this portion of their catalogs.

Somewhere in this section, most colleges include a student responsibility statement. Such a statement places the success or failure of your college education squarely on your shoulders.

RULE SIX: *Final responsibility for scheduling courses and satisfactorily completing curriculum requirements for any degree rests with the student.*

This means that, although you may enjoy the services of an academic advisor, you will find it hard to blame her or him for your failure to complete an academic requirement.

Advisement is a process that introduces the student to the academic programs of the college, the study skills services, career planning services, decision-making skills, and extracurricular opportunities. College faculty serve as academic advisors at most schools and advising, like teaching, is considered one of the duties of the faculty. It is a duty, however, that depends on the amount of cooperation offered by the student. This means that you are responsible for reading the catalog and becoming familiar with the requirements for graduation and other pertinent rules and regulations. The best advisors will work with your needs and preferences to help you decide which are most beneficial for you.

Other significant information in this section may pertain to registration for classes, changing major programs, grades and graduation, scholastic deficiencies and academic suspension, course rules, the right to petition, and the confidentiality of student records. Let's explore these one at a time.

Registration for classes

Nearly all colleges and universities use one of two methods, or a combination of the two, for registration. Many schools register students with the assistance of a computer. By checking the master schedule of classes, a publication that tells which classes will be offered during the coming term and where and when they will meet, you choose courses and then submit your request to your college. The college will notify you as to whether or not you've been admitted to those courses. If you are permitted to pay fees in advance, you need do nothing else until classes start. Most large colleges as well as many smaller ones use this method.

The second way to register is to show up on certain days set aside by the college and sign up for classes in person. If you attend a large school and other students have already registered by computer, you may find yourself standing in long lines, only to discover that the most popular classes and times are closed. Smaller colleges may be able to register you under this system with little or no difficulty, and some colleges combine this method with computer registration.

RULE SEVEN: *Find out which registration system your school uses. See your advisor well in advance, and follow the posted directions, and you'll have fewer headaches.*

Changing class schedules after registration

For a limited time after registration, many schools permit students to change class schedules. Changes may include dropping a class, adding a class, or changing one section of a class to another that is at a more convenient day or time. Such changes can only be made early in the term. Once the deadlines have passed, you won't be allowed to make course changes, except with special permission. All change actions, furthermore, require certain official signatures, usually from your advisor, professors, departments, and/or deans. The catalog and academic calendar will answer most questions concerning changes, but you might also want to check with your academic advisor.

Students are also permitted to change their programs or majors with the approval of college officials. Please be cautious about making such a change, though. If you should transfer from one college to another in the same university, you'll probably find that the requirements for graduation are very different. This may cause you to fall behind in your earned academic credits because courses you completed in one college may not count toward graduation in another. For example, an introductory required engineering course may not count toward a degree in history.

RULE EIGHT: *If you become dissatisfied with your major for any reason, see your advisor immediately to discuss alternatives and to determine what a change will mean to you. Also, see an advisor for the program you wish to enter.*

I want to be honest with you. Many college students choose a major that is unrealistic for them; they base their choice on where they believe the jobs will be after graduation. Some select engineering without finding out what an engineer does for a living or what courses they have to complete to earn the degree. In fact, many students fail to investigate a major and weigh its potential against their career goals until after they're enrolled in college classes. If you enter college as an undeclared major, it is even more important for you to investigate all the choices in the catalog and to seek academic and career counseling from the college. (See Chapters 7 and 8.)

Grades and graduation

Most colleges introduce you to their grading system in some detail, and most schools try to maintain the same grading system to avoid confusion. In addition to the A-B-C-D-F scale, many schools add pluses and minuses (B+, C−, and so on). Other grades are given for withdrawing from a course, for work not completed during the term assigned, and for courses taken on a pass-fail system.

Your grade point average (GPA), sometimes called the grade point ratio (GPR), is computed on the basis of the number of hours you attempt during a term for credit. Each grade represents a certain number of points. At most colleges, the point system goes like this:

A = 4 points D = 1 point
B = 3 points F = 0 points
C = 2 points

By multiplying the number of points for your grade by the number of credits for the course, you can determine the total points you have earned in that course. Add the points for all courses taken that term, then divide this total by the total number of credit hours attempted that term. This is your GPA or GPR. With a high average, you will make the college's honor roll or dean's list. If your average is high enough at the end of your college career, your transcript and perhaps your diploma will indicate that you graduated "with distinction" or "with honors." Check your catalog for specific rules regarding graduation, dean's list, and becoming an honor graduate.

Scholastic deficiency and academic suspension

At any point in your college career, you will be in either good or bad academic standing. No single rule defines "bad standing" at all colleges. But most catalogs use phrases such as "unsatisfactory progress," "scholastic deficiency," and "scholastic ineligibility" to describe the condition. Catalogs also explain at what performance level you would be subject to academic suspension or dismissal. If you're suspended for academic reasons, you must remain out of college until you're permitted to enroll again.

RULE NINE: *It is your responsibility to remain in good academic standing with the college.*

When you know you're having academic problems, see your advisor for help immediately!

Rules concerning college courses

Many students who fail to read and understand the rules and regulations concerning their course work claim they were misadvised. But regardless of who made the error, the final responsibility for complying with the rules is yours. You should know and live by these rules, but remember to ask questions if you don't understand them. Of particular importance to you will be rules covering acceptance of transfer credits, final examinations, correspondence courses, course numbering systems, repeating a course, course load per term, substituting courses in your program, class attendance, and enrolling in summer school. Here are several tips to help you with the most misunderstood of these rules.

- *Tip 1: Transfer Courses.* Transfer credits will not be entered on your record until the dean's office has evaluated them. Don't expect them to appear automatically. If you have questions, contact the dean's office.

- *Tip 2: Course Numbering.* Most freshman and sophomore courses are numbered at the 100 and 200 level. However, there is no rule that states "The higher the course number, the more difficult the course." To some students, the lower level courses are more difficult since many of them are survey courses that attempt to cover many things in one term. Courses carrying higher numbers often narrow the topic to be studied and, although you may receive more information on the subject, you will have the entire term to master the material.

- *Tip 3: Repeating Courses.* No rule states that a student must repeat every course he fails. If you fail a course that is required for your major, you must, naturally, repeat it. But, if your catalog tells you that you may substitute other courses for the course you failed, do so—don't repeat the course unless you prefer it to the substitutes or are positive your grade will rise significantly. Don't repeat a course simply to remove a lower grade from your transcript without checking with your advisor, because some colleges don't allow higher grades to replace lower ones.

- *Tip 4: Attending Classes.* Class attendance policies vary dramatically. For some reason, many college students believe they will always receive a certain number of class "cuts" each term. Although some colleges allow you to miss class occasionally, their catalogs discuss excused and unexcused absences and never mention the word *cut*. Many more good reasons exist for attending a class than for missing one. First, many professors and departments establish a tougher attendance policy than the one in the catalog. Second, some professors say they never take attendance, but add that a majority of the material necessary for passing the course will be in the lectures. Third, a direct relationship exists between class attendance, how well you learn the material, and the final grade you receive.

The first few classes in the term are among the most important. Many schools allow you to change your schedule during the first few days of class. Since most professors tell students what the requirements for passing the course are during the first few sessions, you can decide right away whether or not to stay in the class or switch to another. Start college properly by attending all classes. If an illness or emergency occurs, notify your professor or advisor. If you know in advance that you'll be missing a class, your professor may appreciate knowing, too.

- *Tip 5: Attending Summer School.* Your advisor, and often your dean, must approve in advance any courses you wish to take in summer school, especially if you will be attending a different school during the summer. Tell your advisor you wish to take summer classes and find out how to get the classes approved.

The right to petition

At some point during your college education, you may wish to fulfill a requirement in a way that differs from the catalog description. In such a case you may wish to petition the school to allow the exception. Unusual situations for which students may petition include: substituting one class for another, seeking readmission to college after academic suspension, attending another college and transferring those credits to the school where you plan to graduate, and seeking a waiver of any other academic rules and regulations due to extenuating circumstances such as prolonged illness. Many colleges have a petition process that must be followed step by step and that includes review by a petitions' committee. Be certain you understand the process at your school, but don't be frightened of it. Petitioning can often save you both time and money.

The privacy of student records

In 1974, Congress passed the Family Education Rights and Privacy Act. As a result, you are considered an adult when you enter college and your records are considered confidential. At your school, your academic file is kept in the student records or registrar's office. Usually, this file contains everything from your admissions application and high school transcripts to your grades for each college term. The 1974 act allows you to review and challenge the accuracy of all information in your file, and also assures you that none of the information will be released to others without your written consent, except in emergencies. Your college catalog will explain this rule in more detail, but in effect, only college or university officials will have copies of your grades so they can advise you more accurately.

Degree programs, curriculum outlines, and course descriptions

This is the second "need to know" section of your catalog because it tells you what degrees your school offers and which courses you must complete for graduation. Following a list of all degree programs at your institution, the catalog will probably contain an alphabetical listing for each major along with the required courses for that major. Finally, you will find a course listing and description of every course offered by the school.

Be aware that course descriptions can never be current. New courses are always being added and others dropped. Just because a course is listed in the catalog is no guarantee that it will be offered each term.

Understanding your degree program

Most undergraduate programs award a bachelor's degree, which takes four years to complete if you're a full-time student, pass all your courses, and don't withdraw from school. To complete your degree, you must fulfill all academic requirements in the catalog regarding course work. The first block of courses you will be required to take are called "core courses," "basic requirements," "general education requirements," or "distribution requirements." Usually all students in a particular college, regardless of major, must take such courses during the first and second years. More specifically, these courses may include requirements in English, history, social science, humanities, science, and math. Learn the requirements for your program and follow them.

The second group of courses constitutes your major. After you have satisfied all prerequisites for courses in your major, you will be permitted to take courses that more closely correspond to your educational goals. Your college catalog will identify for you all prerequisites (that is, courses you must complete before moving on to higher courses). Some majors allow you a choice of courses to fulfill certain requirements, and some colleges allow you to have a double major, or complete all major courses for two different programs. Since your major is directly related to what you want to do after graduation, you should choose it carefully and select courses that will help you reach a specific career goal.

A third group of courses in your program is your minor or cognate, a group of courses that supports your major and is approved by your advisor or dean. Not all college programs include minors or cognates. If yours does, remember to choose it wisely so that it also contributes to your educational and career goals.

Finally, you will have an opportunity to choose "free electives" to round out your program. Electives are courses that are not required for your program, but that will count toward your degree. Be careful when choosing them.

> RULE TEN: *Some academic programs have few free electives, and your dean may refuse to count in this category certain courses at your university.*

You are responsible for ensuring that all courses you choose will apply to your degree.

In the section that outlines degree programs, many colleges include a curriculum outline or suggested program of study for the student to follow. You should remember that these outlines are merely guides, and that most were designed for the full-time student. However, you must also realize that some courses in your degree program are more important than others and must be completed early in your college career, especially if they are prerequisites for other courses. Many majors are now divided into upper and lower divisions, and entrance to the upper division often depends on successful completion of all lower division courses. Check with your advisor!

The final item in this section of the catalog is the list of course descriptions. Unfortunately, many students spend more time studying these descriptions than trying to understand degree requirements or academic rules. The main things to check in this section are the number of credits the course carries and the prerequisites, if any, for each course. Here are four tips to help you pick courses.

- *Tip 1: Talk to a student who is currently taking or has taken the course you want.* Ask what the requirements for the course are, as well as information about who teaches the course. Ask about tests, class attendance policies, and the professor's grading system.
- *Tip 2: Go to the campus bookstore and look at the book or books required for the course.* Are they interesting? Check the books of students taking the class.
- *Tip 3: Go to the source.* Ask the faculty member teaching the course to describe the course to you. Many faculty encourage students to speak with them, although most students avoid this potentially meaningful contact.
- *Tip 4: Check out the course with your academic advisor.*

Student activities/student services

This information may fall into the "nice to know" or even the "need to know" category. I divide student services into two types: academic and nonacademic. Although I'm often soundly criticized for this oversimplification by friends who provide these services, for my purposes, the labels work.

Academic services include: teaching library skills, reading skills, note-taking skills, test-taking skills, writing skills, and time management; and academic advising. Nonacademic services include: career planning and placement; orientation; student employment/volunteer services; financial aid; housing/residence; health counseling, and other forms of personal counseling. Many of these services have different names in different catalogs.

Every college or university provides a number of student activities. Many take place in the student center or union. Activities are represented by clubs, organizations, fraternities and sororities, student media, student government, and intramural sports. The range of activities is nearly unlimited. Some are more valuable than others since they may help you get the job you want after graduation. A career counselor and academic advisor can help you select meaningful activities that may be fun as well. (See Chapter 16).

In conclusion, let me repeat five important things you should do to prepare yourself for a meaningful college career. First, get a current catalog as soon as you enroll. Second, be sure you know who your academic advisor is and where you can find him or her. Third, read the catalog. Learn the "need to know" and "nice to know" information in that order. Fourth, ask your advisor to help you build a sample program of study for your major; recommend courses and professors; explain any rules, regulations, or terms you don't understand; and recommend services and activities that might help you. Finally, attend class, study, and graduate!

I hope you can see how easy all of this can be if you apply a little time and effort. Master the material in your catalog, and it will be much easier for you to master college.

Decoding Your Professors

John N. Gardner
and A. Jerome Jewler

From a combined twenty-five years of teaching college students, we have developed many insights into the relationship between students and professors. Little did we suspect, when we were college students, that our professors really had an interest in teaching us something or that they might have appreciated our dropping by for a chat. Office hours, we now know, are for students—and we've often wondered over the years why we weren't smart enough to take advantage of them.

The extent to which you'll be successful in college will be determined, in part, by how successful you are in acquiring certain attitudes, behaviors, and skills in relating to your professors. We've tried to make you aware of at least some of them in this chapter, and we hope they help you avoid making the same mistakes we did.

They're supposed to be smart, because college professors have to be. Yet some of the things they say and do in class make you wonder. They rush through pages of notes, so it's impossible to remember all the important details. They give too many quizzes, and expect too much from you in return. It doesn't matter to them whether it's homecoming weekend, or the big fraternity/sorority rush week, or

33

the day you just *have* to go home because it's your birthday. They still expect you to be in class, and on time.

Do your college professors really understand you? Sure they do, but if you expect them to act, think, or even dress the way your high school teachers did, you may be in for a rude awakening.

Furthermore, you might be surprised to know that many of your college teachers are extremely interested in your well-being, and hope you'll earn high grades in their classes. These same individuals, however, may be quick to disagree with your ideas, ready to correct you when you answer a question in class, and extremely demanding about the amount of work they expect from you. If that scares you as you begin your college career, hold on. Establishing a positive relationship with your college professors, in the way we're about to discuss, can be one of the most rewarding experiences, not only of your college years, but of your entire life.

Teachers are people who once were freshmen

As you warily approach your professors during your first semester in college, remember that they have one thing in common with you: Each was once a freshman, too. Your professors are also human beings who respond to many of the same kinds of needs, goals, rewards, aspirations, gestures, and praise that you do. While you need to generate some empathy for them, many of them—despite what you think—have even more empathy for you.

Your college professors are probably teaching because they love their disciplines and love to communicate to others what they know best. They certainly did not choose their profession for the money! To find out what kind of people they are, you might begin by studying their offices. Usually, you will find them decorated to reflect the interests and personality of each teacher, and you will most certainly find them filled with books. Professors read voraciously, and they like to talk about what they have read. Some may mention articles from the *New York Times* or the *Washington Post*. Others may quote from trade or professional journals, such as *Advertising Age* or the *Chronicle of Higher Education*. Some may speak of travels abroad, or to other parts of the United States, where they have lived, taught, or attended college. If you have lived in the same area of the country most of your life, you can learn much from your college professors about the rest of your country and the world.

They weren't trained to teach

You might be surprised to learn that most of your college professors have never taken an education course in their lives. Instead, they chose courses in their academic disciplines that taught them how to acquire new knowledge and to understand that knowledge. They did not learn how to communicate that knowledge to you, or how to entertain you as they did so. In fact, you might find a few professors who would much rather be doing nothing but research, but must teach to justify their salaries. Others have left professional careers in various fields in order to teach their professions to college students. You'll find lawyers teaching law, physicians teaching medicine, newspaper editors teaching journalism, and corporation executives teaching business management.

Professors who pursued several advanced degrees in graduate schools or spent many years working in a profession have learned the virtues of diligence, patience, and persistence, and of the ability to ask, process, and handle enormous amounts of minute detail, so they'll probably expect you to do the same.

Your professors may be very different from your high school teachers

Your professors probably won't spend much time in class teaching you the textbooks, and they won't base their tests exclusively on them either. If it were enough to teach you the book, there would be little need for professors to work very hard. But your professors have their own ideas about their discipline, and one of their goals is to help you learn as much about their subject as you can. This usually means that a textbook is only the basis for all else in the course, and you'll probably work harder than you ever did in high school to absorb all the material they give you.

In high school, your teachers filled you with knowledge and information accumulated by others. Their task was simply to pass it on to you. Naturally, your college teachers also want to pass on the knowledge accumulated by others, but many professors feel the need to create new knowledge of their own. As a result, many of them will talk to you about the research they are doing, in the hope that you'll find this interesting and will want to learn more.

Your high school teachers probably checked your notebooks to see that they were neat, took attendance regularly, and checked up on you to make certain you were doing all your work. In college, some professors will take roll, but others never will. It isn't that they don't care whether you come or not—they do. But they also feel you should be treated as an adult. They hope, of course, that you're taking adequate notes, but they won't be checking to see that you do.

And while your professors may frequently praise your school and many of its activities, they may not always get excited about the football and basketball teams or the homecoming celebration you've been waiting for all season. They just express their enthusiasm in different ways.

They believe in education for its own sake

To college professors, a solid education is more than a means of getting a degree and a job. Becoming an educated person is in itself something they prize, and they hope you'll take the same pride in education. Consequently, many professors will be idealistic, and not as practical as you might like. You probably can't change that, but you can try to appreciate their zest for knowledge, and to understand how vitally it affects their lives.

They're interested in you

Many college faculty will take a personal interest in you as a student and as a person. Professors like this chose teaching because they genuinely wanted to help others. However, they may not take the initiative to ask you to come see them. You will have to do that. Faculty try to treat students as adults. They don't want to babysit, but they do appreciate a friendly visit. One of your greatest opportunities for learning in college will come from the kind of one-on-one interaction you can experience with a professor outside of class. Professors are required to keep office hours, and that's the time to make an appointment to see them. Don't feel as though you're bothering them. It's part of their job to make time for you.

They love what they're teaching

If they don't love what they're teaching, they're probably not very good professors. In fact, good professors love their subject so much they may become excited and enthused about its significance. They may speed up their lectures because they want to tell you so much, and you just can't keep up. That's when you should raise your hand and ask them to slow down. Just because they're rushing through the material doesn't mean they're not willing to listen to you. Many professors get carried away by their own thoughts and must be brought down to earth by a student.

Why they chose college teaching

How does one explain what draws an individual to teaching on a college campus? The hours are long, the pay is only fair, and the frustrations are many. Perhaps it begins with a love of the "college experience" as a student and a desire to someday return to that intellectually stimulating environment. For some, it may involve a desire to learn more about a favorite subject while imparting that knowledge to others. Many professors love research, and find it rewarding to uncover new ideas about people and the world. Others are talented in the arts—in writing or music or painting—and want to develop those skills further while passing them on to others.

Deep within nearly all college professors is the desire to use their knowledge and life experiences to affect the lives of others in a positive way. After all, they were probably affected in the same way by certain professors while they were students. Ask several of your professors why they chose teaching. You'll find as many answers as the number of people you ask.

What college professors do

One of the most common myths about college professors is that they lead easy lives of quiet contemplation while teaching one or two classes every week. College professors do much more than go to class. In fact, the time they spend in classroom instruction takes up a relatively small part of a typical workweek. The average professor spends between six and fifteen hours in the classroom weekly, compared to the thirty hours or more a high school teacher spends. Yet that same college professor works from sixty to eighty hours a week.

Since it is important that they remain current in their field, professors spend part of that time reading, reading, reading. That leads to additional hours during which they revise and update their class lecture notes. It takes far longer to prepare notes than to deliver them in class. Professors may spend time conducting experiments, reviewing manuscripts, and writing, writing, writing. They may be called upon to speak to community, civic, and professional groups, or to assist such groups in the development of a project. They may do consulting for private corporations and government agencies for extra money. They may be writing books, book reviews, journal articles, or papers for delivery at conventions. They may be writing plays or music, or creating paintings or sculptures.

When they're not doing any of these things, you'll probably find them advising students. Many spend considerable time in individual and group conferences with students to help them plan their academic programs for the coming term, reach career decisions, deal with personal problems, or find ways to improve their grades.

And with the time that's left, your professors are asked to perform administrative duties, serve on academic committees, or become involved in special college or university projects. A typical college professor may serve as chairperson of a college advisement committee (to devise ways to improve student advisement); be a member of an awards committee (to set up procedures for nominating and selecting outstanding students); serve as a faculty senator, or representative, in a university-wide governance system; and be called upon to participate in a special task force to evaluate the current student disciplinary system.

When not in the classroom or in the office, professors are still working: behind closed doors in committee sessions or at home grading papers and preparing for tomorrow's classes. To accept this sort of schedule willingly, they must feel very strongly about the importance of the college experience.

Making the most of the student-professor relationship

Remember what we said earlier about professors being people who respond positively to the same things other people do, such as politeness, consideration, tact, smiles, attention, compliments, affection, and praise? If you will remember this, you can do a few simple things to cause your professors to think more positively about you.

First, come to class regularly and be on time. Many students don't do this, so your exceptional behavior will stand out. Take advantage of office hours and see professors when it's appropriate. Realize that professors are not people to be avoided at all costs, and that you will not be criticized by your peers if you're seen talking with them. In fact, it's very likely that these same peers have already talked with them. Use their office hours to get to know your professors and let them make you a significant person in their life, too.

What else can you do to make your professors think highly of you? Come to class well groomed and properly dressed. A sloppy appearance suggests you can't be very serious about their lectures and discussions. Read all the assigned material before class. Ask questions frequently, but not to the point of annoyance or distraction. Show interest in the subject. Remember, your professors are extremely interested in their subjects and for that reason they'll appreciate your show of interest.

Sit near the front of the class. A number of studies have shown that students who do so tend to make better grades. To your professors, this will indicate your heightened interest in their ideas. Never talk or whisper while professors are lecturing. They'll interpret this as an uncaring or even rude gesture, which, indeed, it is!

Finally, don't hand your professors a lot of "bull." They've been hearing this drivel for years, and can spot phony excuses a mile away. If you're sincere and give honest reasons for missing class or work, they're more likely to respect you for it, and may even bend their rules about late work and grade penalties.

Academic freedom

Academic freedom is a condition and a right most college faculty enjoy at the majority of private and state-supported institutions. Simply put, it is the freedom to pursue intellectual inquiry and research, or to raise questions that are legitimately related to scholarly interests and professions. The concept of academic freedom allows professors to raise controversial issues without risk of losing their jobs. It doesn't give them total immunity from pressure and reprisals, but it does allow them more latitude than teachers you knew in high school.

Academic freedom is a long-established tradition in American higher education and has its origins in the development of intellectual history, dating back to the Middle Ages. Colleges and universities have found it desirable to promote the advancement of research and knowledge by giving their scholars and professors virtually unlimited freedom of inquiry, as long as human lives, rights, and privacy are not violated. This same assurance of freedom from political intervention and pressure is one of the appealing things to faculty about the collegiate lifestyle. It allows a professor to enjoy a personal and intellectual freedom not possible in many other professions, and opens the door to less conventional thoughts and actions.

Such thoughts and actions may surprise and even anger you at times. Your professors occasionally may articulate some ideas and opinions that offend you. You won't like them because they'll be contrary to some of your basic values and beliefs. Professors may insult a politician you admire, may speak with sarcasm about cherished American institutions such as the presidency, or may look with disdain upon organized religion.

Sometimes, they may be doing this just to get a reaction from you. They may believe that, in order to get you to think, they must disrupt and provoke you out of your "intellectual complacency." On the other hand, your professors may actually believe those statements you find outrageous. You need to realize that professors are highly independent, intellectually and personally, compared to the average American. Since college professors may be free thinkers, you may hear ideas from them that are at variance with many of the conventions of society. This does not mean you must agree with them in order to get good grades. It does mean, however, that you must understand such views, examine them rationally, and be prepared to defend yours if you still believe you are correct.

Tenure

The notion of academic freedom is related to something called "tenure." This is the award a college or university gives to professors once they reach a certain point in their professional development that promises them lifetime employment. While untenured faculty also have academic freedom, tenured faculty theoretically have more of it. Tenure, in effect, means that a professor may not be terminated from employment except for these extraordinary situations:

1. *An act of moral turpitude.* Such an act would be a gross violation of the legal code or of any code of conventionally acceptable behavior. As current standards for conventionally accepted behavior become increasingly more tolerant, the range of behaviors involving moral turpitude become narrower.

2. *Insubordination.* Since a professor enjoys academic freedom, it is very difficult to define, let alone prove, insubordination. Very few professors, therefore, are terminated for this infraction.

3. *Incompetence.* Once again, who is to prove that the faculty member is incompetent? Obtaining the consensus of one's peers is virtually impossible, although complaints by students may be effective here.

4. *Bona fide reduction in staff.* If your college experiences severe financial hardships, the institution could decide to eliminate faculty positions, departments, or majors, and the reduction in staff might include tenured faculty.

You won't be able to tell if your professors are tenured just by looking at them. The existence of tenure is a support of the general climate of free expression and free inquiry into the pursuit of ideas, which makes higher education an uplifting experience, for professors and their students.

Rank

Not all professors are "professors." A subtle yet significant pecking order exists among college professors, reflecting enormous differences in power, authority, prestige, income, and special privileges. Here is how it works.

First, there are instructors and lecturers. Next come assistant professors, followed by associate professors and full professors. Most colleges have probationary periods of employment for faculty that they must complete before applying for promotion to the next highest rank. When promotion comes from assistant to associate professor, it may also include the award of tenure. Full professors generally teach fewer classes, have fewer students, and are more likely to be working with graduate students.

This pecking order may not be important to you at first, but it could become important if you should decide to seek advanced degrees. A recommendation for employment or graduate school from a senior professor can carry more weight than one from a lower ranking professor, especially if your senior professor is well known in the field.

Academic standards and belief in education for its own sake

While it's difficult to generalize about college professors, since they exhibit so many personal and intellectual differences, it's relatively safe to assume that most of them believe in the value of a liberal arts education.

You've probably heard that a liberal arts education is important because it makes you more marketable in the job market. To your professors, its value goes far beyond that. The word *liberal* is a direct reference to the ability of education to free your mind. Indeed, the word itself comes from the Latin *libero*, a verb meaning "to free." The goal of a liberal arts education is to free you from the biases, superstitions, prejudices, and lack of knowledge that characterized you before you came to college.

To free you of these restraints, it may be necessary to provoke, challenge, and disturb you by presenting you with new ideas, beliefs, and values that differ from your previous perceptions. Keep that in mind the next time your college professors say something that surprises you. In college, as in life, you'll have to learn to tolerate opinions that are vastly different from yours. Note that you need not always accept them, but you should learn to evaluate them for yourself instead of basing your responses on what others have always told you.

Because your professors want you to grow intellectually, they'll probably demand more of you than your high school teachers did. You'll probably have to study more to get good grades, because your professors may be inclined to give fewer A's and more F's than teachers in high school. Most college professors believe students who enter college are woefully underprepared to do college work—many through no fault of their own. As a result, they'll challenge you to raise your standards to theirs, instead of lowering theirs to meet yours.

It often comes as a great shock to students who made high grades in high school with little or no studying, to find that they must study for hours to earn a high grade on a college exam. As a rule of thumb, you may need to spend two to three hours preparing outside of class for every hour you spend in class. This means that, if you're carrying fifteen hours a semester, you should be spending an additional thirty hours each week studying, for a total workweek of forty-five hours, which is similar to the amount of time you'll be spending when you begin your professional career.

What professors want from their students

Good professors frequently have students approach them at the end of the term to tell them how much they enjoyed the class. Professors appreciate that, but what they really want to hear is, "I really learned a lot from you and I want to thank you for it." Enjoyment should result from the positive learning experience; it shouldn't result from enjoyment for its own sake. Frankly, the pleasure of learning new ideas should constitute enjoyment in itself, and that is what your professors want to hear. Remember, they're not primarily entertainers but teachers. If they entertain out of proportion to teaching, they may be less than adequate in their profession.

Much has been written about professors who don't really care about students, but are dedicated in their desire to teach them new ideas. It's difficult to see how these two ideas are consistent with one another. Some level of caring must exist before learning can be passed from one individual to another. If you doubt that your professors "care" about their students, ask them. The question may be revealing to them and the answer may be revealing to both of you.

Finally, remember that professors will like you more, even though they may not show it, if you participate in class discussion, complete your assignments on time, ask questions during class, make appointments to see them, comment on lecture materials, or simply smile and say "hello" when you meet on campus. They'll appreciate you if you maintain frequent eye contact with them during class, share a story or anecdote, joke with them or the class, and show you realize the value of what they're teaching you.

During the remainder of your life, you'll meet many admirable, stimulating, exciting, unique, remarkable, inspiring, perplexing, frustrating, and challenging individuals. Few will be more complex than your college professors. One or two of your college faculty may help counsel or guide you as you pursue your life goals, and may indeed affect your entire life significantly. For that reason alone, it pays to get the most out of them during your four years in college, which, after all, is probably the most significant period of change in your entire life.

Suggested activity

Interview one or more of your current professors to find out whether they fit the descriptions provided in this chapter. You might ask them how they chose their academic discipline, what motivated them to teach on a college campus, what they regard as the ideal student, and what irritates or bothers them most about college students today. To gain an even more complete picture of college professors, share your interviews with other students, and have them share theirs with you.

Using the Library:
A Ticket
to Success

Charles Curran, *Associate Professor of Library and Information Science*
University of South Carolina

Joe Lewis, *Social Sciences Reference Librarian*
Old Dominion University Library

I remember how angry the student was. I had just helped him find some extremely useful stuff, lots of it, but he was furious because he was a junior. Why had it taken three years before someone told him about all that useful material in his major, political science? His complaint was that he could have learned a lot more and received better grades, too, if only he'd known how easy it really was to get at so many valuable sources of information.

In this chapter, Joe and I will give you an action strategy for using your college or university library. I really believe this strategy is a survival skill, and it's a strategy that will work for you. Guaranteed. But don't expect this chapter to contain the names of every book and magazine you'll ever want to consult on any subject imaginable. Our purpose here is much more modest: to give you firsthand experience with a successful and realistic information-retrieval project that you can use as a model next time you get an assignment that requires you to use the library. And make sure you do use your college library; it's your ticket to success.

Aware of it or not, like it or not, all of us—you, Joe, and I—are smack in the middle of a crisis. How we deal with that crisis will determine the quality of our survival as students, family members, and workers.

Here's the problem. Information and knowledge are growing at an astonishing speed, resulting in an explosion of records in paper, micro, and electronic formats. That's the good news. The bad news is that it's getting tougher and tougher to keep up, even in a very narrow area of knowledge. Besides that, organizations whose job it is to manage information are finding it increasingly difficult to acquire, store, and disseminate information.

Even as a beginner at the college and university game, you don't need anybody to point out the obvious—that you need information but at the same time are faced with so much of it that you don't know where to begin. You need somebody to help you help yourself manage information, and that's where Joe and I can lend a hand.

Joe is a reference librarian at Old Dominion University. He manages information in the social sciences for a living. At the USC College of Library and Information Science I teach people like Joe how to become information managers. Joe and I have worked together on many an information problem, and together we'll give you a survival skill that will make you successful students and competent retrievers of information.

In fact, if you read this chapter and run through the simple steps it suggests, you'll know more about the library and how to use it than most of the Ph.D.'s walking around campus. That's *important* and that's *possible* and that's *good*.

You need to know more

That's *important* because you *have* to know more than Ph.D.'s do. Most Ph.D.'s know a great deal about a tiny little subject—like green mold. You, on the other hand, have to know about computers, English, history, math, physics, marine science, Spanish, and/or a host of other subjects you're taking. The Ph.D. who wants to know when his bread is too fuzzy to eat asks a colleague or studies the *Mildew Journal,* the magazine in the field. His or her interests are so well defined and narrow that an information search is simple. But you're a beginner who has signed up for five subjects!

If you go through the simple steps outlined in this chapter, you'll find out how information in many subjects is organized, and you'll learn how to get at it. Remember, the Ph.D. expert in penicillin doesn't have to know about Chaucer or Theory Z management, but you don't have the luxury of being unfamiliar with a variety of subjects. You've signed up for five different courses! This chapter starts you on the road to becoming an information manager.

And that's *good*. If you use the library well, you'll learn more and you'll earn better grades. You'll learn to use sources that even your professors don't know exist. And you'll learn there's more than one perspective or way of looking at a topic. The information explosion is so massive that a substantial chunk of what is now known in your professors' fields was not known when they were in school. You are about to learn how to gain access to the latest, most authoritative, and most significant information that's available, and you'll be able to display these discoveries in your course papers, exams, and recitations.

You must want or need to learn

A word of caution is in order. Here comes the fine print in the guarantee. If you don't want to or need to learn more about the library right now, skip this chapter—come back to it when you do. Joe and I guarantee favorable results *only* if you either want to or need to learn about information management. If your course requirements include only taking lecture notes, reading a text, and writing an essay or objective exam, read no further. But if you think you have something substantial to gain from learning how to use your information center right now, here comes your two-step package, backed by a lifetime warranty and money-back guarantee.

Step one

First, as information is created and goes into the record, it assumes a variety of different forms and gets packaged differently. Your understanding of this phenomenon of information flow is necessary if our lesson is to work.

Information may have its origins in the spoken word, passing on after that into the forms of reports, journals and magazines, books, and encyclopedias. Information is newest when it is in its oral and report forms, and oldest when it is in book and encyclopedia forms. New is not necessarily good, though, and old is not necessarily bad. A 1921 article on space exploration probably needs some updating, but a 1921 article on Teddy Roosevelt may be fine, depending on the kind of information required.

Second, you can manage your information need by learning how to use each of the following information sources:

- Encyclopedias
- Dictionaries

- Books
- Bibliographies
- Indexes and Abstracts
- Librarians

This is not just a list; it's an outline of a strategy for retrieving needed information. Learn what each category delivers, and you'll develop successful search strategies.

1. *Encyclopedias give useful basic information on a topic.*

   If you are beginning a search on an unfamiliar topic, a general or special encyclopedia can give you the foundation you need to understand some pretty complex issues. Because these sources frequently get misused (copied from or never gotten beyond), they get a bum rap. So footnoting an encyclopedia, even a renowned one, may be discouraged or forbidden. OK, but remember that these sources may give you a super introduction to your topic even if they win you no "points." Remember too that there's a special subject encyclopedia covering almost every discipline. Here are a few examples: *Encyclopedia of American Religions, Encyclopedia of Bioethics, Encyclopedia of World Art, Encyclopedia of Food,* and *Encyclopedia of Sports.*

2. *What you should know about dictionaries.*

   In addition to what you already know about dictionaries, you should know that when you need a word defined in a very special context, there's probably a special subject dictionary available to you.

3. *Books are books.*

   As you build upon information found in encyclopedia articles, you will expand your search to more sophisticated and detailed sources, like books. The key to a library's book collection is its catalog, sometimes available in card form. The subject key to a library's catalog is its list of official subject names. More on this later.

4. *Bibliographies are lists.*

   Bibliographies supply you with more sources to consult. Normally, you look in a bibliography to see if any sources on your topic exist, and then you check the library's catalog or magazine holdings to see if the cited sources are available. Bibliographies can be in magazines and in books. Sometimes a whole book is devoted to bibliographies on one or more topics. Librarians will show you how to find bibliographies in your subject.

5. *Indexes and abstracts put you in touch with magazine and book articles on your topic.*

   You're already familiar with indexes in the backs of books. The term is used differently here. "Periodical indexes," because they refer you to articles in magazines and journals, offer you access to recent information. A book can soon become dated and obsolete, but a magazine may be a monthly or weekly publication and can stay abreast of contemporary developments. Some indexes, like the *New York Times Index*, cover information on a *daily* basis. Abstracts refer you to currently produced information and also include a synopsis, summary, or critique of the referred-to source. The library in which you are doing your search will probably have most of the sources to which the indexes and abstracts refer—that's why they subscribe to them. There are indexes and abstracts covering virtually every field of inquiry. Some are general, like *Readers' Guide;* others are specialized, like *Social Science Index, Art Index,* and *Business Periodicals Index*. One helpful feature of indexes is that you can easily find the opinions or thinking that existed at a specific time. To check views on isolationism from 1930 to 1940, for example, just look at the appropriate index for those years.

6. *Librarians are hired to make information available.*

Librarians have a special job: to help you directly. Most of those who pick that job do so because they like to help you, and most of them are pretty good at it. You have a right to the very best service they can give, and when you ask questions, you help them do their job. Their business is you—not books—and if it weren't for you, they wouldn't have jobs. Librarians are an important source of information and should be considered important links in your search strategy chain.

Approaching a librarian is an important step in seeking information. It's a simple step, yet some people find it difficult. Librarians may look busy all the time, even grouchy once in a while, but they really do enjoy helping people. Otherwise, they wouldn't be in the business. Librarians are paid to provide service, first and foremost, and that means that helping you is more important than anything else.

Librarians are not surprised at your questions or judgmental about your needs; in fact, librarians often ask other librarians how to find stuff, too! So, when you ask for help, you're exercising your right and allowing a librarian to do his or her job. Walk right up to a librarian, smile, and ask your questions.

Before you take step two, review step one. Be sure you understand the six parts of this outline of sources. What kind of information is contained in each part? Note that you may not always follow that sequence exactly and that you may go back and forth between librarians and the various other parts in a different order from that given. You may even begin your search with an inquiry of the librarian. That's OK. Just be sure you understand the kind of information you'll get from each of these different sources.

Step two

If this is going to work for you, you have to have an information need. Joe and I are going to supply that need. We ask you to imagine that you have been assigned a term project on "communes in the United States." Later you can use the strategy we advise and plug in your own topic or need. But for now, use the topic we suggest and you'll learn how each type of source can help you.

Encyclopedias

Encyclopedias may be single-volume or multivolume, general or specific subject. *Americana* is a multivolume general encyclopedia. The *International Encyclopedia of the Social Sciences* is a multivolume subject encyclopedia. The first step in using encyclopedias is to turn to the index, which is usually at the end of the set, most often in a separate index volume. Your chances of finding data in an encyclopedia are increased significantly when you use the index. That's because all information on a topic can't be conveniently packaged alphabetically. Think about all the important information about "automobiles" that cannot be keyed with words that begin with A. Consider "car, Detroit, Ford, gasoline, highways, petroleum, transportation, and spontaneous combustion," all of which are important and related to "automobile," and none of which begins with A and, therefore, may not appear in the A volume. Note how this works with your "commune" topic.

Check the index volume of the *Encyclopedia Americana*. In the 1981 printing that will be volume 30. Note that the entry "Commune (U.S.):" refers you to "Utopian Societies 27–845." That means that in volume 27, page 845, you'll find information you need. Note that this information is not in the C volume. Careful use of the index protects you against overlooking valuable information. Notice also that your "Utopian Societies" article is followed by a bibliography of sources for additional information on the topic. And make a note of the "Utopian Societies" subject heading because you might find additional information using the same heading in other sources.

Now check the index of the authoritative multivolume *International Encyclopedia of Psychiatry, Psychology, Psychoanalysis and Neurology,* a specific subject encyclopedia. In volume 12, the index volume, you'll spot the entry "Communes I:428." This means that on page 428 of the first volume (not the C volume but the A volume!) you'll find a reference to your subject, in this case in the article entitled: "Alienation: College Students," which gives some reasons for the establishment of communes that you would never learn if you hadn't consulted the index volume.

Dictionaries

Like encyclopedias, dictionaries can be general or specific. *Americana* is a general encyclopedia; *Webster's* unabridged is a general dictionary. The *Interna-*

tional Encyclopedia of Psychiatry, Psychology, Psychoanalysis and Neurology is an example of one of the many specific subject encyclopedias. There are also many specific subject dictionaries and a number of them are in the social sciences. Check around in the HM 17 section of the reference area (if the library uses Library of Congress classification; otherwise ask your librarian where the social science dictionaries are.)

Books

Having introduced yourself to some basic information on communes by consulting the indexes of encyclopedias and dictionaries, general and specific, you may now be ready to pursue your topic in books. The library's key to books is its catalog, and in order to know what subject to pursue in that catalog, you should first check the list of authorized terms, which will provide you with the language you need.

In the case of most academic libraries, that subject list will be the *Library of Congress Subject Headings,* in big orange/red volumes. Check your subject— communal living in the United States—and you'll find a reference: "Communal settlements See Collective settlements." That means that the legal term you want is "Collective settlements," not *Commune* or *Communes.* It also means that you should go back to "Collective settlements." There you'll find listed a lot of "sa" references. Since "sa" means "see also," you now have lots of additional legal terms to pursue, "Collective farms, Harmonists, and Religious communities" among them. *Legal* simply means "official."

Now that you have the authorized terms, you're ready to go to the card catalog. In some libraries you'll find the card catalog in the older, familiar format: on cards. In other libraries the card catalog appears in a different format, such as in a computer print-out or in microform. No matter. They all have the identical function of identifying books by author, title, and subject. You have your subjects.

Here are two books you're likely to find:

COLLECTIVE SETTLEMENTS—UNITED STATES

HX
654   Fairfield, Richard, 1937–
.F35   **Communes USA**

COLLECTIVE SETTLEMENTS—UNITED STATES

HX
653   Houriet, Robert
.H67   **Getting back together.**

Two books on the subject "Collective Settlements—United States," one entitled *Communes USA* and the other *Getting Back Together,* each with call numbers, or identifying numbers, that begin with HX, are owned by your library. If you had not consulted the authority list and had merely looked under "Communes," you may not have found both these books, only the one that happens to have "Communes" as the first word in its title. Find a chart or sign that tells you where the HX's are in your library. When you get to the HX section, look around for the subsection of books that have 653 and 654 as the next part of their call number (see the second line of the call numbers of our example books). When you find this section, look around at other books with the same numbers, as these may also relate to your topic. Check their titles, tables of contents, and indexes to determine this.

Bibliographies

Bibliographies are excellent sources because they offer lists of related books, magazine articles, reports, and other materials on individual topics. We continue our search by checking *Bibliographic Index (BI)* which is an annual compilation of bibliographies on many subjects. It's up to date, extensive, and easily accessible, and it's usually located in the reference stacks or tables in the reference area. *BI* is arranged by general subject headings.

Select the 1979 volume of *BI* and look under the heading "Communes" on page 112; you don't find "Communes," but you do find "Communal settlements," and you are referred to another heading, "Collective settlements." This is a cross reference for you to follow.

COMMUNAL settlements. See Collective settlements.

Turning to page 109 and looking under "Collective settlements" as directed, you find seven potential useful listings, one of which is:

Miriampolski, H. Communes and utopias past and present; a bibliog. of post 1945 studies. Bull Bibliog 36:119–27 + J1 '79

Let's follow up on this title.

H. Miriampolski's *Communes and Utopias, Past and Present: A Bibliography of Post-1945 Studies* looks like a comprehensive and timely list. While the author's name and the title of a work are fairly easily understood, the rest of the citation may not make much sense to a beginner. For example, what is a "Bull Bibliog" and what do all of those numbers mean?

You'll find out in the "Prefatory Note" on an unnumbered page at the very front of the *BI* volume in hand.

SAMPLE ENTRY:	Muir, John, 1838–1914
Periodical Articles	Lynch, A. T. Bibliography of works by and about John Muir, 1869–1978. Bull Bibliog 36:71–80+ Ap '79
Explanations	A bibliography of works by and about John Muir entitled "Bibliography of works by and about John Muir,

> 1869–1978," by A. T. Lynch, will be found in the periodical *Bulletin of Bibliography,* volume 36 pages 71–80 (continued on later pages of the same issue), the April 1979 issue.

So your Miriampolski item is in the *Bulletin of Bibliography* (an abbreviation list can also be found in *BI* prefatory pages), volume 36, pages 119–27 and continued, in the July 1979 issue.

To determine whether your library subscribes to the *Bulletin of Bibliography,* you consult the library's magazine holdings list. Ask the librarian where this list is and how to use it. You might find an entry in the magazine list like this:

Bulletin of Bibliography
v.36-
1979-
Call Number: Reference Z 1007 .B94

That means your library subscribes to the *Bulletin,* has it from volume 36- and 1979- on, and shelves it in the Reference Z collection. Find the Z section in the reference area, select volume 36, turn to the July 1979 issue,.and check page 119 for the start of Miriampolski's text. What you now have found is a list of sources on your topic. Some will be books and some will be magazine articles. The card catalog will tell whether the library owns the books, and the magazine list will tell whether the library owns the referred-to periodicals or magazines.

Indexes

Indexes are the primary means for finding magazine or periodical articles about a topic, and magazines offer timelier, briefer, more narrowly focused, and more specific-event related information than books. So, while the card catalog helps you locate information in books, indexes help you locate contemporary individual articles within whole issues and volumes of periodicals.

Many libraries place indexes on tables that are centrally located in the main reference area. When you look through indexes for periodical articles, it is helpful and important to remember the steps you took in searching *BI.* Here are some reminders:

- *Subject headings.* Have several in mind, check all of them consistently, and look for new ones as you search each source. Make a list. Include common-sense, everyday language terms. Consult the Library of Congress list. Add new headings as encountered. Always carry this list with you. Remember, some sources use headings that other sources don't include. Occasionally, an index will switch over the years from one heading to another heading. Always be alert for new headings and variations.

- *Sample entry or explanatory key*. This tells you what information is contained in each entry, thus eliminating guesswork.
- *List of abbreviated terms and symbols*. Those funny little letter combinations do mean something. Check for an explanation in the front of the index.
- *List of abbreviated periodicals*. You have to know the full title of a periodical before you can find it in the library. Check the key to abbreviations, usually found in the front of the index.
- *Microfiche reading machines and fiche cards*. Here you find out if your library has the issues of the periodicals you need and the call numbers assigned to these sources.
- *Location signs*. These tell where those call numbers you've listed can be located within your library.

With practice and experience, following this routine checklist will make searching magazine and periodical indexes faster and easier.

The *Readers' Guide to Periodical Literature (RG)* is a good basic subject index to popular (as distinguished from scholarly) periodicals. Let's see what it offers on our topic. If you select the March 1974–February 1975 volume of *RG* and look under the heading "Communes" on page 259, you are referred to "Collective settlements."

COMMUNAL living. See Collective settlements.
COMMUNAL settlements. See Collective settlements.
COMMUNES. See Collective settlements.

Turning to page 248 and looking under "Collective settlements" as directed, you find fourteen potentially useful listings in ten different periodical sources. Here's one:

COLLECTIVE settlements
Barn-building, fence-mending, goat-raising, well-digging women; Country women collective in Mendocino County, Calif. J. Westin, il Ms 3:22 Ag '74

Using a procedure similar to the one you followed in *BI*, you note that the title of the article on communes is "Barn-building, fence-mending . . . in Mendocino County, California," by J. Westin. It is illustrated (il) and appears in *Ms*, volume 3, page 22 of the August 1974 issue.

Check the magazine list to see if your library subscribes to *Ms*. You may find an entry in the serials list like this:

Ms.
vol. 1-
July 1972-
Call Number: HQ 1101 .M741
Current volume displayed on main floor

Now check the HQ stacks to find your issue. Issues for 1972 will probably be bound in yearly volumes and shelved in the stacks. Current issues, however, are likely to be displayed elsewhere. Find out where.

Social Sciences Index (SSI) is a different kind of index, but only in that it covers different types of periodicals or magazines—the more scholarly ones in the social sciences. Otherwise, it follows a format almost identical to the *Readers' Guide* arrangement.

You are now basically acquainted with searching periodical and magazine materials, so use our same checklist formula to explore the *Social Sciences Index*. Selecting the April 1980–March 1981 volume of *SSI*, begin the search. Looking for "Communes" on page 188 yields foreign headings and a referral to "Collective settlements."

COMMUNAL SETTLEMENTS. See Collective settlements.

COMMUNE DE PARIS, 1871. See Paris, France—History—Commune, 1871.

COMMUNES (OPSTINA). See Administrative and political divisions—Yugoslavia.

But "Collective settlements" on page 181 offers only five listings under the subheading of "Israel" and no articles relating to the United States. Look for yourself.

COLLECTIVE SETTLEMENTS
See also
Collective farms
Experimental communities
Israel

Note that you are told to "See also" the headings "Collective farms" and "Experimental communities." Turn to page 336 and you find three entries in *Futurist* magazine under the latter heading.

EXPERIMENTAL COMMUNITIES

Prototype communities of tomorrow; Arcosanti, J.C. Glenn, il Futurist 14:35-Je '80.

Prototype communities of tomorrow; Auroville, J.C. Glenn, il Futurist 14:35-9+ 0 '80

Prototype communities of tomorrow; Findhorn, J.C. Glenn, il Futurist 14:44-51 Ag '80

To see if your library subscribes to *Futurist*, check the magazine list.

Now you are ready to search two very helpful *abstracting* services: *Sociological Abstracts (SA)* and *Psychological Abstracts (PA)*.

For *Sociological Abstracts* get the index, volume 25, for 1977 and turn to page 1619. There in column 2 you'll find "Commune -s, -al, -alism, -ality." This means that the following fifteen titles listed all have the words *commune, communes, communal, communalism,* or *communality* in them. Each title is followed by a number such as 77S06859, the one after the second entry: "Communal groups." You'll find that number on page 615 of the 1977 *SA*. Use the numbers on the back (spine) of *SA* as guides to which volume has which article number. Note that you have located a citation to the paper by Hall, which your library may have and which is also available from *SA* for $1.50, *and* that you have located an abstract of that article. Prefatory explanations available in *SA* will explain entries.

If you decide you'd like to see the larger article from which the abstract you just found has been taken, follow a procedure similar to the one you used with indexes. To find a book, check the catalog. To find a periodical or magazine article, check the magazine holdings list. From the catalog or list you'll get call numbers for books or magazines owned by the library. Your next step is to find your books and magazines in the stacks. If you have any questions about how to locate a needed item, *always* ask for help.

Now check page 290 of the July–December subject index to volume 60 of *Psychological Abstracts (PA)* to discover what *PA* offers on your topic. In column 1 you'll see "Communes" and three citations. That third entry looks promising because it refers to viability and failure of U.S. communes and cites #859. Again, using the spines of volume 60 to guide you, you'll find #859 on page 104 of the July–September 1978 *PA*. Your article, by Shey, appears in *Journal of Marriage and the Family,* volume 39, number 3, pages 605–613, August 1977. You know how to determine whether your library gets that journal, so do so. That is, check the serials list and get the call number for *Journal of Marriage and the Family.* Note that the specific indexes and abstracts you've checked all have runs (a "run" indicates that the indexes or abstracts consist of *many volumes*), so always go through the entire set of volumes, or at least through those years that are suitable to your investigation. Sometimes there are cumulative indexes that cover many years, so you won't always have to check year by year.

After you've checked all the relevant encyclopedias, books, indexes, and abstracts known to you, remember that there may be other sources that would be helpful. So ask for help. When you do, you'll find that the librarians appreciate your being able to tell them what you've checked so far. So it's important to check the Library of Congress subject list and to have ready the names of the indexes and abstracts you've checked, along with their inclusive dates. They'll ask if you've checked the card catalog and the *Readers' Guide,* for example.

Computerized information retrieval

One way we've devised to deal with the information explosion is to computerize information retrieval. The very same indexes and abstracts you search manually are contained in large computer data bases, which can be searched electronically. For example, you can search *Sociological Abstracts, America: History and Life,* and *Psychological Abstracts* through a data base.

The computerized search process can be simple. You and a librarian survey the language or terms (usually in a printed thesaurus) used by each source, select the most useful key words, and make a list of these. The librarian then enters appropriate terms through the computer, which responds by citing or listing articles/reports containing the key words.

If the citations are not what you want, you adjust strategy and terminology until more relevant articles appear. You can even get abstracts (or summaries) of the citations printed either on-line (during the search) or off-line (at the computer site and shipped to you within a week). The librarian will advise you about the cheapest and swiftest alternatives. Some searches are more expensive than others.

The major differences between manual and computer searching are time and money. But often time *is* money, and vice versa. Some people feel the quality of information obtained in both searching procedures is the same. So, by having an on-line computer search made you're simply saving time; the computer gets the same or similar citations in a matter of minutes that you would need days or weeks to locate when searching manually. An important question, though, may be whether or not your pocketbook can afford that service on a given assignment.

Put your librarian to work

Librarians, part 6 in your Information Sources model, earn their living by knowing about information, all kinds of it, and putting you in contact with it. Librarians can show you lots of current information and new developments in a variety of areas that are useful in a search about communes, your sample topic. For example, a librarian can point out: (1) the wide differences in viewpoints about communes; (2) alternative information sources; (3) relevant sources in other media formats (such as films, tapes, slides); (4) community activities; (5) unpublished studies; (6) ongoing research; (7) local and national experts; (8) other students studying similar topics; (9) new magazines that aren't indexed in standard sources; (10) other libraries housing hard-to-find materials; (11) utopian fiction; (12) local or regional newspaper articles; (13) new communal trends (such as the "friends as family" surge in big cities); (14) groups like the Briarpatch Community, a national communal business network. Is there any other single source where you can find such a diversity (and gold mine) of data? Probably not. Put your librarian to work for you.

Other things to know

At the beginning of this chapter, Joe and I told you that this was not *the* definitive list of sources. We haven't attempted to tell you everything, and we haven't set out to lecture you or make librarians of you. If you learn to use libraries well, you'll have a better time of it with your assignments. Your work will improve because you'll be able to accumulate and use more materials quickly and intelligently.

Eventually you'll need to use micro materials, newspapers, maps, directories, government documents, pamphlets, films, tapes, and other library materials. Each kind of source is likely to be housed in a special place. Government publications, for example, are usually kept in documents departments, and the documents librarian will help you with the indexes that identify needed sources for those.

Joe and I hope this exercise helps give you confidence in retrieving needed information from your college or university library. We know it will if you give it a shot. We also know that learning to use the library is an essential survival skill.

Suggested activity

Skill at retrieving information is an intermediate kind of skill. Some librarians argue that for too long students have been taught these kinds of skills at the expense of higher level ones, like what to do with information after it has been retrieved. Joe and I tend to agree that putting retrieved information into a usable form should be emphasized as much as retrieving it has been over the years. Because of the information explosion and because of improved control mechanisms, the problem facing most of us is how to be precise about what we want and what to do with it once we get it.

Nevertheless, you may wish to search another topic, either because you find "communes" dull or because you'd like to make sure of your retrieval skills. It might not be a bad idea to test one or more of the following topics. All of these can be searched with the model Joe and I have given you, and you may find yourself using different indexes and abstracts, like *Art Index, Nursing Index, Police Science Abstracts,* or *Chemical Abstracts.* That may be good practice. Ideally, you'll soon put the model to work with a *real* assignment; it works best when you really need it.

Here are some practice topics:

adoption	cybernetics
capital punishment	drug abuse

electronic data processing	pop art
future	property taxes
Montessori method	recidivism
New York City	stress management
nuclear energy	symbiosis
Oriental philosophy	Woodrow Wilson

Suggested readings

Your reference librarian will be glad to give you some pamphlets that show how the library is organized. Read a general guide like this. If you really want a grasp of the problem and opportunity the information explosion has created, read selectively in these three books:

Morse, Grant W. *Concise Guide to Library Research*. New York: Fleet Academic Editions, 1975.

Naisbitt, John. *Megatrends: Ten New Directions Transforming Our Lives*. New York: Warner Books, 1982.

Toffler, Alvin. *The Third Wave*. New York: Bantam Books, 1981.

Study Skills: Planning and Preparing

Jim Burns, *Director, Academic Support Center*
College of Applied Professional Sciences
University of South Carolina

When I arrived at Shaw University in Raleigh, North Carolina, I knew that I was ready for college. I had done very well in high school. My careless study habits had somehow worked for me there, so why shouldn't those same study habits work for me in college? My very first class was a mathematics course at 7:30 A.M.! I couldn't understand why the human body had to be subjected to such torture so early in the morning. I studied infrequently and failed the very first test. I was crushed because I had never failed anything in my life, and my roommate had made an A. That experience taught me that I didn't have the kind of study habits that would make me a successful college student. I saw that, instead of putting my clothes on top of my pajamas, going to that 7:30 class, and going back to bed afterward, I needed some kind of time management. The painful experience of failure made me see that college success and good study habits are synonymous.

As director of a developmental reading and writing skills center, I try to impress upon students the importance of developing good study skills, reading skills, and writing skills. No matter what profession you choose, time management, reading, and writing are three skills that will serve you well.

In this chapter, I want to introduce to you some of those skills that worked for me when I was in college—and are working for my

61

students today. Build a solid foundation by planning, preparing, and performing. Your efforts will be worth it!

Getting started in college is an entirely new situation for you, and sometimes adjusting to new physical surroundings and new emotional and academic responsibilities isn't easy. With your new situation come new freedoms and responsibilities. How you handle them will determine how well you do in college. Which choices will *you* make?

1. Will you prepare a time management schedule, or will you study only whenever you feel it's necessary?

2. In reading your class assignments, are you just one very small step *behind* your instructors; or have you read the assigned material before they discuss it?

3. Do you feel that reading any class assignment just once is sufficient, or are you committed to reviewing after you've read for clarity?

4. Is it a waste of your time to have a dictionary handy when you're reading, or do you find that looking up unfamiliar words helps you understand the assignment?

5. Are you a scanner and a skimmer who can never remember what you've read, or do you follow a logical program for reading and retention?

6. Does your mind wander *while* you read? Does your mind wonder *what* you read?

7. Do you underline or take notes when you read?

8. Do you seek to find a *logical* relationship between class lectures and your reading assignments for that class?

9. Do you try to write down every single word spoken in class, or have you learned to distinguish between major and minor points made by your professor?

10. When do you review your class notes? Only at test time, or shortly after you take them as well?

11. What do you do when you find large gaps or incomplete ideas in your notes?

12. What are the important steps in preparing for a test, and do you follow them?

This chapter will help you evaluate these questions. But first, you must learn commitment. Commitment is the key element for study skills success, and it begins with an effective method for managing your time wisely.

Time management

One of the most important decisions you'll have to make in college is how to organize and get the most out of your study time. You're going to have to say no to your friends sometimes, but it's very important that you stick to a schedule. A time management schedule helps you develop a weekly routine that will allow you to be successful both in your college work and in your leisure activities. To find out how beneficial time management can be, review the sample schedules (Figure 5–1 and Figure 5–2) planned by two students for a week's activities.

As you can see, the first student has carefully planned his activities for the week, making use of time before and after classes to review notes, and scheduling specific study activities in the evening. The second student has not been nearly as thorough. Even though he intends to "study," he has not allocated time for specific classes or assignments and may end up with those I-have-to-cram-for-my-finals-blues.

A time management schedule is useless if you don't have good study habits, and the key to good study habits is not how long you plan to study, but the quality of time you spend.

Is your problem just getting started—sitting down at your desk to begin your work? By carefully adhering to your schedule, you'll develop the study habit, and it'll become easier for you to begin your routine. For example, suppose you've allotted Mondays through Fridays from 9 to 11 P.M. as study time. Even if you don't have anything to study on Friday, study something anyway! Review your notes! Read a book! Don't get out of the study habit.

Don't use your valuable study time *getting* prepared. When it's time for you to study, *be* prepared. Have all of your materials (books, notes, typing paper, references, and so on) ready at your allotted time. Next, consider where you're going to study. Do you need absolute quiet when you study? Some students can study with music blasting in a crowded room, while others can tolerate no distractions at all. This is a very important decision that only *you* can make. Choose an area (the library, your dorm room, the student lounge) that makes you feel comfortable, but not so comfortable that you'll take a nap!

Have you considered study partners? Working with others who have made the study commitment can help you. Talk with students in your classes, and maybe you can help each other. Learn to share the art of studying. Work out a mutual schedule, and choose study times that will benefit all of you. Remember to choose your study partners wisely, for chances are you'll become more like them. Group studying *can* work. Besides developing a good atmosphere for studying, studying with partners can help you make new friends.

	MONDAY	TUESDAY	WEDNESDAY	THURSDAY	FRIDAY
8:00					
9:00	PSYCHOLOGY 101	REVIEW SOCIOLOGY NOTES	PSYCHOLOGY 101	REVIEW SOCIOLOGY NOTES	PSYCHOLOGY 101
10:00	STUDY: READING ROOM (RR) PSYCHOLOGY NOTES	SOCIOLOGY 104	STUDY: READING ROOM (RR) PSYCHOLOGY NOTES	SOCIOLOGY 104	STUDY: READING ROOM (RR) PSYCHOLOGY NOTES
11:00	ENGLISH 102		ENGLISH 102		ENGLISH 102
12:00					
1:00	MATH 140	REVIEW HISTORY NOTES	MATH 140	REVIEW HISTORY NOTES	MATH 140
2:00	REVIEW MATH NOTES	HISTORY 114	REVIEW MATH NOTES	HISTORY 114	REVIEW MATH NOTES
3:00	← ————— BAND ——————————→				
4:00	← ———— REHEARSAL ———————→				
5:00			FRATERNITY MEETING ↓		
6:00	OUTLINE PAPER FOR ENGLISH (DUE NEXT WEEK)	WRITE DRAFT FOR ENGLISH PAPER / READ SOCIOLOGY		STUDENT GOVERNMENT MEETING	
7:00	↓			↓	
8:00	↓	↓		PROOFREAD DRAFT FOR ENGLISH PAPER	

Figure 5–1   First Student's Schedule

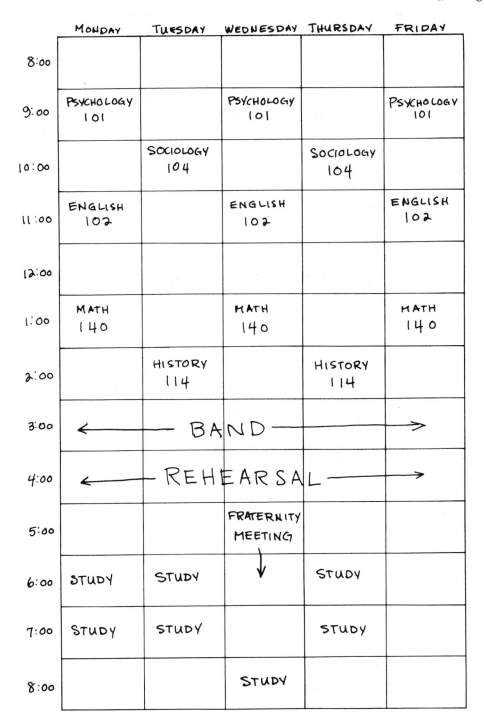

	MONDAY	TUESDAY	WEDNESDAY	THURSDAY	FRIDAY
8:00					
9:00	PSYCHOLOGY 101		PSYCHOLOGY 101		PSYCHOLOGY 101
10:00		SOCIOLOGY 104		SOCIOLOGY 104	
11:00	ENGLISH 102		ENGLISH 102		ENGLISH 102
12:00					
1:00	MATH 140		MATH 140		MATH 140
2:00		HISTORY 114		HISTORY 114	
3:00	← BAND →				
4:00	← REHEARSAL →				
5:00			FRATERNITY MEETING		
6:00	STUDY	STUDY	↓	STUDY	
7:00	STUDY	STUDY		STUDY	
8:00			STUDY		

Figure 5–2   Second Student's Schedule

Reading textbooks

The next stop in the process of gaining the study habit is learning how to get the most out of what you read. Your teacher cares what you get out of your reading assignments, but the chief reason you read is for *you* to learn something about yourself and the world in which you live. Remember that books, especially your textbooks, are a permanent record of your college experiences. Even more important, reading provides you with information that makes you a more intelligent and interesting person, one who is better equipped to make the most of opportunities.

So first, develop a positive attitude about reading. Remember that reading introduces you to new experiences. If you want to be informed, read. If you want to develop skills as a conversationalist, read. Reading encompasses all of the communications skills you'll need to meet your career goals. Television, movies, and music are all excellent forms of communication, but you're only a passive listener. Reading makes you an active participant in the world of communication. To read is to think. If you believe you can get something out of what you read, then you will. Reading raises your level of understanding and expands your capacities to retain information.

Pay close attention to the following tips. They were designed to help you get the most out of what you read.

1. First, *preread* your assignment. Skim the chapter to find out generally what you are going to learn. If the chapter has a summary and/or study questions at the end, read them first so that you'll know what to look for in that particular assignment. You'll find that this procedure will shorten the time it takes to read and understand the material. After you have skimmed the chapter, make note of any questions that come up so you can look for the answer when you read.

2. Then, *read* the assignment. As you read, make notes on a separate sheet of paper, or in the margins, of elements in the chapter that seem important to you and that you want to remember for class. Make sure you're familiar with the information called for in the study questions at the end of the assignment.

3. Finally, *reread*. When you've finished reading, look back over your notes and any questions you wrote down to be certain they've been answered. Now skim the chapter again, rereading the marked portions. Be sure you see how all the ideas relate to each other.

It's always a good idea to review your assignment just before class. This is especially useful if you've read the chapter several days in advance. You'll be surprised at how great it feels to be able to intelligently discuss the day's lesson when you get to class.

Taking notes

The next step toward perfecting the study habit is maintaining good notes for your classes. Your classes are going to be different than they were in high school. In high school, you probably had the benefit of small classes and readily available teachers. Now you may be in a college lecture hall with 200 other students, sharing your sociology instructor with all of them. This means that you'll need to shoulder even more responsibility when it comes to taking class notes.

The key element for note taking is organization. Keep a separate notebook or separate divisions in a large notebook for each course. Follow these tips for developing and maintaining good note-taking skills:

1. It's impossible to write down everything that's mentioned in class, but write as much as you can, especially information that is (a) repeated, (b) preceded by a word like *important,* or (c) written on the chalkboard. Don't worry about neatness. Your notes are for *your* benefit. You may even want to develop your own abbreviated writing or shorthand.

2. Listen carefully at the beginning of the class for the teacher's outline of the day's discussion. Then try to jot down your notes in outline form so that you can see how the information given is related in meaning and in importance.

3. If the teacher takes the time to emphasize certain information, make sure *you* emphasize that information in your notes. Ideas that are emphasized and/or repeated are more than likely to appear on an examination. It is important for you to match class notes with the information in your textbooks. Work out a system. Use your imagination.

4. After class, don't allow your notes to get too "cold" before you review them, especially if you write poorly. As soon as possible, look over your notes while the material is still fresh in your mind.

5. If you find that recopying your notes helps you to remember, do it.

6. After reviewing your notes, you may find that you missed something. Check your notes with your teacher or a reliable classmate.

Taking tests

The last step in the study habit is learning how to take tests. Tests are a very important evaluation of your work in a course. Often it is the tests alone that will determine what your final grade will be. Review the following steps in preparing for a test:

1. *Study your notes.* Even if you think you know the material, spend some time going over it again.
2. *Discuss class notes and lectures with members of the class.* You may even want to prepare practice test questions with your classmates. (Remember my suggestion about study partners?)
3. *Don't spend the entire night before an examination cramming.* Go to bed early so that you'll feel refreshed the next morning.
4. *You may even want to get to class a little early* so you can relax and get comfortable. Taking deep breaths helps you relieve the anxiety of taking an examination. (See Chapter 13 on anxiety management.)
5. *Bring all of the necessary materials to the test.* Last minute preparation, even sharpening your pencils, may heighten the anxiety of taking an examination.

You've studied. Now you're ready for your test. The professor will usually announce beforehand what kind of test you'll be taking. Many professors give objective tests, which may include true-false, multiple-choice, completion, or matching questions; others give essay examination questions. Here are examples of these types of tests:

True-False
_____ 1. Shakespeare is the author of *Romeo and Juliet.*

Multiple-Choice
_____ 1. As conceived by Freud, the total personality consists of all but
　　　　a. ego
　　　　b. impetus
　　　　c. superego
　　　　d. id

Completion
1. Sociology is the study of _____.

Matching
1. noun_____　　　　　　a. modifies a noun or pronoun
2. verb_____　　　　　　b. names
3. adjective_____　　　　c. joining word
4. conjunction_____　　　d. expresses action or a state of being

Essay Examination
1. Analyze Martin Luther King's vision in "I Have a Dream."

True-false

When preparing for true-false questions, always look for key words because one word can change the meaning of a sentence. Look for words like *some, all,* and *always*. You have a 50–50 chance of choosing the correct answer. Don't let a statement that *seems* to be true confuse what you *know*. If you've studied well, you'll be able to answer true-false questions. Unless a penalty is announced for guessing, *answer every item.*

Multiple-choice

Multiple-choice tests ask you to select the best answer from three or more possibilities. Always remember to read the directions carefully. Read the question and read *all* the choices. If a multiple-choice question contains three to five possible answers, you can usually eliminate one or two right away. Then select from the remaining choices. Don't go for the first correct answer you see. Sometimes professors will ask you to select the *best* answer from a list that may include other correct answers.

Completion

Sometimes you may be asked to take completion examinations, which require you to fill in the blanks. Usually one or two words will complete the blank left in a sentence. You can sometimes find hints in the words that are given. For example, sometimes the words provided will let you know whether or not the answer is singular or plural.

Matching

With matching questions, be sure to read *both* columns first. Then read the left column and find the answer in the right column. To make your next selections quicker, cross out the correct answers as you go along.

Essay examinations

Essay examination questions call for both writing ability and good, clear organization. The key to a successful essay examination response is planning and writing. Use the following tips as an outline for writing a good essay examination response:

1. *Read over the entire examination first.* When you have read the directions and the examination, decide how much time you have for each response.

Remember to budget your time! If a choice of questions is given, eliminate the question(s) that you know the least about. Always save some time to proofread your response.

2. *Analyze the question.* In an essay examination, the verb is usually the most significant word in the question. Verbs like *summarize, analyze, compare, contrast, define,* and *evaluate* provide the key to your response.

3. *You're ready to write.* If your teacher allows you to answer the questions in any order, begin with the question(s) you know best. This strategy will increase your confidence.

4. *Write a brief, informal outline of your response.* Don't waste too much time outlining. Jot down the main points that will help you write a well-organized response.

5. *Never take for granted that your teacher will fill in any holes in your response.* Your teacher will grade you for what you say, not for what she or he *thinks* you're saying. Assume you're the expert and you're writing to inform your instructor who knows nothing about the subject.

6. *Proofread carefully.* Make sure your response sticks to the main idea, explores the idea concretely, and shows how your sentences are tied to each other and to the main idea.

7. *Use standard English.* Check for spelling, punctuation, subject–verb agreement, and sentence fragments. For example, an incomplete sentence is an incomplete idea.

Conclusion

It's important that you acquire a study system that works for you. Remember to:

1. *Budget your time.* A time management schedule will help you. Why not make a time management schedule *now?*

2. *Get the most out of your studying.* Find a study area that suits you. If it's helpful for you, get a reliable study partner.

3. *Get the most out of your textbooks* by prereading, reading, and re-reading.

4. *Develop note-taking skills* that will help you get the most out of class lectures and reading assignments.

5. *Know the kinds of tests you may take.* Be prepared for anything!

Now look back at those questions at the beginning of this chapter. *Now* is the time for you to make the right choices if you're genuinely interested in getting the most out of your college experience. I know you can do it! One additional word of advice: ask your instructors, advisors, or academic skills center about the many books on the subject of study skills. If you feel you need further help, use one of these books and see if their recommendations help.

Suggested readings

Elbow, Peter. *Writing Without Teachers*. New York: Oxford University Press, 1973.

Elbow, Peter. *Writing with Power*. New York, Oxford University Press, 1981.

Gilbert, Helen W. *Pathways: A Guide to Reading and Study Skills*. Boston: Houghton Mifflin, 1982.

Joffe, Irwin. *Opportunity for Skillful Reading, 4th ed*. Belmont: Wadsworth, 1977.

Kagan, Corin E. *Coping with College: The Efficient Reader*. New York: McGraw-Hill, 1982.

McWhorter, Kathleen T. *College Reading and Study Skills*. Boston: Little, Brown and Company, 1980.

Pauk, Walter. *How to Study in College*. Boston: Houghton Mifflin, 1974.

Sotiriou, Peter Elias. *Integrating College Study Skills: Reasoning in Reading, Listening, and Writing*. Belmont: Wadsworth, 1984.

Spargo, Edward. *The Now Student: Reading and Study Skills*. Providence, R.I.: Jamestown Publishers, 1977.

Walter, Tim, and Siebert, Al. *Student Success: How to Do Better in College and Still Have Time for Your Friends*. New York: Holt, Rinehart and Winston, 1981.

A WORD OR TWO ABOUT WRITING

Editor's note: I doubt if anyone has ever determined whether reading or writing is the more important study skill, but as someone who has made his living as a writer, I know that people who have trouble setting their thoughts down on paper are likely to be the same ones who have not read extensively.

So my first suggestion to you on writing is, *read!* Read magazines and newspapers. Read fiction and nonfiction. Stay away from the trash. (If you can't tell the trash from the good stuff, ask a fellow student or one of your professors.) The other thing I want to share with you about writing is that you must always remember that writing is not only (a) the means by which we record those transient thoughts drifting about in our heads, but can also be (b) a means to create new ideas.

Peter Elbow, in his two books, *Writing Without Teachers* and *Writing With Power,* uses a number of exercises designed to reduce the causes of writer's block (also known as "blank paper anxiety") and help individuals learn to enjoy the process of writing. Let me share just a few of these with you, and ask that you practice them, either individually or in your class.

Specialists in writing at the Bard College Institute for Writing and Thinking have determined that most college freshmen lack the feeling that they have anything important to say. Therefore, when they're asked to write an essay based on their own experiences, the results are grammatical, predictable, and dull. To overcome this attitude, students must rethink the writing process. For example:

1. Students must respect the rules of grammar, spelling, and syntax, but *not* when generating their early drafts of a paper.
2. Students can help each other improve their writing by listening to one another's words, and thereby help the writer understand what he or she is communicating.
3. Students need to temporarily clear their heads of all the traditional rules, and simply write.

Are you ready?

First, try some *freewriting*. The rules are simple. Just begin writing about whatever strikes you. Don't worry about spelling, grammar, or anything. No one will see this writing except you. If you can't think of anything to write, don't stop and stare at the ceiling. Simply write, "I can't think of anything to write," until your thoughts return. Write for about ten minutes. Discuss this experience with others.

Next, choose a topic and try some *focused freewriting* on that topic. A topic that might help you in your writing: "What I do that makes it difficult for me to write."

If you're writing this in class, it might be helpful to have everyone in the room read his or her paper to the others. Hearing what others have to say about a topic helps you crystallize your own ideas on that topic. Responding in a positive way to what others have said ("I have that same problem, too;" "I solve that problem in this manner;" "Could you explain that a little more? I didn't quite understand what you meant") also helps the writer rethink his or her piece.

The next step, after hearing the comments of others and reviewing your writing, is to write a second draft of the piece. Your final draft, of course, should also correct those errors in spelling, grammar, and syntax. But Elbow and his group suggest that such correcting should constitute the final refinements in what is essentially a series of thought processes.

Try these simple exercises the next time you have a writing assignment. I think they'll help you gain confidence in your writing. For more ideas on writing, consult either of the books by Elbow.

JERRY JEWLER

6

How Rational Thinking Affects Student Success

Foster E. Tait, *Associate Professor of Philosophy*
University of South Carolina

I wasn't born rational and neither were you. Being rational means being able to reason correctly. I became interested in correct reasoning when, as an undergraduate, I took several courses in logic and philosophy and discovered just what a poor reasoner I was. I saw that I'd been guilty of a number of fallacies in my thinking and in papers I'd written. Even my valedictory address to my high school seemed riddled with thoughts that didn't properly support one another.

In graduate school I majored in philosophy and took additional courses in logic. The more I studied these subjects, the more aware I became of the problems I had in reasoning. It was then that I started applying the rules of logical reasoning to all my work. After receiving my doctorate, I left New England to teach at the University of South Carolina. There I found students who couldn't write any more coherently than could I as an undergraduate—and I began to emphasize the fact that we all need structure in our writing as well as in our general approach to life. I taught concepts of logic even in courses not specifically designated as logic courses. I emphasized correct reasoning as a means of establishing continuity in one's thoughts. All of this has helped me considerably in that I now have students who write better papers and can state a thesis and defend it. I'm still learning as well and hope to improve the logical consistency of my own writing and reasoning.

What follows is a guide to avoiding commonly found errors in reasoning. Writing a proper paper, discussing ideas in class, and not just surviving, but flourishing, at a college or university, require that you understand the difference between correct and incorrect reasoning. Thinking, as well as writing good term papers, requires that you make the proper connections between your thoughts. You can do this only by following the rules of valid thinking and avoiding the use of common fallacies.

The need for correct reasoning

Successful students generally become successful and productive people in society. This isn't surprising, since the habits and talents of successful students are similar to those required in business and professional life. If you can't understand what you read—or remember what you've read or heard—you're not likely to succeed at any very demanding kind of life. The same is true of minimal mathematical skills and a knowledge of the basic principles of grammar—you can't succeed without them.

Conditions like these are necessary for success in school and in society, but they're not all you need. Most teachers know students who can write crisp, nicely formed sentences and who can do mathematics and can read well, but who still can't write a logical paper or answer essay questions properly.

What's the problem? In many cases, the students can't relate one idea to another, or put ideas together to form a central theme, or thesis. In other words, they haven't learned the basic rules of reasoning—the rules that enable you to connect your thoughts in a logical fashion. The words may be appropriate and the grammar perfect, but what emerges is a lot of independent thoughts or sentences, not a cohesively written report, quiz answer, essay, or term paper.

Connecting your thoughts properly is more an art to be learned than an inherited characteristic. While the ancient Greeks defined human beings as "rational animals," they didn't believe people were rational from birth, only that they had the ability to reason correctly.

What is correct reasoning? The answer isn't easy. We'll begin our discussion by looking at some examples of correct and incorrect reasoning. Next we'll discuss the value of having a thesis upon which to base your comments, the importance of correct methods of argumentation, and how you learn or fail to learn through arguments. Finally, we'll examine how you can recognize and use correct reasoning so that your term papers, essays, quiz answers, and classroom participation improve—and your grades go up!

Reasoning: correct and incorrect

Most famous scientists and mathematicians probably made lucky guesses at one time or another about the truths they're credited with discovering. But the reason for their fame is that they were able to *prove* their discoveries to others. You may experience an important insight, but unless you can prove to others that it's new as well as valid, not many people are going to accept it. Insights, no matter how profound they may be to those who experience them, must be backed up by evidence. Basic college geometry, for example, is modeled on that developed twenty-three centuries ago by Euclid. He defined his terms carefully and proposed statements that were readily acceptable to the scientific community of his day. Based on these statements, Euclid was able to arrive at some very useful conclusions. Every carpenter and mechanic today recognizes that the sum of the angles of a triangle must equal two right angles and must total 180 degrees. The applied science of surveying is based in great measure on such truths.

The astronomer Edmund Halley, for whom a comet was named, observed his comet in 1682 and recorded data concerning its motion through our solar system. Based on this data, Halley concluded, in a work published in 1705, that the comet would return at approximately 75-year intervals. Indeed, Halley was able to infer from his own observations, together with the work on gravitation published by the physicist-philosopher Isaac Newton, that the comet would return sometime in December 1758. Halley died in 1743, but fifteen years later, on Christmas Day 1758, the comet appeared. What a success, and what a triumph for reason! Halley's observations, coupled with Newton's theory, taken as axioms and postulates, allowed him to calculate a prediction accurate to one month in seventy-six years. Thus, the motion of comets, which had previously been considered erratic and even mysterious, was resolved to a system of laws that could predict their behavior.

The logic of correct writing: the thesis

The examples in the preceding section have several things in common. First, they state a thesis, which is something to be proved (you've probably already heard your English teacher refer to "the thesis statement"). In Euclid's case, the thesis was actually a large number of statements, known in mathematics as theorems, which he was able to prove. In Halley's case, the thesis was the prediction that the comet would return at a specified time.

A *thesis,* then, refers to something you want to prove. In any paper, the thesis is the central point—it represents what must be proved within the context of the paper. A paper without a thesis would be like a geometry with no theorems, or a work on astronomy that maintained only that a certain comet might or might not return. Such a paper would be useless. Science requires more of its practitioners, and so do teachers in any subject you can name. *A paper of any merit always states a thesis.* The thesis is always expressed as a statement, and it must be proved by correct, logical reasoning.

When you present a thesis and then give reasons why it should be accepted, you almost always ensure that your sentences and paragraphs, indeed your entire paper, will progress logically. To many college professors, the most poorly reasoned papers they receive are those where nothing is being argued and a simple comparison is made. If you do make comparisons between two authors, you should do so within the context of a thesis that states what you are comparing and why that point is important to an understanding of one or more works of the authors. You should then defend the thesis, which means introducing evidence to support it.

The logic of learning

A thesis may be thought of as a conclusion. Reasoning works through argumentation, and each argument must have a conclusion. The conclusion or thesis is then defended by providing evidence in its favor. The evidence, in the form of basic statements, or premises, must be readily acceptable to your audience. If it's not, you should prove to your audience that the premises are acceptable to experts in the field. This applies to all theses: the main thesis as well as any minor theses (which may serve as premises for the principal thesis) that might exist.

In establishing a thesis, not only should the premises used to support it be considered true, but the steps you take in reasoning from the premises to the thesis must be correct. At this point, the science (or art) of logic enters the picture, because this discipline, which stems largely from the Greek philosopher Aristotle, is concerned primarily with connecting evidence (premises) to conclusions (theses).

Aristotle presented rules for inferring conclusions from premises. When used correctly, these rules will lead you from true premises to true conclusions—not to false conclusions. Euclid and other mathematicians have used such rules for centuries. Halley, Newton, and all other recognized scientists have used some version of these rules. Indeed, calculus, which holds needless terrors for many of you, is basically an application to mathematics and science of logic and its rules.

Learning through arguments

As you must now realize, what we call an "argument" is a process of reasoning that takes us from premises to a conclusion. An argument in this sense is certainly not an emotional "happening," where somebody gets bruised or bloodied. Newton, Euclid, Halley, Einstein, and other famous thinkers were known for their powers of reasoning, not for their physical prowess.

So what is an argument? An argument is one or more premises, and at least one conclusion. As arguments are communicated from one person to another, they exemplify the use of reason. But not all arguments are good ones. Some are missing the proper connection between premises and conclusions, and others don't support, or lack acceptance for, their premises.

Arguments whose conclusions follow closely from their premises, and whose premises are well established, lead to increased knowledge. If we accept the premises as true, or correct, then logically correct arguments, such as those of Euclid, force us to accept the truth of the conclusions. If we accept the truth of the premises, but don't accept the conclusions, then we commit a contradiction, such as admitting that the sum of the angles of a triangle is equal to two right angles, yet not equal to 180 degrees.

The acceptance of contradictions is known as "being irrational," since we know they're false. It is inconsistent to believe something is true when we know it's false. For many centuries, consistency has been considered the primary condition for being rational. Your teachers will certainly demand consistency in your essays and papers.

Let's look at an example of a correct argument, where the conclusion follows from the premises:

1. Either truth is purely subjective or it is objective in at least some sense.
2. If truth were purely subjective, it could be true that $2 + 2 = 5$, simply because someone believed it.
3. But it is not true that $2 + 2 = 5$. Consequently, it follows that
4. Truth is not purely subjective. Thus we see from these premises, as well as from the fact that
5. We all know that just wishing to make something true, such as wishing that there were actually a Santa Claus, is not enough to make the belief true; that
6. Truth is objective in some sense.

In this example, the statement (6) that truth is objective in some sense is the major conclusion or thesis of the argument. Let's go through the reasoning process in this argument: Sentences (2) and (3) function as premises for (4), which might be termed a preliminary conclusion or a preliminary thesis. Sentence (4), together with sentences (1) and (5), provide evidence for the principal thesis (6).

Note how the use of expressions such as "consequently it follows that" and "thus we see that" help show us that we have an argumentative structure—that a process of reasoning is occurring.

Such expressions, commonly known as "argument indicators," help tie sentences together so we can see a logical progression. The use of such indicators can help assure your reader or listener (or the professor grading your paper!) that you are not just producing a mere collection or jumble of sentences, but that there is some determined meaning behind their arrangement. A long paper, a thesis, or a dissertation should include a number of supporting arguments for the principal conclusion. It will ordinarily also propose arguments against any opposing points of view. Just remember that your arguments have to be clear and logical if they're going to support your views and refute any conflicting views.

Failing to learn through arguments: some common fallacies

We've seen that in defending a thesis (conclusion), we need two things: (1) accurate evidence to serve as our premises, and (2) correct reasoning from our premises to our conclusions. You might not agree completely with the premises, but, given those premises, the conclusions follow.

Most people—including most of you—are a little better at collecting evidence for premises than in using that evidence correctly to establish a conclusion. The reference librarian can help you find the data you'll need to put together premises. Please use this person and her or his valuable skills if you don't know where to find the information you need for a project! (See Chapter 4.)

Unfortunately, libraries aren't equipped with resident Newtons or other logicians who can help you reason from your data to correct conclusions. So it might help you to enroll in one or more logic courses during your first semesters at the university, or at least to have a logician look at your arguments. Most universities have people in the philosophy or mathematics departments who are trained in logic. Look for the names of these people in your catalog and call for an appointment.

Now, let's look at some common ways that people go wrong in reasoning from premises to conclusions. These methods of incorrect reasoning have been recognized for centuries. Using any of them will never help you support your thesis.

Argument directed to the man (argumentum ad hominem)

When you attack other people's positions, make sure it's their arguments you're attacking and not the individuals themselves. When very controversial questions, such as the legalization of abortion, are at issue, and strong emotions are involved, people often get caught up more in their arguments with the character or reputation of their opponent than with the content and meaning of the opponent's argument.

If you're arguing for a woman's right to have an abortion, and you're arguing against someone like Claire Boothe Luce, who has given many talks opposed to abortion on request or on artificial means of birth control, don't say something like, "We all know where Mrs. Luce stands on these issues because she's a Roman Catholic." Such a statement has no bearing on your task of proving her wrong, but it might influence your audience, listeners, or readers, depending on their biases.

Appeal to force (argumentum ad baculum)

The famous seventeenth-century physicist and astronomer, Galileo, adopted the Copernican theory that the earth was not the center of either the solar system or the universe. With the aid of the telescope, which he had developed, Galileo was able to prove some of the views held by Copernicus. Copernican theory, however, contradicted centuries of church teachings, which held that everything revolved around the earth. For this reason, Galileo was condemned for heresy by the Inquisition and threatened with burning at the stake if he didn't change his position. The argument used by the Inquisition was basically: Your ideas are wrong, and you must see that this is the case or we'll condemn you to burn at the stake. Galileo did change his position, but the argument posed against his views was hardly a legitimate one. It appealed to force.

Your parents may have reasoned this way at times; they may have made you admit they were right on some issue by suggesting that unless you did you might not receive your allowance for the month or the car on Saturday night. Students use such arguments against teachers when they threaten to give them a poor evaluation. Teachers use the argument on students when they threaten to fail them for not agreeing with them.

Teachers can also use these techniques more subtly; for example, they might pick on certain students who don't agree with them. And students use this reasoning when they talk, read a newspaper, or work on an assignment for another class while the teacher is trying to lecture. This behavior is intimidating to most teachers because they want to communicate with their students, and they frequently see such behavior as a rebuff. Nothing you do can ensure a teacher's dislike more than practicing this sort of behavior. (See Chapter 3)

Appeal to pity (argumentum ad misericordiam)

"Please, officer, don't give me a ticket because if you do I'll lose my license, and I don't deserve to lose my license because I have five little children to feed and won't be able to feed them if I can't drive my truck."

What is at issue here is whether or not the driver deserves to lose his or her license. None of the driver's statements offer any evidence, in any legal sense, as to why he or she shouldn't be given a ticket. The driver is making an appeal to pity. This isn't the way to reason with your instructors in your papers—and it's not a proper way of reasoning when a question of guilt is involved.

Either you did something or you didn't. If the "something" is a crime, then no matter how unfortunate your position and the circumstances involved, you either committed the crime or you didn't. Once it's been established that a crime was committed, some appeal to pity may be appropriate to lighten the sentence. If you can't finish an assignment on time, be honest and tell your teacher why. If you have problems in your family, state them. But don't say it's not your fault the paper is late because, poor you, this and that has happened. Instructors frequently get together and discover that the same student has had a maternal grandmother die two or three times in the last year. Admit fault, but also explain truthfully the circumstances that prevented completion of your assignment. Be frank and honest. Never, never say, "I don't deserve to be punished for such and such." Always try to communicate your problems to an instructor before an assignment is due. Teachers are usually understanding, and in those rare occasions when they're not, other methods of appeal may be open to you.

Appeal to authority (argumentum ad verecundiam)

This incorrect argument occurs when you hold that your position is correct and you base your claim on the authority of someone who quite possibly isn't an authority on the topic. And even if the person you cite is an authority, most people would rather learn your reasons in support of your claim rather than those of another.

Advertising abounds with *ad verecundiam* reasoning. Sports stars who are not doctors, dieticians, or nutritionists appear before us daily, urging us to eat a certain cereal for breakfast. Glamorous women who aren't mechanics tell us that a certain transmission will help our cars run better. Don't fall for this kind of advertising or this kind of argument. The expertise of most of these people is irrelevant to what you might be concerned with, be it nutrition or a better transmission.

Students frequently fall into the *ad verecundiam* trap by putting great weight on what other students say about teachers or courses, or by consulting a friend about proper answers for a class assignment. The best person to consult about courses is your academic advisor. If you're having problems in a course, the best person to consult is your instructor. Please don't forget that the "stuffy" professor a friend told you not to take might just possibly teach you more than most of your other professors.

Appeal to popularity (argumentum ad populum)

You've never seen a very heavy man model a bathing suit. You've never seen a woman with very heavy or very thin legs model pantyhose. Why not? The answer is easy! People want to associate with the people who tell them to buy things. So advertising looks for the "beautiful people" in a society—those who have looks, financial success, or sports fame. Studies by psychologists on such phenomena as the "halo effect" indicate that people generally listen more to popular people than to others. In other words, we believe more what we're told by successful and attractive people than what we're told by those who aren't so successful or attractive.

One of the worst kinds of reasoning you can follow is to imitate the commercials and base your arguments on a person's popularity. Establish your conclusions on facts, not on beauty, financial success, or political fame. Students frequently choose their classes on the basis of such irrelevant things as a teacher's looks or popularity. Please remember that some teachers need to be popular; they want to be stars. They'll provide lively class sessions, but you may not learn much.

Argument from ignorance (argumentum ad ignorantiam)

A common argument takes the form: "My position is correct because it hasn't been proved incorrect." Go to a bookstore and you'll find dozens of books, usually paperbacks, detailing close encounters with flying saucers, flying cigar-shaped objects, beings from outer space, and so on. Almost all of these books describe the person who has had the "close encounter" as beyond reproach in integrity and sanity. And, the description goes on, although they've had their statements questioned by the military, or by unrelenting reporters and editors, these critics could not disprove the claims of the witnesses. Therefore, the events really occurred. Even in science, few things are ever proved completely false, but evidence can be discredited. Outside the realms of pure mathematics and logic, complete or demonstrative proof for the truth or falsehood of claims is seldom, if ever, possible. If you go to your instructor and argue that your claim is correct because he or she hasn't proven it false, the instructor can turn the tables on you by using the same fallacy. *Ad ignorantiam* arguments work both ways, and both ways are incorrect.

False cause

Frequently, we think that just because one event occurred that was followed by another event, the first event must have caused the second. This reasoning is the basis for many superstitions. The ancient Chinese once believed that by ringing a large gong they could make the sun reappear after an eclipse. They knew nothing about eclipses, but they did know that on one such occasion the sun reappeared after a large gong had been struck. It's not surprising to us today that the sun reappeared, because we realize that eclipses are only temporary. Yet we also commit the same fallacy quite frequently.

You go shopping and an inconsiderate person blows smoke on you in an elevator. You become ill that evening and place the blame on the smoker in the elevator. Yet the blame might be based more properly on the deviled crabs you ate at that charming little restaurant on the dock. It's difficult to establish causal relations, and some scientists maintain it can never be done. A single encounter with something isn't sufficient for assuming a causal relation.

All too often, students tend to put the blame for their failure on a teacher. Yet students often cause their own failure. If you don't read your notes after class, don't ask questions, and don't take notes while you read, chances are you won't do well in a course. Don't blame your failure on your instructor; to do so would be to commit the fallacy of false cause.

Hasty generalization

Statisticians realize that no accurate generalization about the real world can be made on the basis of one or even a few samples. If someone selected one green marble from an urn containing 100 marbles, you wouldn't assume that the next marble would be green. After all, there are still ninety-nine marbles in the urn, and you know virtually nothing about the colors of those marbles. Given fifty draws from the urn, however, each of which produced a green marble after the urn had been shaken thoroughly, you would be much more willing to conclude that the next marble drawn would be green—what seems to be a fairly large series of random samples has produced the same results.

So please, don't jump off in hasty generalizations on your papers. Don't assume that just because one course you took in sociology or biology was boring, all courses in those subjects will be boring. Don't assume that just because you did poorly in one course in a particular subject, you'll do poorly in others. Quite frequently, the least interesting and, in some respects, most difficult course in a subject is the introductory one.

Correct reasoning and how to accomplish it

We've examined examples of correct and incorrect reasoning. What distinguishes them? Correct reasoning won't lead you from correct evidence (premises) to false conclusions. Correct, or valid, reasoning preserves the truth of your premises in the inferences made from them. Incorrect reasoning, as displayed in the fallacies we've just examined, is a haphazard affair that frequently will lead you to infer conclusions that are false and irrelevant to your premises. A thesis can't be defended by the use of fallacious reasoning, and a paper that uses such reasoning can't display the proper amount of logical progression and connection between its ideas. To test your reasoning, ask this of your arguments: If the conclusion inferred from my premises is false, isn't it likely that one or more of my premises is also false? If you're convinced the answer is yes, you probably have a proper argument. If your answer is no, try another argument, for the chances are you've committed a fallacy in your reasoning.

In writing a paper, always state the thesis representing your principal argument as early as possible. Provide evidence for your thesis and relate the evidence to the thesis by means of correct arguments. If there might be any doubt about the evidence for your final conclusion, you must provide arguments to establish the truth of that evidence. Be very sure of the reliability of any source you use for your evidence, thus avoiding the fallacy of *argumentum ad verecundiam*.

Suggested activities

1. Read an article in a journal or a chapter in a book and see if you can determine what its thesis is. Next, examine the evidence provided for these theses. Is the evidence convincing and are the arguments leading from the evidence to the conclusions correct?

2. Select a topic that interests you. Such a topic might deal with busing to achieve racial equality, a woman's right to abortion, or the death penalty. State your thesis (basic position to be defended). Find evidence for your thesis and argue for it from your evidence. Try your arguments on some of your friends and ask a teacher to look at them.

3. Look at articles in professional journals and see how their theses are supported. Ask several teachers to name the journals they consider to be most important in their fields. Journals in philosophy are good places to look because these journals almost always require a clear statement of a thesis plus logically correct supporting arguments. The *Journal of Philosophy* might be a rewarding place to start.

4. Consult a text in logic, such as Irving Copi's *Introduction to Logic*, and examine what it describes as correct and incorrect forms of reasoning.

Suggested readings

Copi, Irving M. *Introduction to Logic*. 6th ed. New York: Macmillan, 1982.

Giere, Ronald N. *Understanding Scientific Reasoning*. New York: Holt, Rinehart, and Winston, 1979.

Ruggiero, Vincent Ryan. *Beyond Feelings: A Guide to Critical Thinking*. Sherman Oaks, Calif.: Alfred Publishing, 1975.

Walter, Tim and Siebert, Al. *Student Success*. 2d ed. New York: Holt, Rinehart, and Winston, 1981.

Part Three

GETTING COMFORTABLE WITH YOU AND OTHERS

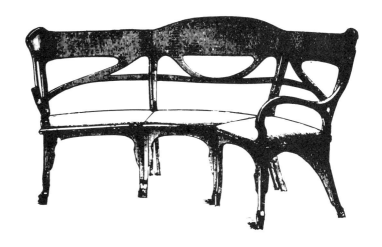

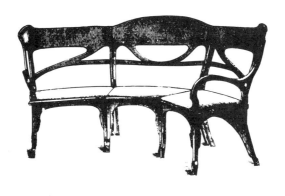

7

Choosing a Major, Planning a Career

Linda B. Salane, *Director of Placement*
and Barbara G. Alley, *Associate Director*
University Career Center
University of South Carolina

Over the years Barbara and I have done a lot of things, held many different jobs, and seen our goals change. When I was young, I always wanted to be an actress or a dancer—something glamorous and exciting. No one talked to me about career planning or helped me explore my dreams, my skills, my potential. I had to figure it out for myself. What was I interested in? People, and why they behave as they do. What was I good at doing? Making presentations and really listening to people. I'm a crusader—I believe in all the issues concerned with equality and quality of life: civil rights, feminism, consumerism. At the same time, I valued the home, family, and community, and wanted roots. I wanted to change the world to reflect my values and so I held many jobs to this end: social worker, residence hall director, women's center director. And through all this, I grew to appreciate my strengths and to understand that many jobs would meet my interests, values, and skills. Finally, I decided to help others learn this, to help others explore their career potentials.

Barbara's been working since she was thirteen years old. She began teaching dancing classes, and moved on to modeling for local groups. Eventually, though, she decided to go to college and major in elementary education. She chose this field because she knew she had the skills, liked children, and would be able to get a job—lots of teaching jobs were available in the late fifties. Besides, it was "normal" then for a woman to be a teacher, and this was important to her since she'd always been criticized for being different. Barbara has learned over the years, though, that life is too short to

89

spend your time doing things you're not interested in and don't en-joy. She became a teacher and loved it, but gradually her interests changed—and she followed them: full-time mother and homemaker, real estate agent, organizational development consultant, and now administrator in higher education.

We've both achieved our individual dreams and find our lives filled with excitement, meaning, and creativity. A young friend of Barbara's, Josh, recently summed it all up: "Mommy," he said, "when I grow up I want to be just Josh." We believe the career-planning process can enable you to identify career fields that will give you the joy of being your own "just Josh." And we hope this chapter helps you begin to put it all together.

When most people think of career planning, they think of choosing among career fields, deciding whether or not to take a job offer, or deciding whether to change employers. These are important issues, but college students face more immediate decisions. Choosing an academic major, selecting elective courses, and deciding which activities to get involved in at college are also career decisions.

There are no right or wrong choices. You'll decide what's right for you. If you make your decisions with a full understanding of your personal priorities and of the realities of the job market, your decisions can lead to an array of exciting career fields. You'll understand why you made the choices you did, and you'll realize that you can change your career direction as your priorities change. Begin to establish those priorities now, as you read this chapter.

Just as college is only the beginning of the rest of your life, so choosing a major is but the first step in planning your career. For some of you choosing a major is a simple decision, but most of us enter college not knowing which major will lead us to the career we're best suited for.

If you find yourself facing such decisions right now, stop and ask yourself the following questions:

- What kind of work do I want to do?
- Which career fields offer opportunities for this kind of work?
- What role will college play in my future career plans?
- Are there specific things I can do to enhance my chances of getting a job when I graduate?
- Do my career goals complement my life goals and work values?

Career planning involves the exploration of these questions to discover how they relate to one another and to find the answers you'll need to make effective career choices.

Workplace and work's place

The reward of career planning is that it can help you find your place in the world of work. You've probably met people who tell you how much they love their jobs and even marvel that they're being paid to do something they enjoy. You've probably also met people who dislike what they do, count the days until Friday, and are always looking for another job. We might say that the latter group has a place to work while the former group has work that has a place in their total lives. Career planning can help you identify the kind of work that will "fit" or have a place in your life.

The career-planning process stresses the importance of knowing enough about yourself, specific career fields, and your personal values system so that you can consciously and intentionally make the decisions involved in choosing a satisfying career. This process has all the potential for helping you find work that is both interesting and makes use of your abilities and skills. It can also help you examine your values (what is important to you) in relation to your work and personal life and to explore ways of meeting needs based on those values.

If your goal is to identify work that will "fit" or be a vital part of your life, you obviously need two kinds of information. First, you'll need information that can be obtained from self-assessment: your personality type, interests, values, aptitudes, skills, and goals. Second, you'll need information that can be obtained through career research: information that will help you determine which career fields can provide opportunities for exploring your interests, exercising your values, demonstrating your aptitudes, using your skills, and fulfilling your personal goals.

Before you actively begin the career-planning process, though, let's explore some false assumptions that may keep you from making a sensible career decision.

The major myth

Most college students think a matching academic major exists for each specific career field, and that it's impossible to enter most career fields unless they choose that matching major for undergraduate study. This is not true!

The relationship of college majors to career fields varies. Obviously, some career choices dictate that you choose a specific undergraduate major. If you want to be a nurse, you must major in nursing. Engineers major in engineering. Architects major in architecture. There's no other way to be certified as a nurse, engineer, or architect. However, most career fields don't require a specific major, and people with specific majors don't have to use them in ways most commonly expected. For example, if you major in nursing, history, engineering, English, or many other majors, you might nevertheless choose to become a bank manager, sales representative, career counselor, production manager, or a number of other things. Your awareness of the relationship between career fields and college majors can play a vital part in your choice of academic major, minor, and elective courses.

Going beyond your major

In most cases, a college major alone is not sufficient for getting a job. The increased number of college graduates has produced more competition in the job market. To be competitive in today's market, you need the experience and competencies related to your chosen career fields. Internships, part-time jobs, and extracurricular activities can provide numerous opportunities for you to gain experience and develop the competencies required by your career choices.

Therefore, you should plan your college curriculum so that you can study what you enjoy learning about, what you can do successfully, and what will serve as groundwork for the future you want for yourself.

The most common question college students ask is, "What can I do with my major?" Career planning can help you focus on a different question: "What do I want to do?" This question leads you to explore yourself and career fields that provide opportunities for you to achieve what you want, not only from your college major, but from life as well.

In attempting to answer what you want to do, you'll find that the choice of an academic major takes on new meaning. You're no longer concerned with the prescribed route of specific majors. The search becomes one of finding the best academic program for your chosen career goals. We can compare this process to mapmaking. You actually begin to chart your college career, using your career goals as the basis for decisions about your academic major, minor, elective courses, internships, vacation jobs, leadership commitments, and extracurricular activities.

Map reading and mapmaking

Map reading can be very appropriate if you're looking for the shortest distance between two points, or if the scenery and experiences along the way are the ones you want. Many people tend to look at academic majors as maps. They choose a major, read about what other people with the same major are doing to earn money, and, without further thought, decide to look for the same kind of job when they graduate. How many times have you heard someone say, "I'm majoring in English so I guess I'll teach"? If you question them further, you might learn that the person doesn't like anything about teaching except the subject matter. Obviously, this person began with the question, "What can I do with my major?" and chose to follow someone else's map. Such behavior is typical of map readers, those who view academic majors as maps.

In contrast are the people who view the choice of an academic major as one part of a map they're making in order to reach their chosen career goals. Mapmakers know what they want to do and where they want to go, so they make decisions that will help them get there. They're ready to begin the journey.

The remainder of this chapter is designed to help you make that map for the journey to your career choice.

Career planning and you

Before you begin a journey—whether to the beach for spring break, or home for the weekend—you do a quick assessment of what you have and what you'll need to make the trip a good one. You automatically determine whether there's enough gas in the car, where and when to meet your ride, what clothes to take, and so on. As you do this, you automatically begin to set priorities. You may have a closet full of clothes you could take, but you pack only what you have room for.

The same processes of assessment and decision making are the major components of career planning. Instead of considering factors such as gasoline, distance, money, and weather, though, you evaluate important factors about yourself: your interests, skills, aptitudes, personality characteristics, life goals, and work values.

You are a unique and complex individual. You bring to college a maze of different characteristics forged by your previous experiences. You have developed and will continue to refine a picture of who you are, which is your self-image. Some people have a very definite and complete self-image by the time they enter college, but most students are in the process of defining (or perhaps redefining) themselves. The complexity of all these factors makes the assessment a difficult task. Often, students see themselves as puzzles.

To begin understanding this puzzle, consider each factor separately and then consider the impact each has on the others. Let's begin.

Interests

Interests develop from your previous experiences and from assumptions you formed in the context of the environment in which you have lived. For example, you may be interested in writing for the college newspaper because you did it in high school and loved it, or because you'd like to try it even though you've never done it before.

Throughout your lifetime, your interests will develop and change. Involvement may lead you to drop old interests and add new ones. It's not unusual for a student to enter Psychology 101 with a great interest in psychology and realize halfway through the course that psychology is not what he or she imagined.

How do you identify what you're interested in? First, you can take many standardized personality inventories or tests through the counseling services at your school. You can also help identify your interests by doing the following:

1. Read through your college catalog and check each course that sounds interesting to you. Ask yourself why they sound interesting.
2. Make a list of all the classes, activities, clubs, offices, and so on you enjoyed in high school. Ask yourself why you enjoyed these things.

Skills

Skills are things you do well. To claim something as a skill, you must have proof that you do it well. You can't claim to be a good writer, for example, unless you've written something good. You can measure your current level of skill by your past performance.

Note the reference to "current level of skill." Skills, like interests, can be developed. You may be a poor writer now, and you may choose to work on that skill. By using resources available to you at college and by practicing, you can become a better writer.

Use the list in Figure 7–1 to help you determine your best skills. First, check the skills you think you presently have. Then, identify the five skills you are most confident about, those about which you could say to anyone: "I am good at this." Circle those five skills. Finally, place an "X" next to the skills you would like to develop while you are in college.

Aptitudes

Aptitudes are inherent strengths. They may be part of your biological heritage or they may have emerged from your early learning environment. Aptitudes are the foundation for skill development. High aptitudes generally produce the

___ writing	___ socializing	___ being neat
___ reading	___ making a team effort	___ keeping records
___ conversing	___ explaining	___ being accurate
___ reporting information	___ helping others	___ asserting self
___ interviewing	___ teaching	___ taking risks
___ being creative	___ entertaining	___ negotiating
___ making machines and mechanical things work	___ public speaking	___ selling
	___ being sensitive	___ winning
___ applying technical knowledge	___ learning	___ being friendly
___ building things	___ analyzing	___ motivating
___ repairing things	___ evaluating	___ managing
___ operating tools	___ handling money	___ directing others
___ observing	___ planning	___ adapting
___ listening	___ problem solving	___ encouraging
___ coming up with ideas	___ scheduling	___ other
___ cooperating	___ following through	___ other
___ being tactful	___ getting results	___ other

Figure 7–1   Skills Checklist

potential for higher skill levels. In discussing skills, we said that through practice and the use of available resources, you could improve your writing. Now we can add that if you have an aptitude for writing and couple that aptitude with practice and the use of resources, you'll probably become a better writer than someone who doesn't have a strong writing aptitude.

Having an aptitude for something doesn't ensure success. But aptitude coupled with high motivation and hard work breeds success. At the same time, high motivation and hard work alone may not be able to compensate for low aptitude. A student may study calculus for hours and still barely make a C.

Each of us has aptitudes we can build on. It makes sense to build on your strengths. Strengths are clues to those areas where you will be most successful. Check the aptitude areas below which you believe are strong for you. Strike through those you know are weak areas. Put a question mark by those you are not sure about. Then, identify your strongest aptitudes. Are they in the same family as the skills you previously checked?

___ Abstract reasoning	___ Mechanical ability	___ Language usage
___ Verbal reasoning	___ Clerical speed	___ Spelling
___ Spatial relations	___ Clerical accuracy	___ Numerical ability

Personality characteristics

What makes you different from others around you? Obviously, each of us is physically unique. But we're all psychologically unique, too. The personality characteristics you've developed through the years make you *you*, and those characteristics can't be ignored in the career decision process. The person who is quiet, orderly, neat, calm, and detailed probably will make a different work choice than the person who is aggressive, outgoing, argumentative, and witty. Many psychologists believe that working in an occupation consistent with your personality can make you feel more successful and satisfied with your work.

What ten words would you use to describe yourself? Using the list in Figure 7–2, place a checkmark next to the adjectives you think best describe you. Then, ask your parents, your brother or sister, and a close friend to write down ten words they would use to describe you. How do the lists compare?

___ academic	___ cooperative	___ idealistic
___ active	___ courageous	___ imaginative
___ accurate	___ curious	___ independent
___ adaptable	___ daring	___ individualistic
___ adventurous	___ deliberate	___ industrious
___ affectionate	___ determined	___ informal
___ aggressive	___ dignified	___ intellectual
___ alert	___ discreet	___ intelligent
___ ambitious	___ dominant	___ inventive
___ artistic	___ eager	___ kind
___ attractive	___ easygoing	___ leisurely
___ bold	___ efficient	___ light-hearted
___ broadminded	___ emotional	___ likeable
___ businesslike	___ energetic	___ logical
___ calm	___ fair-minded	___ loyal
___ capable	___ farsighted	___ mature
___ careful	___ firm	___ methodical
___ cautious	___ flexible	___ meticulous
___ charming	___ forceful	___ mild
___ cheerful	___ formal	___ moderate
___ clear-thinking	___ frank	___ modest
___ competent	___ friendly	___ natural
___ competitive	___ generous	___ obliging
___ confident	___ good-natured	___ open-minded
___ conscientious	___ healthy	___ opportunistic
___ conservative	___ helpful	___ optimistic
___ considerate	___ honest	___ organized
___ cool	___ humorous	___ original

Life goals and work values

Most people want two things from life: success and satisfaction. Each of us defines these words in our own way, and one person's perception of success and satisfaction may be the opposite of another's. Defining these concepts is complex and very personal.

Two things influence our conclusions about success and happiness. One is knowing that we are achieving the life goals we've set for ourselves. The other is finding we value what we're receiving from our work.

Figure 7–3 is a list of life goals some people have set for themselves. This list can help you begin to think about the kinds of goals you may want to establish for yourself. Read each goal and check the ones you would like to have as part of your ideal life. Next, review the goals you have checked and circle the five you want most. Finally, review your list of five goals and prioritize them (1 as most important, 5 as least important).

The chart in Figure 7–4 includes typical work values, or reasons people say they like the work they do. This list can help you begin to think about what you want to receive from your work. Read each definition and check the items you'd

___ outgoing	___ resourceful	___ teachable
___ painstaking	___ responsible	___ tenacious
___ patient	___ retiring	___ thorough
___ peaceable	___ robust	___ tolerant
___ persevering	___ self-confident	___ tough
___ pleasant	___ self-controlled	___ trusting
___ poised	___ sensible	___ trustworthy
___ polite	___ sensitive	___ unaffected
___ practical	___ serious	___ unassuming
___ precise	___ sharp-witted	___ understanding
___ progressive	___ sincere	___ unexcitable
___ prudent	___ sociable	___ uninhibited
___ purposeful	___ spontaneous	___ verbal
___ quick	___ spunky	___ versatile
___ rational	___ stable	___ warm
___ realistic	___ steady	___ wholesome
___ reflective	___ strong	___ wise
___ relaxed	___ strong-minded	___ witty
___ reliable	___ sympathetic	___ zany
___ reserved	___ tactful	

Figure 7–2   Adjective checklist

like to have as part of your ideal job. Then review the items you've checked and circle the ten items you want most. Finally, review your list of ten items and put them in order of importance (1 as most important, 10 as least important).

My life goals include:

____ the love and admiration of friends.

____ a healthy life.

____ lifetime financial security.

____ a lovely home.

____ international fame.

____ freedom within my work setting.

____ a really good love relationship.

____ a satisfying religious faith.

____ recognition as the most attractive person in the world.

____ a happy family relationship.

____ complete self-confidence.

____ an understanding of the meaning of life.

____ success in my chosen profession.

____ a personal contribution to the elimination of poverty and sickness.

____ a chance to direct the destinies of a nation.

____ freedom to do what I want.

____ a satisfying and fulfilling marriage.

____ (other)

____ (other)

____ (other)

____ (other)*

Figure 7–3   Life goals checklist

____ *Help society:* Do something to contribute to the betterment of the world.

____ *Help others:* Be involved in helping other people in a direct way, either individually or in a small group.

____ *Public contact:* Have a lot of day-to-day contact with people.

____ *Work with others:* Have close working relationships with a group, as a result of my work activities.

____ *Competition:* Engage in activities that pit my abilities against others where there are clear win-and-lose outcomes.

____ *Make decisions:* Have the power to decide courses of action, policies, and so on.

____ *Power and authority:* Control the work activities or (partially) the destinies of other people.

____ *Influence people:* Be in a position to change the attitudes or opinions of other people.

____ *Work alone:* Do projects by myself, without any significant amount of contact with others.

____ *Knowledge:* Engage myself in the pursuit of knowledge, truth, and understanding.

*Adapted from Human Potential Seminar by James D. McHolland. Evanston, Illinois. 1975. Used by permission of the author.

___ *Intellectual status:* Be regarded as a person of high intellectual prowess or as one who is an acknowledged "expert" in a given field.

___ *Creativity (general):* Create new ideas, programs, organizational structures or anything else not following a format previously developed by others.

___ *Supervision:* Have a job in which I'm directly responsible for the work done by others.

___ *Change and variety:* Have work responsibilities that frequently change content and setting.

___ *Stability:* Have a work routine and job duties that are largely predictable and not likely to change over a long period of time.

___ *Security:* Be assured of keeping my job and a reasonable financial reward.

___ *Fast pace:* Work in circumstances where there is a high pace of activity, and work must be done rapidly.

___ *Recognition:* Be recognized for the quality of my work in some visible or public way.

___ *Excitement:* Experience a high degree of (or frequent) excitement in the course of my work.

___ *Adventure:* Have work duties that involve frequent risk taking.

___ *Profit, gain:* Have a strong likelihood of accumulating large amounts of money or other material gain.

___ *Independence:* Be able to determine the nature of my work without significant direction from others; not have to do what others tell me to.

___ *Location:* Find a place to live (town, geographical area) that is conducive to my lifestyle and affords me the opportunity to do the things I enjoy
most.

___ *Time freedom:* Have work responsibilities that I can work at according to my own schedule; no specific working hours required.*

Figure 7–4 **Work values chart**

This systematic assessment is a necessary first step in career planning. Otherwise, you're pulling career choices out of thin air and may run the risk of choosing poorly and being dissatisfied. Some students can easily evaluate their strengths and weaknesses. If you're one of those students, you're probably ready to begin exploring career choices.

But if you had difficulty with this section, it may help to talk with a career counselor at your school. Career counselors are trained to help you identify your strengths and order them according to what is most important to you.

---

*Figler, Howard E. PATH: A Career Workbook for Liberal Arts Students. Cranston, R.I.: The Carroll Press, copyright © 1979. Reprinted by permission.

What are your career choices?

The federal government lists more than 31,000 career fields. How many can you name? If you're like most college students, your list begins to get sketchy beyond thirty-five or fifty occupations. Most students admit they don't know much about occupations. Few have accurate information about typical on-the-job activities, necessary skills, occupational outlook, salary, methods of entry, or related fields—even for their most likely occupational choice. Obviously, you can't make a good choice if you don't understand what your choices are.

You certainly can't explore all 31,000 plus career fields, either, but you can focus your research on the most appropriate careers for you. Many reference works can help you focus on these careers. Some emphasize the need to analyze your skills. The *Dictionary of Occupational Titles* (DOT), published by the U.S. Government Bureau of Labor Statistics, is organized by the level of skill with people, with data, and with things that a career field requires of a worker. Other systems emphasize interests.

Dr. John Holland, a psychologist at Johns Hopkins University, has developed a system based on several factors that are important about individuals and that are designed to help you identify career choices. Dr. Holland separated people into six general categories (see Figure 7–5), based on differences in their interests, skills, values, and personality characteristics—in short, their preferred approaches to life. His categories include:

1. *Realistic*
   Characterized by competitive/assertive behavior and by interest in activities that require motor coordination, skill, and physical strength. People oriented toward this role prefer situations involving "action solutions" rather than tasks involving verbal or interpersonal skills. They like to take a concrete approach to problem solving rather than rely on abstract theory. They tend to be interested in scientific or mechanical, rather than cultural and aesthetic, areas.

2. *Investigative*
   Prefer to think rather than to act; to organize and understand rather than to persuade. They are not apt to be "people-oriented."

3. *Artistic*
   Value self-expression and relations with others through artistic expression. They dislike structure, prefer tasks involving personal or physical skills, and are more prone to express emotion than other types. They are like investigative people, but more interested in the cultural-aesthetic than the scientific.

4. *Social*
   Seem to satisfy their needs in a teaching or helping situation. In contrast to investigative and realistic people, social types are drawn more

to close interpersonal relationships and are less apt to engage in intellectual or extensive physical activity.

5. *Enterprising*

Verbally skilled, they use this skill in persuasion, rather than in support of others. They also value prestige and status and are more likely than conventional people to pursue it.

6. *Conventional*

Don't mind rules and regulations and emphasize self-control. These people prefer structure and order to ambiguity in work and interpersonal situations. They place value on prestige or status.

In choosing several categories that are most like you, don't let one or two factors keep you from making a choice. Choose the ones that have the *most* true statements about you.

Holland's system organizes career fields into the same six categories. Career fields are grouped according to what a particular career field requires of a person (skills and personality characteristics most commonly associated with success in those fields) and what rewards particular career fields provide for people (interests and values most commonly associated with satisfaction). As you read the following examples, see how your career interests match the category as described by Holland.

- *Investigative:* urban planner, chemical engineer, bacteriologist, cattle-breeding technician, ecologist, flight engineer, genealogist, handwriting analyst, laboratory science worker, marine scientist, nuclear medical technologist, obstetrician, quality control technician, sanitation scientist, TV repairer, balloon pilot.
- *Artistic:* architect, film editor/director, actor/actress, cartoonist, interior decorator, fashion model, furrier, graphic communications specialist,

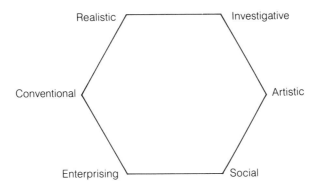

Figure 7–5   Holland's hexagon

jewelry designer, journalist, medical illustrator, editor, orchestra leader, public relations specialist, sculptor.

- *Social:* nurse, teacher, caterer, dental assistant, social worker, genetic counselor, hair stylist, home economist, job analyst, marriage counselor, parole officer, rehabilitation counselor, school superintendent, theatre manager, production expediter.
- *Conventional:* accountant, statistician, census enumerator, data processor, dental assistant, hospital admitting officer, instrument assembler, insurance records supervisor, keypunch operator, legal secretary, library assistant, linotype operator, mail clerk, office coordinator, reservation agent.
- *Realistic:* agricultural engineer, barber, dairy farmer, electrical contractor, ferryboat captain, gem cutter, heavy equipment operator, industrial arts teacher, jeweler, navy officer, health and safety specialist, radio repairer, sheet metal worker, tailor, waitress/waiter.
- *Enterprising:* banker, city manager, employment interviewer, FBI agent, health administrator, industrial relations director, judge, labor arbitrator, personnel assistant, TV announcer, salary and wage administrator, insurance salesperson, sales engineer, telephone interviewer, travel guide.

At first glance, Holland's model may seem to be a simple method for matching people to career fields. It was never meant for that purpose, however. Your career choices ultimately will involve a complex assessment of the most important factors about you. To display the relationships between career fields and the potential conflicts people face as they consider them, Holland's model is commonly presented in a hexagonal shape. The closer the types, the closer the relationships among the career fields. The further apart the types, the more conflict between the career fields.

Using Holland's model can help you answer the question of career choice in two ways. First, you can begin to identify many career fields that are consistent with what you know about yourself. Once you've identified potential fields, you can use the career library at your college to get as much information as possible about those fields. When making career decisions, you should research career fields for information about:

- daily activities for specific jobs
- interests and abilities required
- preparation required for entry
- working conditions
- salary and benefits
- employment outlook

Second, you can begin to identify the harmony or conflicts in your career choices. This will help you analyze the reasons for your career decisions and be more confident in yourself as you make choices.*

The chart in Figure 7–6 can help you determine at a glance which career fields complement your interests, personality skills, and aptitudes. Review the career research you've done and list the five career fields that are most appealing to you *now*. Indicate with a check whether or not the career field offers interests, satisfaction, personality fit, and use of current skills you want to develop, as well as the opportunity to exercise and develop your aptitudes.

College students often view career choice as a monumental and irreversible decision about their lives. The *choice* haunts some students as they decide on a college major. Others panic about "the choice" as they approach graduation and begin to look for a job. The assumption is that "the decision" will make all the difference in their lives.

This assumption is false, for in its broadest sense career means life path. A career is the sum of the decisions you make over a lifetime. There is no "right occupation" just waiting to be discovered by you. Rather, there are many career choices you may find fulfilling and satisfying. The question to consider is, "What is the *best* choice for me *now?*"

If you want to make the *best* choice *now,* we can help you begin. You've already identified five career fields you would consider as potential career choices. The next step is a bit more complex and involves your consideration of the effect of these choices on your life goals and work values. An exploration of

Potential Career Choices	Interests Satisfaction	Personality "Fit"	Skills Usage	Aptitude Usage
1.				
2.				
3.				
4.				
5.				

Figure 7–6   Career Interest Chart

---

*Adapted and reproduced by special permission from *The Self Directed Search Manual,* by John L. Holland, Ph.D. Copyright 1978. Published by Consulting Psychologists Press, Inc., Palo Alto, CA 94306.

life goals and work values allows you to measure the information about the career field you've chosen against what you need in order to feel satisfied about your work.

The chart in Figure 7–7 can help you determine whether or not your potential career choices will enable you to fulfill your value needs. List your top five potential career choices from Table 7–6 in the appropriate column. List your ordered life goals and work values from Tables 7–3 and 7–4. Place a check in the box to the far right of the listed goal or value if you feel that the potential career choice will enable you to satisfy that goal or value.

This comparison of information about yourself, career information, and the role of life goals and work values is what makes career planning an effective decision-making process.

Career planning isn't a quick and easy way to arrive at what you want to do with your life, but we think it can be a most effective means to help you discover the best career choice for you now in the sense that the *now* choice will be appropriate in terms of your personal characteristics and goals and will lay the groundwork for future career choices. Career planning *can* help you find your place in the world of work. Take advantage of it.

Suggested activities

Throughout this chapter we've suggested things you can do to gather information about yourself and about the world of work. We hope you'll follow up on the exercises suggested; we believe they'll help you clarify the most important issues involved in your choice of career and academic major. After you've worked through the exercises in this chapter, here are a few other activities that may help.

- *Career exploration:* Once you've selected possible career fields, talk with people working in those fields to get a clear idea of what life is really like as a social worker or accountant or office manager.
- *Choice of a major:* Talk with faculty members about the skills and areas of expertise you'll develop in studying the discipline they're teaching.
- *Skill development:* Choose to get involved in work experiences and/or campus activities that will allow you to develop skills and areas of expertise useful to your career plans.

Potential Career Choice	Prioritized Life Goals	( )	Prioritized Work Values	( )
1.	1.		1.	
	2.		2.	
	3.		3.	
	4.		4.	
	5.		5.	
2.	1.		1.	
	2.		2.	
	3.		3.	
	4.		4.	
	5.		5.	
3.	1.		1.	
	2.		2.	
	3.		3.	
	4.		4.	
	5.		5.	
4.	1.		1.	
	2.		2.	
	3.		3.	
	4.		4.	
	5.		5.	
5.	1.		1.	
	2.		2.	
	3.		3.	
	4.		4.	
	5.		5.	

Figure 7–7 Comparing careers to goals and values

Suggested readings

Bachhuber, Thomas D., and Richard K. Harwood. *Directions: A Guide to Career Planning*. Boston: Houghton Mifflin, 1978.

Bolles, Richard N. *The Three Boxes of Life*. Ca.: Ten Speed, 1981.

———. *What Color Is Your Parachute?* Berkeley, Ca.: Ten Speed, 1983.

Campbell, David. *If You Don't Know Where You're Going, You'll End Up Someplace Else*. Allen, Tex.: Argus Communications, 1974.

Carney, Clark G., Cindy F. Wells, and Don Streufert. *Career Planning: Skills to Build Your Future*. New York: D. Van Nostrand, 1982.

Figler, Howard. *The Complete Job-Search Handbook*. New York: Holt, Rinehart, and Winston, 1979.

———. *Path—A Career Workbook for Liberal Arts Students*. Cranston, R.I.: Carroll Press, 1979.

Gale Research. *Directory of Directories*.

———. *Encyclopedia of Associations*. Detroit, Mich. Published annually. (Expensive but worthwhile directories.)

Garrison, Clifford B. et al. *Finding a Job You Feel Good About*. Allen, Tex.: Argus Communications, 1977.

Harris-Bowlsbey, Joann, James D. Spivack, and Ruth S. Lisansky. *Take Hold of Your Future*. Towson, Md.: American College Testing, 1982.

Jackson, Tom. *The Perfect Resume*. Garden City, N.Y.: Anchor Books, 1981.

———. *28 Days to a Better Job*. New York: Hawthorn Books, 1977.

McLaughlin, John E., and Stephen K. Merman. *Writing a Job-Winning Resume*. Englewood Cliffs, N.J.: Prentice-Hall, 1980.

Occupational Outlook Handbook, 1982–83 ed. Washington, D.C.: U.S. Department of Labor, 1980.

Paetro, Maxine. *How to Put Your Book Together and Get a Job in Advertising*. New York: Hawthorn Books, 1979.

Pearson, Henry G. *Your Hidden Skills: Clues to Careers and Future Pursuits*. Wayland, Mass.: Mowry Press, 1981

Powell, Randall C. *Career Planning and Placement Today*. Dubuque, Ia.: Kendall-Hunt Publishing, 1978.

Stair, Lila B. *Careers in Business: Selecting and Planning Your Career Path*. Homewood, Ill. Richard D. Irwin, 1980.

About Being an Undeclared Major

James L. Lancaster, *Director*
Center for Undeclared Majors
University of South Carolina

As I look back, I believe I went to school during one of the luckiest times ever! The United States was booming in a decade of unparalleled economic growth and social change. Prosperity meant plentiful scholarship money from both government and private sources and almost limitless opportunities for good jobs. The students of the 1960s could afford the luxury of studying whatever we enjoyed most and planning to work at whatever occupation we found most personally fulfilling.

Not only did I not have to worry about money for going to school almost as long as I wanted to go, or about getting an interesting job, but there was also in those days a general consensus that people went to college to "get an education." We weren't always clear about what that meant, but we spent our first two years satisfying the "general education requirements" and sampling both the subjects and the faculty. Lots of us soon learned that it was far more important to "major" in good teachers, whatever their courses, than to select a departmental major, no matter how interesting or useful the curriculum might look in the catalog.

I finally selected history simply because I liked it most and the professors were so outstanding. But I also minored strongly in English and religion for the same reasons. The undergraduate major didn't matter to me at all in terms of preparing for a job, since that was why I would be going to graduate school. But even when I began doctoral study in American history at Princeton, my goal was not to specialize in a specific period so much as to continue becom-

107

ing broadly educated in order to repeat the process with students of my own.

After I got my doctorate I started teaching history at the University of South Carolina. Later I became administrator of the Center for Undeclared Majors—something I'd never heard of until being an undeclared major somehow became the exception rather than the rule in higher education. Now it's the undecided student who needs special attention; in "my day" it was the other way around! My work allows me to be an advisor and mentor not only for the students in my classes, but for literally hundreds of students. At the same time, I continue to write history, read mystery novels and romances, play the pipe organ and collect classical records, teach Sunday school, and raise Shelties.

I'm still an "undeclared major."

Although most students and their parents experience a great deal of anxiety about it, being undecided about educational and career goals is the current condition of most college freshmen. In fact, for most of you, admitting you're "undecided" is the most positive decision you can make. While different degrees of "undecidedness" exist among students, more than 70 percent of you won't graduate in the major you pick as freshmen. Why, then, are openly "undeclared" or undecided students still considered exceptional or problematical, and why do so many colleges make little or no provision for addressing their needs?

Perhaps the chief reason is that the attitudes and standards of many teachers and colleges have changed. Today it's expected or assumed that students will have a declared major, that the "norm" is to be "majoring." Only in recent years, however, has this been the case, and it's evidence of an increasing professionalization and vocationalism in higher education, even among the traditional liberal arts faculties.

To be sure, there are practical dangers in being undecided, especially if it means being *uncommitted,* and for too long. But a far more serious danger may result from choosing your educational emphasis unwisely, often with unsuccessful or unhappy results. Despite the admonitions of parents and the expectations of teachers, it may be best for most of you to *decide* to be undecided—to explore, and to seek information and impartial advice about majors, careers, and the process of making good decisions. Perhaps the best advice that any of you can get about choosing a major is: "Just don't worry about it.".

Surely one of the most commonly asked questions on any college campus in the United States is: "What are you majoring in?" Even before you enter college, your "major" becomes an academic ID card, a sort of educational Social Security number. Sometimes, applicants are accepted or rejected on this basis by the colleges to which they apply. At every turn, from the time you become a student (matriculation) to graduation, you're sorted, collated, processed, and occasionally even graded by this magical password.

Lots of pressures are brought to bear on college-bound teenagers to make an early decision about major and career. These pressures come from friends, from high school teachers and counselors, and above all from the family. Often the colleges themselves are co-conspirators. Many admissions offices send out forms that list the majors offered and ask the applicants to check off the appropriate one. This is to suggest, of course, that you *should* have decided on a major, even if you haven't!

But occasionally you're given an opportunity to check a box labeled "Undeclared," "Undecided," or "General studies." If you do so, you're in a minority and are often stigmatized by peers and parents, admissions officers and faculty members, as confused, directionless, and academically marginal. It's quite common for "undeclared" students and their parents to envy the declared majors and *their* parents when they meet at campus orientation sessions. Students think to themselves, "I sure wish I were lucky enough to know where I am going and how to get there," or perhaps, "It would be so much better if I could just say, 'engineering'." At the same time, the nervous parents are thinking, "I'd feel a lot better about paying the bill if only Fran would decide to become a doctor."

Most freshmen actually have no major

The truth is that the vast majority of freshmen *don't know* what they'll major in when they enter college, despite what they indicate on admissions forms and despite the posture they assume at orientation. Studies show that about one student in five (20 percent) changes his or her mind about a major between the times of application and registration for the first class. Over 70 percent of all students change from one major to another while they're in college, many of them more than once. (Few of the latter finish school in four years, however.)

When questioned closely, three freshmen of every four express some degree of undecidedness or uncertainty about their major and career goals, whether or not they have a major. Almost two students in five (about 20 percent) actually graduate in a subject about which they knew little or nothing in high school, and fully 50 percent of all graduates change their career plans after they finish college. That is, they enter a career that has little or no relationship to their major. Yet they are just as satisfied (or dissatisfied) with their work as are the graduates whose jobs are directly tied to their undergraduate specialization.

In view of these findings, those "decided" students who seem so fortunate at freshman orientation don't look so lucky after all. Maybe all the pressure to make an early decision about a career and a major is misplaced and unnecessary. In fact, refusing to be pressured into an unrealistic and premature choice of major may be the best decision you can make. Yet, despite this, it's still the exceptional freshman who has the uncommonly good sense to withstand the pressure and choose to be openly "undeclared."

Why freshmen often make unwise selections of majors

Most college freshmen aren't ready to declare a major and shouldn't be expected to do so. For one thing, most of you don't know very much about the bewildering array of fields offered as potential majors by a comprehensive college or university. I once asked a group of high school seniors to list every possible subject in which they might major. With a little help from me, they came up with twenty-one different fields, three or four of which are not taught at our university. Yet there are well over 70 different majors available to our undergraduates, and I know of one large state university that offers a staggering total of about 350! The students in this high school group had never even heard of about twenty-five of our majors, much less given serious consideration to any of them as an appropriate personal choice.

New freshmen need adequate information about all that a college has to offer, and they need to know the requirements of the different programs of study. Just reading the catalog isn't enough, and for the majority, exposure to a few subjects in high school simply won't serve to introduce or to interpret the college curriculum, which is a smorgasbord of specialization (and, often, of obscurity) by comparison. Before you can make a realistic decision about your major, you must take an informed look at all the possibilities.

A second reason freshmen select majors unwisely is that many of you don't really know what you want out of life. College students always want to start a session with their advisor with the question, "What should I major in?" or "What can I *do* with a major in so-and-so?" But good advisors know that you can't really start with those questions. You have to put them aside until you first think about "What do I want to *be?* What do I really want out of my life? What kind of person am I, so far? Where do I really want to go with myself?" I know that such questions seem rather vague and "philosophical," and I also know that most students find it uncomfortable, or at least difficult, to talk about them—and that's precisely my point.

Making a wise self-assessment

Most high school students have made only tentative, halting explorations of themselves and what they really want most from their lives and their work. But an adequate, conscious assessment of yourself is essential to making a wise decision about a major and a vocation. Such self-assessment involves several things, including your experiences, abilities, values, and dreams. What clues can you find in what you've already done that might help you make decisions about your future? What have you done that you really enjoyed doing, or that gave you a real sense of satisfaction or accomplishment? What have you been good at doing, in or out of the classroom? Conversely, what has been frustrating or disappointing?

I once advised a student who told me that he wanted to major in engineering. When I asked him about his preparation and aptitude for math, he replied, "I went all the way to fractions in high school, and I was *real good* at them!" We didn't talk much further about an engineering major.

Looking seriously at yourself means weighing your values, or thinking about the things that are of basic importance to you. These might include service to others, working without supervision, security, public recognition or fame, living close to the beach, or making a lot of money.

Such considerations are vital in deciding about a major. One young woman told me that she loved working with little children, and that it was important to her to make lots and lots of money. We talked about a number of majors and potential careers that would incorporate both of those values, but I can assure you that we *didn't* talk about a major in elementary education. When a person's values are at odds with one another, certain very creative compromises must be reached, otherwise one value has to be sacrificed or traded-off for the other. Being realistic with yourself about the opportunities you open and the limits you set by your values is as important in making decisions about your future as knowing what your talents and abilities are and learning something about yourself from past experiences.

Getting help from parents

It's in this area of self-assessment that your parents can be of tremendous help to you. While they probably can't—and shouldn't—tell you what to major in, they know a great deal about you, and a good way to begin the process of self-assessment is to ask your mom or dad, not "What do you think I ought to be?" but something like "How do you see me as a person? Tell me what you know about me." I suspect that after they climb back up off the floor, they'll have a great deal to say! You don't have to agree with all of it, but their perceptions can be a good springboard for your own insight into yourself. Students often make bad decisions about their majors because they simply don't know enough about themselves.

Also, many freshmen know very little about "what's out *there*"—that is, they have only limited information, most of it vague, about the variety of jobs available to them and what these jobs require or involve. The exceptional freshman can name perhaps about thirty occupations or career fields, including the obvious professions: doctor, lawyer, teacher, and so on. And somewhere on everybody's list there will be "businessperson." But there are thousands of kinds of businesspeople, each kind doing a specific type of work. At least half of my own students tell me they're seriously considering a major in business. Only if they say "marketing" or "accounting" or "insurance" do I tend to take the possibility as seriously as they seem to. (You can't be an "undeclared" businessperson.)

More than 31,000 different occupations are listed in a government publication about jobs, yet most people are aware of only a fraction of them. Like knowing about all the majors offered by your college, you need to learn all you can about the potential kinds of jobs related to your own aptitudes and interests. What do they require? Where might they lead? Where does one start off in that field? What are the rewards and restrictions? Good information in this area is essential to making a good decision about your major, yet a lot of young people have only a foggy notion about the range of possibilities, not to mention about how their own parents actually spend their time "working." The key is to not narrow yourself prematurely to one particular goal or occupation or major until you've expanded your horizons enough to include an informed look at the whole occupational landscape. (See Chapter 7.)

"Vocationalism"

Ironically, perhaps the primary reason freshmen choose the wrong major is that so many students concentrate exclusively on studying for a specific "job," as if each job required a certain major. This preoccupation with what we call "vocationalism" is especially powerful among students during uncertain economic times, and it's been fostered by the attitudes of parents, employers, government officials, and educators.

Most students are encouraged from all sides to be "practical" about school. In view of high tuition rates and the prospect of having to invest at least four years of your life in getting a college degree, it seems vital that there be a tangible payoff in the form of a rewarding and secure job after graduation. Most students tell me this is why they're in college in the first place.

You're just being realistic when you consider how your education will prepare you for a job and career. But it's not true in most cases that there's a direct relationship between the major you select and the kind of work you'll do. There are no substitutes for majoring in nursing or pharmacy or engineering if you want to work as a nurse or a pharmacist or an engineer, but most college majors don't offer specific preparation for a single type of work. Instead, they educate you to become almost anything you want to be. Unlike the narrowly vocational subjects, they don't limit you to one type of work.

Preparing you for many careers

College can prepare you for many careers. This is what makes a four-year college education different from the kind of training you would receive at a technical school. There, you might study welding and become a welder. If you wanted to be a plumber instead, you'd have to go back to study plumbing. By contrast, a four-year college education is intended as general preparation for you to become any number of things, depending on your own aptitudes and ambitions. Higher education is geared not toward what you are going to *be* as much as what you are prepared to *become*.

Let me give you an illustration of this very important point. Because students want to be "practical," and because most people work in "business," many of them think they must major in business administration. In most cases, this isn't true, whether the area be insurance, banking, marketing, manufacturing, retailing, real estate, or whatever. Many a bank president majored in English literature, history, or music. Last summer a parent at orientation told me that her husband, an English major in college, is now president of the bank in their city. In any academic discipline, a student may build a personal record of hard work and high achievement, the kind of proven success impressive to almost any future employer because it demonstrates potential for growth and continuing commitment to learning. But liberal arts majors in particular need to develop entry-level marketability, since before they can become bank presidents, they must first get some job at the bank!

Usually, the easiest way to land that first job is to have a skill that's immediately useful to the employer. There are many ways to develop such skills while you're becoming educated: summertime or afternoon work, volunteer experience, extracurricular activities, elective courses, and the like. Once in the field of your choice, you, as a well-educated person, can build your own career and become the generalist, but it requires careful planning to get your foot in the door.

A great deal of the current emphasis on "vocationalism" in education is simple trendiness. Because the newspapers are full of help-wanted advertisements in "hot" areas such as computer programming and data processing, you may feel pressured to major in that field without regard to your aptitude for it or whether or not you'd really enjoy that kind of work. I can't imagine anything more self-defeating than to major in a discipline only because it seems practical, graduate after four years of boring classes, land a job in the field, and dread getting up to go to work every morning for the next forty years. But almost as grim would be to drop out or flunk out of college because you chose a major on such a basis, or to find at graduation that the field has "dried up"—that the "hot" area of four years ago no longer offers any job opportunities. It happens all the time.

To summarize the points I've emphasized so far: Students often choose their majors unwisely because they lack sufficient information about themselves, potential courses of study, jobs and the job market, and—above all—about *how to combine their education with their career goals*. They succumb prematurely to the pressures to decide, commit, and declare. These pressures come from parents, peers, college structures, and academic advisors—many of whom are unsympathetic to the need for tentativeness and exploration except within their own specialties, especially if their enrollments, and job security, are declining! But deciding prematurely on your major may be dangerous.

Some dangers in deciding on a major too soon

To be fair, there are advantages in being able to make an early decision about your major, even before you go to college. For one thing, it's a great comfort to your parents, who are likely to view a college education as the most important entrance requirement for a successful life. More substantially, however, an early decision about what to study can be very helpful in deciding where to go to school. Some fields are so specialized—engineering is a good example—that it's essential to decide on your major early in order to graduate on time. In almost every case, early commitment to an academic concentration is the most direct and surest way to graduate in four years. Being sure about your educational goals is usually a good indication of enthusiasm and high motivation in your work, and often fosters better academic performance.

None of these advantages pertains, however, for the student whose premature decision about a major has been unwise or unrealistic. Instead, he or she faces some very real perils—perils that are at best inconvenient and, at worst, disastrous for success and happiness in college. Let me mention three of them.

Losing credits

The first peril is the danger of losing credits and delaying your graduation by changing from one major to another, especially if the requirements for each are very different and if the change comes after you are well advanced into the first program of study. This danger is underscored by the fact that almost three-fourths of all college students do change from one major to another at some point in their education, many of them more than once. There was a time when almost all freshmen took the same courses to satisfy the common arts and sciences requirements of almost every degree program at any college. Now the core curriculum has been replaced by a small group of general education requirements, and most of them are "selective" in nature rather than specifically prescribed for every student.

The requirements for one major may be so highly structured and involve such early specialization that they are entirely different from those of another major. One student at our school switched after five semesters from engineering to business administration and lost all but six courses in the process. What a waste of his time (and his parents' money). The various degree requirements for the programs offered can constitute a mine field for students who try to negotiate them armed only with a poor initial choice of major. It's clearly wise for you to keep your options open and to follow courses with the broadest possible application until you narrow your decision to the most appropriate specialty.

Failing

The second danger is that of making failing grades in a major for which you have no aptitude or adequate preparation for success. Here is the surest way of all to delay your graduation. Even initial failing grades can so discourage students that they drop out of school before giving another educational track a fair try. And the deplorable aspect of failing for this reason is that it's so unnecessary.

The most difficult students I counsel are those who major for a year or two in a curriculum for which they're totally unsuited and make such bad grades that they can't declare an alternative major of their choice. It must be the most frustrating thing in the world to know what you want to major in and not be able to do it because of a previously bad record in some unwisely chosen field. Almost every week, I talk to students who have been barred from continuing as business administration majors and who come to me for redirection. Their transcripts show consistently poor grades in the required math and economics courses, and by their own admission, basic accounting was a "thundering bore." Why, then, did they want to be business majors? "I didn't especially want to be," is a typical reply. "I didn't know *what* to major in, but Dad said that I should major in something practical, and that with a degree in business I could get a job and make good money and be a success."

Certainly father was well-intentioned, but what Dad didn't say was that none of those things will come to students with no aptitude for business courses, who hate going to the lectures, and who will compete for good jobs against the straight-A students who *were* cut out for that major. Then there's the student who comes in frustrated and defeated by the same kind of record in the basic sciences. "Why did you think you wanted to be a doctor?" I ask. "I didn't want to be," she replies. "I never did like science, especially those labs. But Mama always wanted to have a doctor in the family." Even if such a student doesn't flunk out of school for good, she may never qualify for another competitive, highly desirable major. And even if she does, the legacy of initial failure and defeat can't be erased.

Boredom for life

A third danger in making a premature choice of major is finding yourself on a vocational track that leads to boredom and a lack of personal satisfaction or fulfillment. Students sometimes enter a major with great enthusiasm, make good grades and get excellent recommendations for job placement, only to discover that they've prepared for a field that's not what they expected and that can't sustain their interests and best efforts. Even in college, students become disenchanted with their choice, but find themselves too far along toward graduation to justify (or afford) to change it. Some become dissatisfied with their whole education or disillusioned with their school—and if they were pressured into a premature commitment about the major, perhaps they have every right to be.

Indecision also has disadvantages

None of this is meant to minimize the dangers inherent in being undecided. Undecided students often lack motivation and commitment to successful work in college. Without a clear-cut goal, they're in danger of becoming marginal students and eventual dropouts. The positive advantage of being able to explore the curriculum in order to make or to confirm a realistic educational commitment can easily degenerate into aimlessness. I know students who are majoring in "no major," who avoid having to come to grips with making basic decisions, who avoid setting any goals and sticking to them. They're the students for whom being undeclared will become an academic limbo rather than a special preparation for success, for in "frittering" they'll ultimately compile only poor grades and wasted time, somehow stumbling into a major they can't enter because of its high qualifications.

Undecided students also need to be warned that if they're candid about their indecision, they may face discrimination by colleges that set different admissions and progression standards for the undeclared or prevent such students from taking exploratory courses in certain fields. A final danger in being undecided is that of being undecided for too long. How long students can safely remain in this category varies, depending both on the requirements of the curriculum in which they become interested and on just how "undecided" they are. Some students come to college with little or no idea what to major in, and almost all of them are able to eliminate some of the possibilities when confronted with the list. Others, particularly honor students who are exceptionally talented in several areas, have already narrowed their choices to a couple of areas or have even tentatively committed to one; they simply need to refine and clarify the choice before making it decisive.

To remain undeclared for too long involves, in my judgment, two different dangers to which I have already alluded. The practical danger is that of delaying your graduation unnecessarily, but the other is potentially more serious. This is the danger of avoiding a decision for so long that avoiding decisions becomes a decision in itself, a habit of mind or a failure of nerve that is almost irremediable in some cases. If postponing a decision about your major means evading the necessity of making it at all, then being in college as an undeclared major has merely served to extend the dependent immaturity of childhood.

Advantages of entering college as an undeclared student

Many students approach their college education as if they were locomotives chugging down a one-way set of tracks, and looking neither right nor left, much less backward. To approach your education like this is to approach it with blinders and to cut yourself off at the beginning from a vital part of what a college education should be: the opportunity to expand horizons, to broaden perspectives, to investigate, and to explore.

I'm convinced that most students benefit from the chance to look at the diverse and complex possibilities before committing themselves to a narrow specialization. Yet the truth is that most students want to narrow themselves right away and have to be forced to broaden their outlook. That is, of course, why there's a liberal arts component in every conceivable degree program, why a business major has to take history and an English major has to take chemistry! This is not to devalue the practical and genuine need for specialization, but only to say that specialization without adequate general education is both restricted and restricting.

At colleges that offer even minimal recognition to the undecided among their undergraduates, advisors can help students obtain the information they need to reach an intelligent decision about their academic major. This includes information about the curriculum, career opportunities and prospects, and how any number of different majors may lead into several different occupational choices. Advisors can explain the requirements for a variety of majors. They can explain how almost any major involves the development of certain basic functional skills, which are themselves at the heart of what we mean when we say that a person is educated, as well as the chief prerequisites for getting a good job and for building it into a rewarding lifetime of work. Self-assessment, the need for which we considered earlier, becomes a crucial part of this exploratory process. I don't mean just a casual look at a supposedly magical "aptitude" test, although such instruments can sometimes prove very helpful to advisors and students. If you know that you need information in order to make good decisions, ask for it. Chances are someone on your campus will see that you get what you need.

Being openly undecided as a freshman can also prevent you from taking courses that are inapplicable to all areas in which you are interested. It allows you to responsibly keep your options open while weighing the consequences of your ultimate decisions. Furthermore, to be an undeclared student is to identify yourself with the great majority of your peers—whether they know it or not. In one sense, this is a healthy approach to your first year at college, for only by recognizing indecision can you marshall appropriate resources to help you make a good decision.

At best, undeclared majors are giving themselves the chance to learn how to make decisions and to develop a plan for their education from the very beginning—not after a number of bad choices and false starts have already limited their choices involuntarily. Such a master plan includes self-assessment, career exploration, information gathering, and declaring the appropriate major at the right time. It involves building a practical program for getting your first job, for developing marketable skills while you're getting your education, whatever your major may be. It involves setting some long-range goals for yourself and relating your short-range goals (What should I major in?) to them. Such an open-eyed approach at the beginning of your freshman year can prevent considerable waste, disappointment, and anger by the time you're a graduating senior. Because you make wise decisions at the front door, you won't grope your way from the commencement stage to the Career Planning Office with the question, "What can I *do* with a major in . . .?"

Meanwhile, how can you adequately rationalize this decision to be undecided? You may recognize yourself in some of my remarks, and you may realize that you're in a majority among college freshmen, and you understand that it's an advantage to be undeclared, and perfectly OK. Still, how do you stall your parents? A very good question!

Guidelines about being an undeclared major

1. Don't force the decision. You can't make a good one until you're ready, and then it has to be based on thorough information, and a candid assessment of yourself.
2. Make the decision yourself. Your advisor can be very helpful. Your parents can be very helpful. But ultimately, no one can make your

decision but you. And you must insist on this point, for no one else will bear the responsibility of living with it.

3. Balance your emphasis on specialization and the need to set realistic goals with the importance of getting the broadest possible exposure to the worlds your books and courses and teachers can open to you. Since most people do, expect to change your mind, and provide for that possibility by building as broad a base as possible within the limitations of your curriculum.

4. Major in personal satisfaction. The subject you enjoy most and the career that offers you the greatest chance for happiness will, in the long run, also promise the best chances for success, in life as well as in college.

5. If your college makes no provisions for assisting undecided students, let them know that you're there and that you need guidance. Shake the tree a little! Don't spinelessly accept the first advisor assigned to you if he or she can't help. Ask for another one.

So, despite what you might have thought, being undecided about your major is the rule rather than the exception for college freshmen. Don't be afraid to say that you're undecided, and don't be pushed into making a premature decision. But be sure to use your status wisely and develop a plan for finding the best major as you set the most appropriate goals for yourself. When the time comes, if you've done your homework, you'll enjoy genuine confidence about both.

Suggested activities

1. List some ways in which people most commonly influence high school students in making a choice about a major in college.

2. Use the library to prepare a report on two jobs of interest to you.

3. Conduct a personal interview with an on-campus professional or with someone working in an area of interest to you.

4. Think about the ways in which others (parents, teachers, peers) may try to influence your career choice. How can you make sure the career choice you make is *your* decision?

Suggested readings

Baird, L. L. *The Undecided Student—How Different Is He?* Research Report No. 22. Iowa City, Ia.: American College Testing Program, 1967.

Bonar, J. R., and L. R. Mahler. "A Center for 'Undecided' College Students." *Personnel and Guidance Journal, 54* (1976): 481–484.

Foote, B. "Determined- and Undetermined-Major Students: How Different Are They?" *Journal of College Student Personnel, 21* (1980): 29–33.

Gordon, Virginia N. "The Undecided Student: A Developmental Perspective." *Personnel and Guidance Journal, 59* (1981): 433–439.

Grites, Thomas J. "Being 'Undecided' Might Be the Best Decision They Could Make." *The School Counselor* (1981): 41–46.

Harrington, Fred Harvey. "On Choosing a Major." *Off to College* (1971): 33–34.

Hecklinger, F. J. "The Undecided Student—Is He Less Satisfied with College?" *Journal of College Student Personnel, 13* (1972): 247–251.

Titley, R. W., and B. S. Titley. "Initial Choice of College Major: Are Only the 'Undecided' Undecided?" *Journal of College Student Personnel, 21* (1980): 293–298.

———. "The Major Changers: Continuity or Discontinuity in the Career Decision Process." *Journal of Vocational Behavior, 8* (1976): 105–111.

9

Making Your Ends Meet: Financial Aid and Money Management

Ray Edwards, *Associate Director of Financial Aid and Scholarships*
University of South Carolina

Looking at today's students, I see striking similarities to those of us who were in college two decades ago. It's comforting to know that some things remain the same. At the same time, however, I see some major changes in the environment of higher education today. And one of the most serious changes concerns the financing of a college education.

The fact of the matter is that the economics of going to college are getting out of hand. Educational institutions, like American families, have been seriously affected by the recent economic troubles experienced by our society. Educational costs have risen dramatically in the past few years, and it appears that this trend will continue. It costs a great deal of money to go to college these days, and these costs are creating serious problems for increasingly large numbers of American families. It's not uncommon for the expenses at a good four-year private college to top $10,000 per year, while many public colleges and universities have costs in the $4000 to $6000 range.

This wasn't the case when I went to college. My parents didn't have a lot of money saved for my college education, but they were able to borrow the necessary funds at reasonable interest rates to

121

keep me enrolled. I used a paper route in a hospital to earn money for clothes and spending. Students and their families today face a much bigger task.

The purpose of this chapter is to help you cope successfully with the many aspects of how to pay for your college education, and how to manage your money effectively. The information presented here is certainly not intended to be exhaustive. It should, however, provide you with a basic understanding of the many alternatives you have available, and to present you with a few techniques for succeeding in this important endeavor.

In meeting the new and varied challenges facing you as you begin your college career, none may be more challenging or important than dealing with your finances. For the first time in your life, you may find yourself totally responsible for managing a "household of one." While this can present a number of frustrations and anxieties, especially if you're away from home for the first time, there's no reason to feel overwhelmed by the innumerable demands that will tug at your purse strings. Managing your finances, like most other things in life, can be learned, and the more you learn about how to manage your money the better at it you'll become.

Managing your money is only one aspect of the larger picture of paying for your college education. For, while managing your funds is obviously important, you must first ensure that you have adequate resources with which to finance your education. Paying for college doesn't just happen. It must be planned, and for most students the task is more complicated than simply paying tuition.

In recent years, financial aid programs have meant the difference between going and not going to college for many students seeking a college education. In fact, between 40 and 50 percent of all students nationwide are receiving some type of financial aid each year. With educational costs what they are, and with the likelihood that inflation and other economic factors will continue to force them even higher, it's increasingly important that you familiarize yourself with the process for obtaining financial aid. Millions of students apply annually for the billions of dollars available in federal aid, and although this process can appear to be somewhat confusing and complex, there's really no need to be intimidated by it. Indeed, with a little effort on your part, the mystery often associated with financial aid will easily disappear. Certainly the time and effort required, whether you need to apply as a freshman or later in your academic career, are small when you consider the possible payoff.

Financing a college education

In approaching the task of paying for your college education, no single factor is more crucial than planning. It would be nice to think that every family begins planning for their children's college education years ahead, but this is quite often not the case. Many families are simply not in a position to save very much toward the day their children are ready for college. And many of those who do find that their savings, because of recent economic conditions, are inadequate for current costs. It becomes critical, then, for you to approach the financing of your education in a comprehensive and creative way.

Costs

To deal effectively with college costs, you must first establish what those costs are. In doing this, it's essential that *all* costs be identified. Tuition and academic fees are fairly obvious and generally easy to determine, but many other expenses are also involved, and some of these are more difficult to assess. The following list includes most of the "typical" costs you're going to have to deal with:

- Tuition/academic fees
- Books
- Equipment and/or supplies
- Room
- Board
- Transportation
- Personal or miscellaneous

To go about determining these costs, you should seek help from your college catalog, admissions office, and financial aid office. The aid office of almost every institution will be able to provide you with a copy of what it considers the average comprehensive educational costs faced by most of its students for the current academic year. Based on such average expenses, you can then go about constructing a personalized list of costs. In doing this, you should be conscious of possible ways to keep expenses to a minimum. For example, can you purchase used books rather than new ones? If you must commute is carpooling or public transportation an option to driving your own car? Will you be paying for courses by the credit hour, or can you pay a set tuition fee as a full-time student that allows for a greater number of hours without additional costs? Can you earn course credit through advanced placement examinations? Can you accelerate your program and save money by going to summer school? Is a board plan available that is less costly than paying on a per meal basis? These and other such questions can help you get the most for your money, as well as keep your expenses at a level that's as reasonable as possible.

Once you have a handle on the expenses facing you, it's much easier to relate costs to the resources you have available. After all, the real question is not simply how much an education costs, or for that matter how much you have available. It's how much you need versus how much you have that counts. In order to answer that question, you must analyze your resources just as you did your costs.

Resources

Personal/family resources. In assessing resources, you should first identify personal and, if applicable, family finances available to help you pay for your education. Parental savings, insurance policies taken out for you when you were young, personal savings, trust funds, and summer employment are examples of these types of resources. In addition, relatives are willing in some cases to help you pay for school through direct contributions or loans. Savings from part-time jobs such as babysitting, tutoring, or paper routes can also help. Although financial aid programs and scholarships are available, you should always remember that the ultimate responsibility for financing your college education rests with you and, to the extent possible, with your family.

After identifying the funds available to you from personal and/or family sources, it's a simple matter of comparison to determine if further finances are necessary. If there's a gap between what you have available and what you need, it's time to think about applying for financial aid.

Financial aid resources. Once you have determined that you're going to need aid in order to help pay for your educational expenses, you must successfully negotiate the financial aid application process. Whether you're a freshman or upperclassman, you'll have to reapply for financial aid each year. Negotiating this process is primarily an exercise in completing forms, so you might as well expect to spend some time filling in spaces and checking boxes. The process may appear confusing at times, but it's really quite straightforward. Familiarize yourself with the application procedures and necessary forms, and you should have a fairly easy time completing the process.

Before outlining the basic steps in the application process itself, it should be helpful to first cover some points about financial aid as a whole. What is financial aid? What's it based on? What are the various types of financial aid available? Space doesn't permit a lengthy and thoroughly definitive discussion, but the answers to these three questions should provide you with a general orientation to the ins and outs of financial aid.

What is financial aid?

Quite simply, financial aid is any type of financial support that's available to you to help pay your educational costs. The term *financial aid* may refer to anything from a federal grant to an institutional scholarship. Typically, it can be categorized as either gift aid or self-help aid. "Gift aid" generally means that the student receiving the aid doesn't have to repay the award; "self-help" implies that the student must do something in order to receive the aid. An example of gift aid is a scholarship based solely on academic merit, whereas a student loan is an example of a self-help type of aid, since the student must promise to repay the loan after finishing her or his education. In both the gift and self-help types of aid, "financial need" may or may not be a factor.

What is financial aid based on?

The criteria on which financial aid is awarded vary according to the type of aid under consideration and the educational institution to which you are going. Obviously, all aid programs require that you meet some sort of eligibility standards. Typically, the criteria are academic merit and financial need, or a combination of these two factors. For example, some academic scholarships are awarded solely on the basis of your successfully meeting the required scholastic eligibility criteria and continued as long as the criteria are maintained; other scholarships also require you to demonstrate financial need in order to qualify for the award. For the large federal aid programs, the major eligibility factors are financial need and maintaining satisfactory progress toward your degree. These are the major eligibility standards you'll have to successfully meet in order to receive most forms of financial aid, but there may also be other institutionally determined criteria attached to some programs.

What types of aid are available?

Regardless of how financial aid is categorized (gift or self-help) or on what criteria it's awarded (that is, need and/or merit), there are five basic types of aid programs generally available: grants, loans, work-study programs, scholarships, and benefit programs.

Grant programs don't require any repayment from you, while loans, as the name implies, do require that you repay the amount you received when you leave school. The College Work-Study Program is a need-based financial aid program that allows you to work part-time while going to school in order to earn part of the money you'll need to pay for your educational expenses. Generally, you'll be working on-campus in a college department. However, many institutions also have off-campus College Work-Study job opportunities available that may better serve your needs. In addition to College Work-Study jobs, which are need-based, many schools also offer regular part-time student assistant jobs. In considering whether to work while going to school, you should always remember that your first priority is to succeed academically. If working will not adversely affect your grades, you can gain good marketable job experience by working part-time. In fact, several studies indicate that part-time work actually has a positive impact on students in terms of academics and time management skills. These programs exist at various levels—institutional, state, federal—as well as in many business and corporate settings as benefit programs for employees and their families. Finally, many civic organizations, local clubs and churches, high schools, and private foundations provide monetary assistance in the form of scholarships or loans.

In addition to these types of aid programs, many institutions also offer cooperative education programs that allow you the opportunity to combine an academic program with employment in your area of study. By co-oping, you not only gain valuable work experience that will pay off when you graduate and begin job hunting, but you also have the opportunity to earn money, some of which you may be able to put toward your remaining educational costs.

A number of very helpful publications can help you identify financial aid opportunities. A list of some of these is included at the end of this chapter. However, the best source of information concerning the types of programs offered by a particular college is the institution's financial aid office. There you should be able to obtain information about all aid programs for which you might be eligible.

Financial aid application process

Just as there are various eligibility criteria for the different financial aid programs, so too are there various application procedures that depend on the type of aid you're considering. It's impossible to cover all conceivable application requirements, since they vary as widely as types of colleges. Nevertheless, certain basic elements are common to almost all application procedures.

Needs analysis document

All aid programs based on need require that you complete some type of financial statement. This statement may take the form of a local organization's simple one-page document, or a more thorough multipage form. The large federal aid programs require that you complete one of the federally approved needs analysis forms, all of which ask exactly the same questions regardless of their format. Examples of these forms are the Family Financial Statement (FFS) of the College Scholarship Service (CSS), and the Application for Federal Student Aid (AFSA) issued by the U.S. Department of Education. Any of these financial statements can be used to apply for federal aid.

The purpose of the financial statement is to assess the financial strength of you and your family. By applying a standardized national needs analysis formula to your information, an expectation of what your family is expected to contribute from its own resources toward the cost of your education is calculated. This expectation is called your "family contribution." The institution you're attending uses this contribution figure in determining the amount of your financial aid eligibility.

Institutional financial aid application

Most colleges require some type of institutional application for aid in addition to the financial statement just mentioned. This form generally asks for information not obtained on the needs analysis documents that the school uses in determining its aid awards. Again, it may be a simple one-page application, or it may be two or three pages in length.

Scholarship application

Almost all institutions or organizations that award scholarships based on scholastic merit require you to complete a special scholarship application. These forms can vary widely in their format, but usually they ask about your past academic record, college entrance examination scores, class rank, offices held, honors received, and other similar data used in selecting scholarship recipients. In addition, as part of the application process, scholarship applicants are often required to visit the campus for an interview.

These are the three most common elements in the typical school's financial aid application process, but they're by no means the only ones. Again, the school's financial aid office can provide you with the specific requirements for aid at that institution.

In tackling the financial aid application process you should keep several things in mind. First, early planning is essential. Make sure that you begin as early as possible to determine what application procedures are required for the aid programs you're going to apply for. Remember that deadlines can vary widely, with scholarship application deadlines generally earlier than those for need-based aid programs. Also keep in mind that you probably will have to fill out several forms, and that some of them will require financial information that you may have to gather before you can accurately complete the forms.

Second, time is required for your application(s) to be processed. Depending on the type of program, the processing may take anywhere from several weeks to several months. In any event, you should always find out how long the processing normally takes so you'll be able to check on it if necessary.

The third important thing to keep in mind is that after your application has been received, you may be required to either clarify some data you provided or submit additional information. In order to prevent unnecessary delays in the processing of your application, it's essential that you respond as quickly as possible with the additional information or clarification.

Finally, in order to avoid costly delays, confusion, or other unforeseen circumstances, you should *always* make a photocopy (with the date noted) of everything you complete or send with your application. This simple precaution may save you untold time and agony.

Financial aid awards

The end result of the financial aid application process, if you're eligible of course, is an award letter from the institution's financial aid office. Once your eligibility has been established, the aid office will make an award to you if it has sufficient funding available. The nature of this award depends on the amount you're eligible for, the programs for which you've applied, and the level of funding available to the school. Like you, the institution must also apply for funding to the U.S. Department of Education for its large federal programs. The amount the school receives from the federal government and the size and need of its student population will in large part determine how it awards its funds.

In determining the precise amount and type of aid it offers you, the financial aid office must take into consideration any financial assistance you're receiving from other sources, assistance you're responsible for reporting to the aid office. To this amount, the aid office will add whatever it can in order to meet your financial needs. Some institutions are able to ensure that your total need is met; others have sufficient funding to meet only a percentage of your requirements. If you have a fairly high degree of financial need, it's likely that the aid offer made to you will include awards from more than one financial aid program. This is called a financial aid "package" since it is an individually determined combination of aid funds from several programs the institution has available to it.

Regardless of the amount or types of aid awarded to you, the decision will be communicated to you via an official institutional award letter. This letter will usually show the amount of your eligibility, the amount of aid being awarded to you, the program(s) from which it's being awarded (such as grant, loan, scholarship), and the academic terms for which it's being awarded. For example, the awards for a student at a college operating on a semester basis might appear as follows:

Estimated cost of education	$4,000		
Expected family contribution	$1,500		
Amount of eligibility	$2,500		
Aid awarded	*Fall*	*Spring*	*Total*
School scholarship	$250	$250	$ 500
Federal grant	$500	$500	$1,000
Work-study	$500	$500	$1,000

or			
Federal grant	$250	$250	$ 500
Student loan	$500	$500	$1,000
Work-study	$500	$500	$1,000

Of course, any number of variations is possible depending on the amount of eligibility and types of programs available. Notice, however, that both of these examples demonstrate the "award package" concept. The advantage of this approach is that it provides a great deal of flexibility in meeting the various needs of individual students as well as in allowing the institution to use its funding to the benefit of all.

Disbursements of funds

Once you've signed and returned your award letter to the aid office, you're ready for the final step in the process: disbursement. Disbursement procedures, as with other procedures mentioned throughout this discussion, vary widely from school to school. Generally, however, disbursement is handled by either crediting to your student account the aid you've been awarded or sending you vouchers or checks. The financial aid office at your institution will inform you of the specific disbursement procedures you'll follow.

Managing your funds

Now that we've covered the basics of the financial aid process, it's time to address the remaining essential issue: money management. Whether you're receiving need-based financial aid or paying your way entirely on your own, you must successfully manage your financial resources.

As with the general matter of financing a postsecondary education and dealing with the financial aid process, the key to managing your money is planning. You *must plan* how you're going to spend your money. If you don't, you risk facing some serious problems as your year progresses. And the keys to planning your finances successfully and preventing unpleasant surprises can be summarized in two words: budgeting and discipline.

As I mentioned in the introduction to this chapter, you can learn to manage your finances. Fortunately, learning the techniques of sound money management is not a difficult task. In fact, basic common sense and reason are the foundations for learning how to budget. So let's turn our attention to the school finances management process.

The money management three-step: budgeting made simple

In order to establish a realistic and reasonable budget for yourself, you must determine three basic facts. First, how long a period of time do you want your budget to cover? One semester, an entire year, two quarters? Second, what items must your budget include? In other words, how comprehensive must it be? Are you going to be responsible for handling your total costs, or only ongoing living expenses, while Mom and Dad pay your tuition and room costs directly? Third, how much money do you actually have?

In constructing a budget, the important thing to keep in mind is that it should be as comprehensive as necessary. The whole point of a budget is to establish a plan for allocating the financial resources you have available. It's nothing more than a systematic way of preventing confusion and uncertainty about how you'll spend your money. By planning how you will spend, you can prevent impulsive spending and ensure that you make it to the end of your budget period without going into the red. Several simple steps will ensure a reasonable and comprehensive budget.

Itemize your expenses. The first step in setting your budget is to list all the expenses you can think of. In doing this, keep in mind that you should take *all* anticipated expenses into account. Begin by listing costs for such things as tuition, fees, books, and supplies. Once you feel satisfied you've accounted for your "educational expenses," begin to itemize your anticipated living costs: everything from "soup to nuts," as the old saying goes. It's in this area that you must really be deliberate in your approach. You must not include only such things as food, laundry, clothing, toiletries/cosmetics, and so on, but also social life as well. If you fail to allow for the latter, you may nickel and dime yourself to death with these little items. They may not seem like much, but they can mount up. The whole point here, remember, is to be in control of your money. You can be in control only if you know how much you're going to need to spend, and for what. Chart A should help you in this task of itemizing your expenses.

Itemize your resources. Once you have a handle on your expected costs, you must tackle the issue of how much money you will have, and how and from what sources you will receive it. This is the second crucial step in establishing a budget.

There are probably any number of possible and effective methods for listing your financial resources. For simplicity and comprehensiveness, however, one extremely effective way is the "category approach." That is, list the money you'll have available by categories, such as part-time work, money from parents, savings, student aid, and so on. This way, you not only get a total perspective of what you'll have available, but it will help when it comes time to actually write out your budget. Chart B should help you in this process.

CHART A: *Itemizing Your Expenses*
Time Period: *(Example) Academic Year*
A. Educational Expenses:

Tuition	$ 500
Fees	$ 700
Books	$ 250
Supplies	$ 50
Subtotal	$1500

B. Living Expenses:

Housing	$ 850
Board	$1475
Personal	$ 75
Transportation	$ 300
Clothes	$ 225
Entertainment	$ 175
Subtotal	$3100
TOTAL	$4600

CHART B: *Itemizing Your Resources*
Time Period: *(Example) Academic Year*
A. Savings

Yours	$ 400
Parents	$ 200

B. Parents:

Cash	$ 300
Bank Loans	$1000

C. Work:

Summer $ _____

Part-time during year $ _____

D. Benefits:

Social Security $ _____

Veteran's $ _____

Other $ _____

E. Financial Aid:

Grants $1200 _____

Scholarship $ 400 _____

Student Loan $ 600 _____

F. Other:

ROTC $ 900 _____

Relatives $ _____

Trusts $ _____

TOTAL $5000 _____

Order your expenses. Now that you've itemized all your anticipated expenses and resources, it's time to begin analyzing the budgeting process. Thus, the third step requires you to put your costs into a commonsense perspective. In doing this analysis, you must approach your expected costs from a cold, objective point of view. For clarity and perspective, go through all the costs you've listed and determine whether each can be categorized as discretionary (that is, avoidable or nonfixed costs) or nondiscretionary (that is, unavoidable or fixed costs). The purpose of this exercise is to focus on those expenses such as tuition, books, and residence hall costs that are fixed (those you *must* pay for) and those such as food, clothing, and entertainment that are not fixed (those you have control over).

By categorizing your expenses as to whether or not you have discretion over them, you're in a better position to put your financial situation in perspective. After you have identified your fixed, nondiscretionary expenses, you know exactly how much of your money must be allocated to them. You then face the easier task of reviewing your discretionary, controllable costs in light of your remaining resources.

To deal effectively with discretionary expenses, you must first go through all your expected controllable costs and rank them in order of importance. Obviously, there are a few expenses for which you must allocate part of your resources—food and transportation, for example. You can't stop eating or transporting yourself to campus for classes. Therefore, you should rank these costs at the top of the list with others in descending order of importance. Remember that you do have much greater latitude in deciding how much you're going to spend for these items. You can eat or you can *really* eat, for example. By the same token, if you must commute to class you may be able to use public transportation rather than drive your own car. And if public transportation isn't available, you can generally carpool and reduce your commuting expenses a great deal. Once you have completed this exercise, you can begin the actual process of constructing your budget.

Constructing your budget

Constructing your budget should be a fairly easy process if you've completed the steps just outlined. You should actually make up two versions of your budget. The first should put your financial picture into overall perspective, and the second should be an actual weekly or monthly version of how you're going to spend your money. Based on the previous two charts, Chart C is an example of an overall budget and summary for a student attending a college that operates on the typical two-semester (fall/spring) academic year calendar. This student lives on campus and travels home (which is in-state) for visits and holidays three times each semester. Notice how easily you can put your overall financial situation into perspective by this approach.

CHART C: *Expense/Resource Budget Summary*

I. *Itemized Expenses*			II. *Itemized Resources*		
A.	Educational:		A.	Savings:	
	Tuition	$ 500		Yours	$ 400
	Fees	$ 700		Parents	$ 200
	Books	$ 250	B.	Parents:	
	Supplies	$ 50		Cash	$ 300
	Subtotal	$1500		Bank loans	$1000
B.	Living:		C.	Work:	
	Housing	$ 850		Summer	$

	Board	$1475		Part-time during year	$
	Personal	$ 75	D.	Benefits:	
	Transportation	$ 300		Social Security	$
	Clothes	$ 225		Veteran's	$
	Entertainment	$ 175		Other	$
	Subtotal	$3100	E.	Financial Aid:	
	TOTAL	$4600		Grant(s)	$1200
				Student Loan(s)	$ 600
III. *Summary*				Scholarship(s)	$ 400
A.	Total Resources	$5000	F.	Other:	
B.	Total Expenses	$4600		ROTC	$ 900
C.	Difference +/−	$+400		Relatives	$
				Trusts	$
				TOTAL	$5000

An overall perspective is essential if you're going to deal successfully with expenses versus resources. This approach helps you arrive at the "bottom line"— and that, after all, is what it's all about. However, the second version of your budget—the actual expenditure budget—is equally important if you're going to be in control of your money. Chart D is an example of a monthly expenditure budget for the same student. Keep in mind that the large expenses for tuition, books, and room must be dealt with at the beginning of the semester, while continuing expenses are handled on an ongoing basis. The monthly approach has been used because it's a convenient basic structure for dealing with these expenses. It provides you with a continuing mechanism for keeping track of your money without becoming overly complicated, and since checking accounts run on a monthly basis it's convenient for balancing purposes.

In establishing your monthly expenses, enter the fixed costs first, with the discretionary expenses after. To arrive at the amounts you're going to allow yourself for discretionary expenses, simply divide your total anticipated costs for those items by the appropriate number of months for which you're budgeting. This way, once you have compared that month's costs to resources, you can go back and adjust your discretionary expenses as needed.

CHART D: *Monthly Expenditure Budget*
        Month: *September*

EXPENSES		*RESOURCES*	
Fixed:		My Own	$ 400
Tuition	$ 250	Mom/Dad	$ 200
Fees	$ 350	Federal Grant	$ 600
Books	$ 125	Student Loan	$ 300
Dormitory	$ 425	Scholarship	$ 200
Discretionary:		*BOTTOM LINE*	
Supplies	$ 35	Total Resources	$1700
Food	$ 195	Total Expenses	$1415
Personal	$ 15		
Entertainment	$ 20	Balance	$ 285
TOTAL	$1415		

Again, this is simply an example of one way of budgeting for your expenses. Whatever specific approach you take, make sure that you use a technique that's comprehensive and provides you with an ongoing way of tracking your spending. If you don't keep your financial health and well-being in perspective, you could find yourself writing one of those "Dear Mom and Dad/Uncle Charley, having a wonderful time, please send money," letters.

Conclusion

Financing your college education and successfully managing your money during your college career are formidable undertakings. Recent economic developments have made it increasingly difficult for students and their families to cope with these challenges. Nevertheless, millions of American young people are doing it. It may not be as easy for many as it once was, but it can be done.

In approaching these dual tasks, you must, above all else, *plan* for what you're going to do. Systematic planning is absolutely essential if you're going to succeed. You must be flexible in your thinking and creative in your approach. You may have to change a decision or alter a previously desired plan as a result of this process, but if you do, don't be overly discouraged. As long as you keep your ultimate goals in front of you, you can succeed.

Keep in mind that on every campus there are people and resources available to help you. Use them! The challenges are great, but the payoff is even greater. Above all else, once you've developed your final plan, stick to it. Be confident in what you've done and disciplined enough to make it work. For after all else is said, the only person who can make it work is you.

Suggested activities

1. Determine how much it costs to attend your institution for the academic year.
2. Determine whether you have adequate financial resources to pay for your college education.
3. Explore the types of financial aid programs available at your institution.
4. Itemize your expenses and resources for the current year, using the example in the chapter as a guide.
5. Construct an overall expense/resource budget for yourself for the current year.
6. Construct a monthly expenditure budget for yourself for each month in this academic year.
7. Visit the financial aid office at your school and find out as much as you can about the types of financial aid programs available.
8. Find out how to apply for financial aid at your school, and obtain and familiarize yourself with the application forms.

Suggested readings

The College Cost Book. Published yearly. The College Scholarship Service of The College Board, Princeton, New Jersey 08541.

College Planning/Search Book. Published yearly. The American College Testing Program, Iowa City, Iowa 52243.

Feingold, S. Norman, and M. Feingold. *Scholarships, Fellowships, and Loans*. Arlington, Mass.: Bellman Publishing, 1982.

A Guide for Students and Parents. Published yearly. The American College Testing Program Needs Analysis Service, Iowa City, Iowa 52243.

Leider, R. *Your Own Financial Aid Factory*. Octameron Associates, P.O. Box 3437, Alexandria, Virginia 22303, 1980.

Moore, Donald R. *Money for College! How to Get It*. Woodbury, N.Y.: Barron's Educational Service.

Need a Lift? Published annually. The American Legion, National Emblem Sales, P.O. Box 1055, Indianapolis, Indiana 46206.

Student Bulletin. Published annually. The National Merit Scholarship Program, One American Plaza, Evanston, Illinois 60201.

A Student's Consumer Guide. Published annually. U.S. Department of Education, P.O. Box 84, Washington, D.C. 20044.

Szorady, Mary Jo, and Debbie Talbot. *It's Your Move*. Biospherics, Inc., 4918 Wyaconda Road, Rockville, Maryland 20852, 1981.

How to Integrate Your Living/ Learning Environments: Living at Home, Living on Campus, and Living with Friends

Richard Wertz, *Vice President for Business Affairs*
University of South Carolina

I've always enjoyed my association with colleges and universities. As a student, I loved attending the university. As a career, my work in higher education has been worthwhile and fulfilling. My positive undergraduate and graduate experience had much to do with my returning to the academic world.

I grew up in a small university town in Pennsylvania, and lived there until I finished high school. I had planned to attend Penn State early in my high school career, even though it had an enrollment twice the size of my hometown. I was somewhat concerned about its size, but I wanted very much to go to school there. I lived in a residence hall during my freshman year and this turned out to be a highly supportive environment for me. Good friendships and

139

pleasant experiences contributed to the easy adjustment I made to college life.

Subsequently, I lived in a fraternity at Penn State that housed sixty-two men. This differed from the residence hall in that fraternity members were responsible for managing themselves, paying the house bills, and taking care of matters on their own. The fraternity was a supportive environment with plenty of people to talk to and many opportunities for relaxing after studies were over.

In graduate school, I lived in an apartment off-campus with two other students. Apartment living was very different from life in the dorm and the fraternity house. My apartment mates and I had to do everything on our own, from buying groceries to cooking and cleaning. And, of course, we needed to practice self-discipline since no one was there to make sure we studied!

The three "living" experiences I had in college, along with many other positive experiences from those days, led me to choose college administration as my lifelong career. As I look back, I realize how important it was for me—and how important it is in general—to find the proper residence environment in college, and my aim in writing this chapter has been to make you aware of that, too.

After you have made the decision to attend a particular college or university, the next most important consideration is where to live. Several options are available, and these choices can be narrowed down to three. You may decide (1) to live on campus, (2) to live at home, or (3) to live with friends. At least two of these categories offer a wide range of options that I'll discuss in more detail.

The college experience centers around the academic work your professors require of you. You attend college to learn and develop in the classroom, but an equally important aspect of college is your total development: the sum total learning experience of academic activities; interaction with faculty, staff, and other students; out of classroom time; and the total *living* experience on- or off-campus.

A great deal has been written about "the total development of the student." Colleges and universities have always recognized the importance of academic work and a "formal" education, but during this century higher education has directed more attention to the development of the student as a total person. The process of individual development has reached new levels as those of us in the university setting understand more fully the necessity of enhancing student development.

Because of this recognition of the importance of the total development of individuals, much has been written lately about it. One of the best descriptions or analyses of student development was written by Arthur Chickering, who has studied the development of students for a number of years. Chickering says there are seven steps, or what he likes to call "vectors," that young people confront as they go through college:

1. Achieving competence. This includes intellectual, social, and interpersonal competence as well as physical and manual skills.
2. Managing emotions, of which there are at least two: aggression and sex.
3. Becoming autonomous
4. Establishing identity
5. Forming interpersonal relationships
6. Clarifying purposes that include vocational and recreational interests, vocational plans and aspirations, and general lifestyle considerations.
7. Developing integrity, which is concerned with a valid set of beliefs that serve as a guide for behavior.*

These stages or "vectors" will be a major part of the collegiate living situation; whether on- or off-campus, alone or with friends, with parents or relatives, your living situation will change dramatically from what you were used to previously. What follows is a discussion of the various kinds of living arrangements and what you may expect from each.

Living on campus

For many students going to college means living away from home, making new friends, getting settled in a new environment. Living on campus can be a very exciting and interesting experience as it relates to college life.

Residence hall growth and interest

Dormitories, or residence halls as they are more appropriately called, are a product of the European influence on higher education. The Cambridge and Oxford University models in England were seen as examples of what higher education should be like in America. Residence halls were constructed in American colleges in an attempt to involve students in the academic life of the college and to allow students to meet with, learn from, and live with faculty members.

---

*Arthur Chickering, *Education and Identity* (San Francisco: Jossey-Bass, 1969, pp. 9–19).

This ideal situation occurred at some universities but met with difficulty at many other colleges, where the residence halls were convenient places for students to live, but served no real educational purpose as had originally been intended.

The strong interest in fraternity and sorority houses grew out of this concept and answered a need for students who wanted both a place to live and membership in an organization.

Current residence hall settings

For approximately twenty years American higher education has had a renewed interest in residence halls. Because students spend many hours each day in the residence hall, colleges and universities began taking a closer look at what other activities they could provide for students in these halls.

As a result, institutions began providing "things to do" in the residence halls. These activities have included: informal talks with faculty members invited over for coffee or evening get-togethers; a "free university," which allows practically anyone with an interest or ability in some topic to present that topic; a floor or hall intramural athletic contest; social interaction among the residents on the floor, in the hall, or with other halls; seminars by faculty or staff on campus or by personnel in business and industry off-campus; international cooking nights; guest speakers from on- or off-campus speaking on current topics; and other activities suggested by the residents themselves.

Take advantage of the time spent living in residence halls. Take advantage of activities that may be new to you or that you know nothing about. You may be surprised to find a new area that really interests you or for which you have some real talent.

This setting is a chance for you to excel at no risk. No grade will be given and no stressful expectations are set. Go ahead and try something new. You may actually learn something and have a good time doing it!

What can you expect when planning to live on campus? Several options or choices are available, and you'll need to consider each of them.

First of all, living on campus calls for a different sense of responsibility and behavior. You may be used to parents who expect you home by a certain hour or ask you to "check in" with them by phone. In the residence hall, your counselor or hall director may be around to supervise, but in this day and age generally no one is keeping tabs on you or demanding that you be in at certain hours.

Then, too, in most cases you'll be sharing the room with another person or persons. This calls for an adjustment to the living patterns of others and demands that you show consideration toward others. In most residence halls, a number of people live in a hall, although many residences now feature apartment-style living. This situation means another adjustment—to living with many individuals in the same building and sharing bathrooms, lounges, study areas, and so on.

Living on campus presents you with a great opportunity to associate with other college students and to grow and learn together. A strong feeling of friendship and togetherness develops as students share their college experience together.

Living in a residence hall is a time to learn and study together. It's a time to expand your thoughts about what life has to offer. You'll probably engage in many late "rap sessions" and discuss a limitless number of topics. Students living on campus have the opportunity to explore new frontiers of thinking and thoughts about themselves, their lives, their world at hand. Close friendships very often develop and a sense of belonging prevails. The development of lifelong friendships is not unusual among those who first meet in a residence hall.

In a residence hall, as in any other living environment, you must learn to budget your time. For the most part, it's your responsibility to keep up with assigned academic work and stay current with classes. Looking after personal belongings and keeping your room in some kind of organized fashion is also entirely your responsibility, as are keeping track of room keys, student identification cards, meal cards, and other valuables.

In most cases, an undergraduate or graduate hall advisor will be assigned to your hall. In some cases a full-time college employee will be in charge of the residence hall building. You may seek out a residence hall staff member for many kinds of assistance. The staff member typically is close to the students' ages, and trained to deal with all sorts of situations. Sometimes it's good to be able to discuss a concern or problem with someone who is competent to deal with the situation and is generally a caring, concerned individual. This staff member is usually available to students around the clock, day and night. You should feel free to contact him or her when you need help or just want to talk.

Theme halls

Recently, a great deal of emphasis has been placed on using residence halls as worthwhile educational and learning experiences for students. Growing out of this development has been the establishment of "theme halls" in residence halls that allow students to explore or expand areas of interest. Such theme floors or halls may be "language houses" (such as Spanish, German, French), honors halls, creative arts halls, history halls, engineering halls, architecture halls, and many others. The purpose of the special interest halls is to provide students with certain interests or talents an opportunity to live, learn, and pursue those interests together. These halls can allow you to find out something about yourself and to look at new areas at no risk and with no fear of false expectations. Usually there will be several such programs and you can select those that may appeal to you.

On many campuses, these special interest halls are available during your freshman year, and most campuses allow you to continue the arrangement as you progress toward graduation. As an incoming student, you thus get a chance to look around and match your campus residence to your personal interests. Activities on a special interest floor or hall center around the particular interest or theme involved. Special interest areas may have a relationship to a college major, a hobby or outside interest, or just exist because students want to learn more about, or be involved in, a certain activity.

Coeducational living

Not long ago the only residence halls offered by colleges and universities were strictly men's or women's halls. That is, men and only men lived in men's halls and women and only women lived in women's halls!

This option is still available. However, an option fairly new in higher education over the past ten to fifteen years has been coeducational living. Although students may have roommates of the same sex, the students on the floor above or below, in the next wing, or in the next room, may be of the opposite sex.

This development has led to a great deal of publicity in the media, and the public has often criticized colleges and universities for allowing it to occur. But the coeducation option has now been widely accepted in most sections of the country.

For the most part, coeducational living allows men and women students to get to know each other as individuals and, consequently, a healthy respect develops among students for the opposite sex. Instead of the wild, unsupervised partying many people expected, men and women students have learned to study together beyond the classroom, and brother and sister type relationships have developed. Friendships blossom and individuals are allowed to develop as individuals in a real-world environment.

Student culture in the residence halls

Just as coeducational living has been a fairly recent development, so has the elimination of curfew or restricted hours. In times past, students (especially women, as unfair as that was) were required to be in their residence halls at a certain time each night. For violating these curfew rules, students were "campused"—that is, restricted to their residence hall for a certain period—suspended from college, or expelled permanently.

At most colleges and universities today, there are no curfew hours. You're responsible for your own behavior. With this freedom comes a great deal of pressure from your friends to experiment. Such pressure may force you to decide about your own behavior in relation to drinking, drugs, sex, or some other sensitive area. You need to be prepared for such peer pressure and think about how to handle it. Certainly, peer pressure existed in high school; however, in college the stakes may be higher and the lifetime consequences may be greater.

Decisions about a number of things regarding your personal life will be thrust upon you in college. And living with a group of individuals twenty-four hours a day in a residence hall necessitates more decisions. You need to remember that you are, after all, your own person. You don't need to be pressured into anything and you don't have to do something you'd rather not because a friend or a group of friends is pressuring you. Ideally, the college experience will add to your feeling of independence and to the establishment of yourself as a person. You'll be learning to work through your own decisions and problems more and more as you "grow" through college.

Friends who pressure you into things, as you already know, may turn out not to be friends after all. Friends who stick by you, offer advice and assistance but no pressure may be your best friends. Remember: You become like the people you associate with, so choose your friends carefully!

Going home again

After living in the residence halls for a period of time, you'll probably adjust to group living, learn to become independent, "go it" on your own, and develop as a person. As a result, returning to home and family often brings with it the feeling of change. When you return home, many things may have changed and such changes may alter your relationship with your parents and relatives. In a residence hall, you are achieving full adult status and independence, and this is a natural and very healthy experience. Going home again, however, changes all that. You leave home as a teenager moving into adulthood, and each time you return, you're more of an adult.

You should be aware of these changes and understand the effects they may have on those at home. Your evolving status as an independent adult will be natural and should progress. But you'll need to have patience and understanding, because these changes may be a little difficult for your family to accept.

The situation is not a cause for concern if handled correctly. Tact and diplomacy certainly will be called for, and your patience may be tried when parents, relatives, or friends treat you as a schoolboy or schoolgirl. Remember, though, that their intentions are for the most part good and you'll need to be a little tolerant if they're slow in accepting you into the "adult fold."

So why choose a residence hall? For the friendships that will develop. For the maturity and growth that will help you gradually establish your own identity. For the experience you will surely gain by living with others in a new setting. For the opportunity to take part in activities, programs, projects, and learning experiences that are provided for you, and for the exciting prospect of getting to know yourself as a person through the new people you'll meet, the new experiences you'll have and the opportunity to be taking care of yourself. One more reason is that students living in residence halls tend to stay in college longer than those who don't!

Living at home

The pattern of life in high school is far more regimented and structured than what you will experience in college. High school starts at the same time each day and follows a fixed daily schedule. And the day ends at the same time for most high school students. This is generally not the case in college. Each day may call for a different schedule. Although classes may be in sequence, they usually don't meet every day. There will be days when classes start early or run late, and there will be time between classes. You won't always be able to have lunch at the same time each day, or dinner for that matter, because of class schedules.

Because of such realities, a student living at home will have many adjustments to make. The hours involved will dictate leaving or returning home at times completely different from high school, and the rest of the family as well will have to adjust to this new situation. As these changes occur, patience—yours and your family's—will certainly help.

Resolving issues

It's important to work out in advance any areas that may lead to potential conflict with the family. Although you may have enjoyed a great deal of freedom while living at home in high school, your parents probably felt they still exercised some supervision. As you develop into adulthood, you'll expect less supervision, and living with parents under these circumstances can strain the student/parent relationship!

It's best, then, to discuss "early on" with parents how living at home while attending college will necessitate a different pattern of living for you.

Your coming and going from the house based on scheduled classes, activities, and other interests will surely change from your high school days. Study habits will very often dictate "all nighters" or at least some very late night study sessions. Younger brothers or sisters may need to be "calmed down" so you can get ready for the big exam the next day. The demands of academic work may take you away from traditional family outings, and further strain the family relationship.

Establishing understanding

You can reduce or eliminate some of this stress and strain by reaching an early understanding. Sometimes, though, the conflict may not be resolved while you're living at home. In any event, life needs to go on for the family while you live at home; therefore, sacrifices will need to be made by both you and the other family members.

Since you'll probably have friends attending college who also live at home, it may help to discuss your areas of concern with your fellow commuters to see how they may have worked things out or what they may be doing in situations you're concerned about. You should also become friends with residence hall students, to become acquainted with the lifestyles of students living on campus. Spending time with students in the residence halls is a good opportunity for the student living at home to experience what it's like to live away from home. Remember, at some point, we all leave home!

Living at home with spouse/children

If you're living at home as a husband or wife, a different sort of adjustment is required of the spouse who's a student and the spouse who isn't. Budgeting time for study will be extremely important, and you'll have to allow enough time for academic work while either working or doing household chores. The parent attending college will need to work out a schedule to cope with both college and children's demands, and both parents must come to an agreement about priorities.

For married students budgeting time is extremely important if you're to succeed in college, and the strain of college demands will be heightened when children are involved. Making a schedule that takes into account both of these responsibilities and sticking to the schedule should be an early priority.

Holding down a job

If you must hold down a job while in college, the way in which you budget time is extremely important. The demands of your job in terms of work hours taken away from studying or other activities must be recognized early. There are, of course, only so many hours in the day. By working, you cut down on the number of hours available for other activities, and you'll need to weigh one against the other carefully so that neither academic work nor leisure time suffer.

As in marriage and child rearing, the demands of a job mean complying very strictly to a tight schedule to allow you time for study and other activities.

Living with friends

The student living in the residence halls will be making an adjustment both to living with others as well as to not living at home. Living with friends also requires an adjustment. You'll have many things to consider and work out, and these considerations should be discussed with your intended roommates ahead of time.

Living with friends probably means living in an apartment. Unlike living at home, where the family takes care of meals, laundry, housekeeping, and all of those other chores it takes to keep things running, living with friends will be different.

Adjusting to independence

Life away from home in private quarters off-campus with friends will be challenging. Setting up housekeeping requires that you develop or exercise the ability to perform a number of tasks. First of all, financing the venture will require adherence to some sort of budget. You'll need to set aside funds for items such as rent, food, utilities, telephone, cleaning materials (assuming the apartment is cleaned once in a while), and odds and ends such as dish/utensil replacement, curtain rods, linens, and so on.

Budget planning

It's more than a good idea to work out a budget in advance that everyone can agree with. If a group living arrangement is to work at all, everyone involved must contribute his or her share, and those shares will have to cover all of the expenses involved. What may be taken for granted in a residence hall or at home will have to be provided in the "living with friends" arrangement. Someone in the group will have to make certain that routine bills are taken care of. (See Chapter 9 for more pointers on money management.)

You'll find it necessary to adjust your budget as expenses vary. Cooperation in sticking to the budget is paramount. Sometimes unknown expenses, which are difficult to plan for, will occur and should be taken into consideration when preparing the budget. You may discover the groceries you bought and hoped would last two weeks are gone in five days. Or the utility bill was twice what you budgeted for and you thought you had really tried to conserve energy this month.

Sharing housekeeping duties

Sharing housekeeping duties is also important. If your group is cooking for themselves, grocery shopping will have to be done regularly. If you're all cooking on your own, you'll need to be considerate of each other's food.

You'll also need to take turns cleaning the living areas or assigning regular specific duties to specific persons. How the kitchen is cleaned and the condition it's left in will require cooperation and agreement from all parties. This is obviously also going to be true for bathroom cleaning and general upkeep.

Living with friends off-campus is the most independent lifestyle discussed so far. No parents or relatives or residence hall staff will be around in this situation. Responsibilities for your own actions will be extremely important and expected. Your time demands generally will be greater because the housekeeping chores will require time. This is a good reason to budget time adequately, if time for study and relaxation are to be programmed into the schedule.

Finally, living together with friends will require consideration of others' belongings and possessions as well as their rights and privacy. Without parents or hall staff around, disagreements or conflicts will need to be worked out by the parties involved. Being on your own really means just that when you live with friends off-campus. It can be a very worthwhile and fulfilling experience when handled properly as well as a great deal of fun. Working things out in advance, though, can contribute materially to the success of living off-campus with friends.

Living options: making the choice

We've discussed the various options open to students attending college. Your first year at college in any of these living alternatives will be an adjustment, just as college itself is an adjustment.

Living on campus, at home with parents, or off-campus with friends are the options available to you, and you may experience them all during your college years, as each year offers you an opportunity to rethink living arrangements. If you live in one arrangement during the freshman year, you may wish to change to a different arrangement the next year. A residence hall student, for example, may join a sorority or fraternity and live there until graduation. The student living with parents may decide to move on campus or into an apartment. The apartment dweller may wish to move into the residence halls. The residence hall student may wish to remain in the residence halls, but in a different room, hall, or complex.

The point is that change is possible and that several alternatives will be available. Some students choose to live in a different setting each year while others are more comfortable in the same situation each year. There's no ideal solution to living situations, other than to say that the best arrangement is what's best for you. A setting that allows you to study, to be able to make friends and socialize, and to get the most out of college is what you should seek.

Most assuredly, economic circumstances and other considerations will play a part in this decision. Still, choosing the right living arrangement is extremely important and will have a hand in determining your success or failure in college.

Suggested activities

1. Try compiling a list of questions to be settled with roommates as you think about what it would be like to live with friends off-campus. Try to visualize what might be needed in an apartment, what living there would be like, and how various duties would be done to keep the living quarters orderly.

2. If you live off-campus, interview several students living in residence halls and compare the pros and cons of dorm life to those of off-campus living or living with parents.

3. Arrange a debate in class with students living on-campus, off-campus, and at home, arguing the pros and cons of each situation. Discuss what you learned from this experience.

Suggested readings

Chickering, A. S. *Education and Identity*. San Francisco: Jossey-Bass, 1969.

DeCoster, D. A., and P. Mable, eds. *Student Development and Education in College Residence Halls*. Washington, D.C.: American Personnel and Guidance Association, 1974.

Feldman, K., and T. M. Newcomb. *The Impact of College on Students*. San Francisco: Jossey-Bass, 1970.

Sanford, N. *The American College*. New York: Wiley, 1962.

Establishing Rewarding Human Relationships in College

Mary Beth Love, *Teaching Associate*
School of Public Health
University of Massachusetts at Amherst

Learning to gain support from others has become a challenging and crucial element for me during my adult life. When I'm down, I find a call to a friend, a hug from my housemate, or merely a friendly "hello" from a store clerk can work wonders with my spirit. Positive people seem to feed my spirit just as healthy food nourishes my body. I was reared in a large Irish family, in a neighborhood where each household had a large number of children. So being close to people and part of a community have always been a way of life for me. After I left home, I found it more difficult to fulfill my need to be close to people. My behavior, for some reason, often unwittingly hurt or alienated people I thought of as friends, and I learned the hard way that not everyone was suited to be my close friend, and not every infatuation with a man was a guarantee that we had something in common.

The lessons I learned from these incidents forced me to become more aware of the dynamics of healthy human relationships, and to avoid the frustrations of unsatisfactory ones. From this, I have learned that certain skills and rules of thumb can facilitate love and cooperation among people. Applying these skills has enriched my personal and professional lives. In this chapter, I share what I deem to be important for establishing rewarding human relationships.

151

What is so wonderful is that anyone can learn these skills. I feel that love is essential to human life, and in this chapter I discuss the commitment and skills needed before love can be given or received. Understanding yourself, choosing your friends, and developing healthy partnerships are tremendous challenges and, at the same time, great joys. They are perhaps among the most crucial things we do as adults. It's my hope that this chapter and the suggested readings at the end will provide you with helpful insights into building supportive relationships during your college years—and during your lifetime.

Who is the most frustrating person you have ever known? The one who has caused you more trouble, sorrow, and anger than anyone else? Think carefully, because for most people, the most frustrating relationship they've ever had is with themselves.

Most of us tend to respect our friends much more than we respect ourselves, and we spend time wishing we were as good as, or more like, another person—forgetting that the most wonderful thing about ourselves is that each of us is a unique person! We blame ourselves for things that go wrong, even though the situation is beyond our control. And when someone congratulates or compliments us, we discount the remark, attributing it to luck, or even to that person's bad judgment!

What causes us to be so tough on ourselves? Perhaps part of the answer lies in the values of our society, which teaches us that it's wrong to take pride in our accomplishments. When we confront that attitude in the light of day, how stupid it seems! The most successful people on this earth have learned to love and respect themselves as much as they love and respect others, and one of the ways you can learn to feel good about yourself is to find out who and what you really are.

The search for identity

Throughout life, most of us are involved in an ongoing struggle to define ourselves. Who am I? What can I be? we ask. These questions constitute our search for identity, and it is our identity that serves as a foundation for our relationships with others. Loving and respecting yourself, otherwise known as developing a healthy and positive self-concept, is a difficult but necessary task in your evolving search for identity. The first successful "love affair" you must develop is the one with yourself, because if you can't love and respect yourself, it will be difficult for you to love and respect others.

Who am I?

Discovering just who you are can be difficult, for the self has many different aspects. Each of us has strengths and weaknesses, parts we like and parts we dislike. Knowing and accepting all parts of yourself is crucial to enhancing your self-esteem. An honest assessment of your personal strengths as well as your weaknesses provides the raw material you can use to design who you want to become. Each of us has unique gifts. Discovering yours will help you discover who you are.

Who can I be?

Whereas the answer to "Who am I?" derives from a combination of your natural predispositions and familial influences, the answer to "Who can I be?" emerges from your ongoing adult efforts to capitalize on your strengths and transform your weaknesses. Being realistic about the kind of person you wish to become will help you in the many decisions you face as a college freshman. Some of those decisions will involve choosing friends, choosing a major, and choosing activities. These are all building blocks for the future for you, and you should make such decisions with care.

Consummating your love of self

Not only are self-love and self-acceptance the bases of a happy, healthy person, they are also essential in the pursuit of healthy relationships with others. Self-esteem certainly is not reserved exclusively for people with good looks, intelligence, or loving parents. It's a process that requires attention and energy. Unfortunately, the tools for developing self-esteem are not well established or taught.

Each of us has grown up in a competitive culture where criticism abounds. Unfortunately, most of us have accepted that criticism and competitive spirit. Just listen to yourself for a moment. How often do you tell yourself you're "not OK" or that you're stupid or dumb? If you had to stand in front of a group and share what you don't like about yourself, would it be easier than talking about the good things you can do? Sad to say, most people find it easier to tell others about their weaknesses than about their strengths.

One way to help you like yourself better is to think of yourself as two different people. Accept these two people as caring for and loving one another. They are best friends, and your goal is to foster that love affair. Pay attention to what your two selves say to one another. Do they say things, for example, that you would never say to your best friend?

Here's a personal example. When I first began to monitor my "self-talk," I was surprised at how meanly I treated myself. In a recent racquetball game, I noticed that when my friend made a bad shot or missed an easy point, I would reach out to comfort and encourage him, pat him on the back, or say something kind. Ironically, when I made a bad shot, I would say terrible things to myself. "Get it together!" I would yell. "That sure was a stupid shot!" I would scream silently. Again and again, I would kick myself, saying things to myself that I would never say to my friend.

Such self-talk greatly influences our self-concepts. If we constantly draw attention to our faults, we probably won't like ourselves. If we consistently tell ourselves we're not OK, that's probably what we'll continue to believe. How important it is to be able to give ourselves the same kind of support and encouragement that we afford our friends and loved ones! It can be done.

Fostering your self-love begins with becoming more aware of your relationship with yourself. Realize that you are basically a very likeable person, or can become one if you simply will stop downgrading yourself to you. Pay particular attention to the things you tell yourself. Write them down and read them back. If you feel you deserve a reprimand, express it as a loving and benevolent parent might do to a child. Don't say, "That was a stupid thing to do." Instead, tell yourself, "Instead of doing it that way, it might be better to try this way." The old adage "Love your neighbor as yourself" can be turned around to mean "As you show love to your neighbor, so should you show love for yourself."

Presence

Your efforts to enhance the love affair with yourself will be a worthy investment. The rewards of this investment become part of the somewhat elusive aspect of self called *presence.* What you feel and believe about yourself is somehow transmitted to others, and they like you for it. The self-loving, self-knowing, self-accepting individual is the one most likely to gain understanding and acceptance from others. Another word for presence is *aura,* and some call this characteristic a *charisma.* It means there is evidence of a vibrant life within an individual, and he or she generates that vibrancy, or zest, in all directions.

Transitions can be opportunities

You don't discover, once and for all, who you are when you reach adulthood. Instead, self-discovery is a never-ending process. Each time you begin a new phase of your life, your self-relationship changes. These can be challenging times for you. Like many other new college students, you may have feelings of uncertainty or insecurity as you begin to redefine yourself in terms of new expectations and new friends.

In addition to being challenging, new beginnings add stress to our lives. Stress is inherent in the transition from your known, home environment to the unknown environment of college. Think back to the time when you were anticipating the move from home to college. You probably asked yourself: Will I be liked? Who will my friends be? How will I perform in class? Such questions were probably accompanied by conflicting feelings of anticipation/excitement and fear/uncertainty. Change usually involves such conflicting feelings. On the one hand, you sense the danger in giving up your familiar old friends and ways of doing things. On the other, you sense the opportunity to form new friendships and to establish new ways of doing things.

The transition from family and home to college is unique and challenging. It's a time of new beginnings and new freedoms. It gives you a chance, away from your home environment, to determine who you want to be. If you will honestly recognize your pitfalls as well as your perfections, you can redefine aspects of yourself and your environment so that they project and reflect a presence you can most love and respect.

Relationships

Men and women are social creatures who further their sense of self and the world through the relationships they share with others. I have argued that your self-relationship is the basis for all other relationships. The more you believe in yourself, the better will be your relationship with others. Because your family relationships are the earliest ones you have, they establish the patterns for, and the expectations of, your adult relationships.

If you felt loved and secure in your family, chances are you will feel the same way in your relationships with others. If you felt unloved and insecure, those feelings may affect your current and future relationships unless you take positive steps to change things. Trust, autonomy, initiative, industry, and a sense of identity are personal attributes that add to your ability to relate to others. If your family did not encourage these attributes—and most of us come from families where one or more of them weren't encouraged—you can still work to break those negative patterns and expectations.

When you leave the familiar surroundings of your home for college, you may not know how to develop new friendships initially. Since sharing human feelings and ideas is essential to human life, you may feel particularly lost, alone, and vulnerable at first. It's human at this time to reach out to anyone who can meet your need to relate. But, be careful! True intimacy between two adults—whether parent, friend, or lover—is perhaps the ultimate challenge of adult living. You are building a new world for yourself in college and you should pick your building materials carefully. The relationships you choose today will determine to a great extent the type of world you'll build tomorrow.

The purpose of relationships

"I get by with a little help from my friends" is a popular lyric with age-old wisdom behind it. That people need people is something we have long understood, but more recent research has confirmed the relationship between good health and good social relationships. For infants, the lack of human interaction may actually retard the development of intelligence. Adults who seek supportive social relationships find greater longevity and have less chance of developing a disease.

Most of us don't develop relationships to increase our life spans or to improve our minds and bodies. Such improvements are side effects. Instead, most people seek relationships with others to feel love, gain companionship, or simply to have fun. Mutual interests can be a basis for new relationships. A good way to find new friends is to get busy doing the things you love to do. That way, you're likely to meet more people who share a similar interest and a similar view of the world.

A good relationship helps you feel lovable and capable. It serves as a support system, allowing you to develop your full potential as a person. One of the most wonderful things you can do for friends is to help them develop their self-concept as they help you develop yours. Reinforcing people's positive perceptions of themselves frees them to discover their strengths and to wrestle with their shortcomings. What's even more remarkable is that such reinforcement also helps *you* feel better about yourself.

In other words, when you tell friends about their strengths, two things happen. They feel better about themselves and they want to tell you what they like about you, and that makes you feel better about yourself, too.

Intimacy

The following principles apply to all relationships, but are particularly crucial in establishing a strong romantic relationship. Moving beyond heartthrob infatuation to a relationship based on mutual fulfillment and loving support involves overcoming many obstacles. No easy formulas exist, but following the right principles can help you achieve true intimacy with another human being.

The heart

The romantic image of love created by the mass media creates the illusion that love removes all pain, fear, and anguish from life and ensures that we will all live happily ever after. Television, books, magazines, and other media create the unreal expectation that a romantic relationship involves none of the things we don't like in life.

What we sometimes don't realize in that first rush of love is that much of what we call love is infatuation. Infatuation is the irrational magic you feel when you're romantically attracted to another person. It comes from the heart and makes everything seem smiley and good. Infatuation can be an exciting and wonderful stage in the loving process, but such feelings are not particularly good criteria for establishing a lasting relationship. There's more to intimacy than your loving heartthrobs. There's your head.

The head

Before a love relationship can become serious, it's important for each party to explore the other's views. You do this naturally with friends, and it's even more crucial to do it with a lover. Do you have similar beliefs? Do you enjoy spending your spare time doing the same kinds of things? Are you, in other words, compatible? Do you like the way you feel about yourself when in the other person's company? With the current overemphasis on the romantic side of love, the realistic aspects of relating are often forgotten and can cause great confusion. Relationships are always experiments. Investing the energy to coordinate the intricacies of two personalities, two life histories, and two life goals is what keeps the channels of love open beyond the chemistry of infatuation. If you pursue a partnership strictly "from the heart," you may wind up falling in love with someone you don't like. We need to give and receive both love from the heart and respect from the head.

The mathematics of relationships

Earlier, I spoke about the importance of your relationship with yourself. Often, we pursue a love relationship in order to recapture a neglected part of ourselves. Too often, we're looking for a mother to care for us or a father to provide for us.

The law in mathematics shows that $\frac{1}{2} \times \frac{1}{2} = \frac{1}{4}$. This holds true in the mathematics of relationships. The passionate and dramatic saga of lovers who forever focus themselves on each other, gazing dreamingly into each other's eyes as they travel through a world to which they remain oblivious is unrealistic and, frankly, unfulfilling. Changing the dynamics to $1 \times 1 = 1$ changes that image to two upright, strong individuals standing supportively and lovingly beside one another, with their attention focused outward to the world. Accordingly, the major interest of intimacy should be to grow individually while exploring together as loving friends and life partners.

Overriding purpose and ultimate commitment

The ultimate purpose of an intimate relationship is not to feel passion or to gain security, but rather to feel loved and worthwhile. Sounds obvious, but how easily we miss the point! To commit yourself to another person's well-being is the ultimate commitment. True lovers encourage their partners to be what they are, and simultaneously support them in their struggle to become whom they want to become. True lovers know that if a partner's relationship to himself or herself and to his or her life is positive, then their relationship with each other will also be positive.

Love is no emotion for the uncourageous

Love is a powerful force. The sentimentalization of love by advertisers has led most of us to deal with it in a superficial manner. Loving intimacy is truly human, and it demands honest communication, trust, forgiveness, and responsibility. This is no task for the uncourageous!

The challenge of love demands that you move beyond politeness into an honest sharing of who you are and how you feel. When you feel strong, loved, and loving, honesty is easy. It becomes difficult when you feel weak, unloved, and angry. Being vulnerable, being real, and admitting you're not perfect takes courage, but the reward can be beautiful.

Importance of clear communication

Words help us understand ourselves and build relationships with others. As our cultures become increasingly complex, fast-paced, and mobile, the need for effective expression of our feelings and wants becomes more and more important. Each day, we deal with many individuals whom we know only superficially. Because they know so little about our history, personal lives, work, passions, and so on, they don't understand who we are, either. This is why good communications skills are essential in helping us build and maintain meaningful interpersonal relationships.

Learning clear communication

Becoming a clear and honest communicator requires three personal qualities: personal clarity, a willingness to risk, and good communications skills. Like most skills, this requires patience, practice, and perseverance, but the payoffs are tremendous. Alternate methods of communicating, such as second-guessing, cause hurt feelings and frustrated needs, and are the basis for misunderstanding between people. Being direct and honest can eliminate much of this hurt and frustration.

Personal clarity. To communicate, we first have to know what we want to share. As obvious as it seems, clarity in intimate issues is often hard to attain. Regular reflection and *introspection* (thinking about your own life) helps keep you in touch with your changing needs and desires. Making a conscious commitment to be familiar with yourself can result not only in clarity with others but in a sense of self-understanding and satisfaction. While introspection can't always ward off emotional crises and confusion, it can certainly make such upsets less surprising.

Another useful technique for developing personal clarity is *expression*. When an emotion is inside you and unclear, it tends to control you. As soon as you express that emotion and put words to it, the feeling should become more manageable. When the issues are particularly sensitive, role playing can help. For example, express your serious feelings in private to a chair named "Cathy" before you express them to Cathy herself. When you describe your feelings out loud in a nonpressure situation, you tend to see things more clearly.

Willingness to risk. The second thing necessary for clear communication in a relationship is a willingness to risk. Each time we communicate to another, we risk placing that relationship on the line. Because many of us refuse to take such risks, many of our relationships remain safely and unrewardingly shallow. This fear of losing keeps many of us from striving for true intimate sharing with those we love.

The other risk we take is the risk of being human. We hesitate to admit that, like all human beings, we are sometimes scared, frail, needy, and vulnerable, as well as brave, strong, sufficient, and in control. When we define ourselves to others as strong, and don't allow our weaknesses to show, we lose part of our humanity in the eyes of others. You must be strong to communicate the fact that you are sometimes weak. It takes courage to risk being fully who you are with another human being.

Communications skills. The third requirement of clear communication is practice. Communications skills are like any other new skills. Initially, they may seem awkward and unnatural, but practice makes them seem second nature. Being a good listener is an important communications skill. It may seem odd to consider listening a skill, but few people do this as well as they could. They forget, for example, that nonverbal messages such as eye contact, leaning forward, and a touch can all reinforce communication. Verbal techniques of a good listener include: repeating back to people what you heard them say in order to ensure understanding; asking for clarification so you can understand what a particular speaker is experiencing; and, above all, letting other people know they're OK. Nine times out of ten, all people want is someone who will listen and tell them they're OK.

The communications model used in assertiveness training is excellent and highly effective for expressing needs and making requests both to loved ones and to strangers. See Chapter 12 for more about assertiveness.

If you practice being honest and straightforward with yourself and expressing your needs or complaints in a nonthreatening manner, you'll be well on your way to acquiring the self-understanding and communications tools that facilitate meaningful personal contact with loved ones, friends, and strangers.

Trust

Trust is another pillar in a healthy relationship. Through mutual trust, we gain the confidence to explore, to risk, and to stumble. Establishing and reinforcing trust in your relationship takes nurturing, and begins with the belief that you are loving and trusting and that your friends love you and will not take advantage of you intentionally, or cause you needless pain. Trust must also be reinforced constantly. When you continually express your love through your words, actions, or deeds, you build the confidence your friends have in you, as well as their trust in your loving intention.

Forgiveness

Forgiveness means letting go of judgments and grievances. Since we are never totally in touch with ourselves, with what motivates and stirs us, we often develop grievances that lead us to make choices that hurt us and those who care for us. Forgiveness means releasing those grievances and allowing yourself to believe in the good intentions you trust your partner to have. This doesn't mean you should allow yourself to become a doormat for someone else, but it does imply that you accept the fact that transgressions are part of the human growth process.

Humor/fun

"Humor" in Latin means fluid. Humor is the juice of the mind that gives life such a rich flavor. Laughter and sharing pleasures can be the magic that turns the struggle for intimacy into the adventure of love. Strive to laugh and to share pleasures in your relationships. A laugh can serve as the balm that eases you through the painful phases of being in love.

Sexuality

A primary part of your self-image is your maleness or femaleness, and sexual behavior is the physical expression of that part of our identities. Expressing yourself sexually with another human can be either positive and enriching, or destructive to yourself and to others. Only through awareness, understanding, and responsible sexual behavior can you establish your sexual self-confidence and experience the joy of sex. Sex does not *establish* who you are—it *expresses* who you are.

Read that again. Sex does not *establish* who you are. While sex itself is perfectly natural, bragging about it is usually in poor taste. All too often, college freshmen find themselves listening to all sorts of fanciful stories about the sexual experiences of other college students. It may seem as if everyone in college were a walking encyclopedia of sex! But while talk about sex certainly has become more open in recent years, the act of sex remains a private matter between just two individuals and, while it can be a joyous experience, it's not a prerequisite for success and happiness in life.

Peer pressure can transform sex from expression into obsession, and that can take most or all of the pleasure out of it. No book can tell you what your choices should be, and you shouldn't listen to your friends just because their ideas seem right for them. Sexual feelings and desires are natural aspects of being human, and engaging in sexual intercourse is a personal moral decision. Before you determine the degree of intimacy appropriate in a relationship, you should examine your values and clarify your feelings. Ultimately, nobody else can determine those values for you.

Discrimination in how you express yourself sexually can ward off the guilt, remorse, and self-denial that too often limit the beauty of sharing oneself sexually with another individual. Strong sexual bonding, therefore, is part of an enduring and intimate relationship, and requires all of the characteristics we have described before: self-knowledge, courage, communication, trust, forgiveness, and fun.

For more information about sex, find out whether your college or university offers a course in human sexuality, and take it. You may also want to visit your campus counseling center or peer advisement center. Like everything else in life, sex can be more rewarding if you do your homework before you take the final!

Sexual responsibility: birth control

Although responsibility is the common thread running through all aspects of a healthy relationship, sexual intimacy makes special demands for responsible behavior. Unwanted pregnancies and venereal diseases are potential consequences of sexual activity that you must deal with in a mature and responsible manner. Although most birth control methods were developed for use by women, the responsibility for preventing unwanted pregnancy should be shared by both partners. Resources for further information on contraceptive methods are available on most college campuses. It's important to understand the mechanics, benefits, and risks of all types of birth control methods, so that you'll select a method that best suits your needs and sexual behavior pattern. Here is a brief summary of current contraceptive methods. Contact your health center on campus for more detailed information.

Surgical sterilization. With surgical sterilization, a woman's fallopian tubes are cut, tied, blocked, or removed to prevent the egg from reaching the uterus ("tubal ligation"). For a man, a portion of the vas deferens is removed to prevent sperm from traveling from the testes to the prostate ("vasectomy"). A physician must perform these operations, which have no known side effects and are intended to be permanent; such procedures are seldom recommended until after a couple has had children or are absolutely certain they don't want any. Obviously, it's seldom the technique of choice for university students.

Oral contraceptive ("the pill"). Oral contraceptives, which must be prescribed by physicians, are tablets that contain hormonal substances. Those that contain only synthetic progesterone ("mini pills") do not specifically prevent ovulation and are not sufficiently contraceptive to be recommended for that particular purpose. Pills that contain estrogen and progestogen ("combination pills") prevent ovulation and are the most effective nonpermanent pregnancy preventive presently available. Certain restrictions to their usage exist, but by and large they are safe for 85 percent of the total female population and 95 percent of those of college age.

Intrauterine device (IUD). An intrauterine device, or IUD, is a small plastic or plastic and metal device that sometimes also contains synthetic hormones and is inserted into the uterine cavity by a physician. It probably prevents pregnancy by physically disturbing the uterine lining, but is much less effective when the user has had no children. It carries the chance of unrecognized expulsion as well as a markedly increased risk of deep pelvic infection with secondary infertility. These problems have resulted in a decreased popularity of this method for most women under 25 years of age.

Barrier techniques. With barrier techniques, we come, for the first time, to a place for male participation. In fact, to achieve maximum effectiveness, the male must participate! Additionally, here for the first time we have a pregnancy-prevention technique that also provides some degree of protection against the spread of venereal disease, especially when the male partner gets into the act. There are four major types of barrier contraceptives. We will mention each separately, but it's only when both partners accept mutual responsibility and each uses a barrier simultaneously that maximum protection is attained. This level of effectiveness still falls somewhat short of that provided by oral contraceptives, but consistent use leads to a reasonably close approximation.

1. *Condom (Prophylactic, Rubber):* A condom, a sheath of latex or animal membrane, may be purchased without a prescription and is placed over the erect penis before vaginal entry. Its purpose is to prevent semen from escaping, but it must be applied with a little "slack" at the end to prevent rupture upon ejaculation, and careful removal of the penis from the vagina is essential to prevent spillage. Partial completion of coitus before applying a condom decreases its effectiveness to the level of "withdrawal" alone.

2. *Spermicidal Chemicals:* Spermicidal chemicals include foams, creams, gels, and suppositories that don't require a prescription for purchase. They are inserted into the vagina shortly before intercourse in order to kill sperm as well as block their entry via the cervix into the upper reproductive tract. Inserting the material a long time before intercourse so that its effective time expires or so low in the vagina that it doesn't contact the cervix are common reasons for failure.

3. *Vaginal Sponge:* The vaginal sponge is the newest (and most expensive) of the nonprescription barriers. It has the advantage that you insert it one time in order to get twenty-four–hour dispersal of the same spermicidal material previously mentioned. The polyurethane foam is also shaped to fit closely to the cervix.

4. *Diaphragm and Cervical Cap:* Both the diaphragm and cervical cap must be fit individually by a physician who will supply the unit or provide a prescription for it. Although they are classified together, these should not be confused with one another. The diaphragm has been around for years and has a well-defined record of effectiveness, whereas the cervical cap is not yet universally available and must be considered experimental. The diaphragm requires the accompanying use of a spermicidal cream or gel to achieve adequate protection. Regular inspection for even the smallest of holes and replacement at reasonable intervals are essential. Moreover, an intervening pregnancy or a weight gain or loss of ten to fifteen pounds warrant a physician's reevaluation because of a possible accompanying size change.

Withdrawal (coitus interruptus). As the name implies, withdrawal is accomplished by the male withdrawing from the vagina before ejaculation. Unfortunately, occasional "leakage" of semen may occur without either participant being aware of it, and at other times the emotions of the moment overwhelm one's best intentions. Either event will result in the presence of sperm in the vagina; hence, this method is not very reliable.

Rhythm. The theory of the rhythm technique is that certainty of the time of ovulation (release of an egg) allows a couple to avoid intercourse during a time when conception is most likely. In reality, the practice is much more difficult and requires more stability and knowledge than most young people have had the opportunity to obtain.

Douching. Douching involves washing the semen out of the vagina immediately after intercourse and provides the poorest results of any mentioned. No self-respecting sperm will wait around long enough for this sort of nonsense.

After-the-fact medication ("morning after pill"). There are various types of high dosage female hormones that many doctors recommend for use shortly after unprotected intercourse (a maximum of 72 hours). They prevent implantation of an egg by altering the uterine lining tissue. At present these are not recommended by the Food and Drug Administration and require carefully controlled use.

Sexual responsibility: venereal disease

We now hear not only of "VD" but also of "STD" (sexually transmitted disease). No matter what we call them, many different infections that are spread by intercourse are included in these classifications. Whenever and wherever sexual activity increases, so does the incidence of sexually transmitted diseases. This is true on many college campuses. Our knowledge about such infections is changing so rapidly that it is impractical to attempt to offer specific information here. Nonetheless, sexual activity should be accompanied by individual responsibility toward awareness of the risks, symptoms, and treatment of venereal diseases. Campus or community health centers are readily accessible and are excellent resources.*

Conclusion

During your college years, you will have the opportunity to establish deep and meaningful relationships. The quality of your relationships will determine, to a large extent, the quality of your college experience and of your life. Commitment to growth and integrity in your relationships demands maturity and requires your utmost attention and consideration.

*Special thanks to Dr. William A. Potts of the University of South Carolina Health Center for providing the information on birth control and sexually transmitted diseases.

Suggested activities

1. Projecting Goals: On three different pieces of paper, write your goals for:
   a. the next three months
   b. the next year
   c. the next five years
   Now, hang (a) in a visible place. Place (b) and (c) in envelopes and date them. Exchange envelopes with someone very important in your life—a spouse, lover—who will agree to forward them to you at one and five years into the future.
2. Self-talk: In order to become aware of your negative internal monologues, monitor and record your self-criticisms for three days. Then pick one of these and decide how you will change your behavior to rid yourself of the criticism. For each remaining criticism, write two positive things about yourself and read them once a day for a week.
3. Humor: Memorize three jokes and tell them to friends.
4. Choose a day to compliment three strangers, two friends, and one enemy.

Suggested readings

Boston Women's Health Book Collective. *Our Bodies, Ourselves.* New York: Simon and Schuster, 1971.

Branden, Nathanial, and Devers Branden. *The Romantic Love Question and Answer Book.* Los Angeles: T. P. Tarcher, 1982.

Emery, Steward, and Neal Grogan. *Actualization: You Don't Have to Rehearse to Be Yourself.* New York: Doubleday Books, 1978.

Jampolsky, Gerald G. *Love Is Letting Go of Fear.* New York: Bantam Books, 1979.

Jourard, Sidney M. *The Transparent Self.* New York: D. Van Nostrand, 1971.

Mayeroff, M. *On Caring.* New York: Harper and Row, 1971.

Rogers, Carl. *On Becoming a Person.* Boston: Houghton-Mifflin, 1961.

Sheehy, Gail. *Passages.* New York: E. P. Dutton, 1976.

Standing up for Yourself— Without Stepping on Others

Ruthann Fox-Hines, *Counseling Psychologist*
Counseling and Human Development Center
University of South Carolina

In high school, when I had to talk in front of a class, the paper shook louder than my voice. I have so many "if onlys" when I think back to how I could have handled my college experience differently—how much I missed academically and socially because I wasn't assertive. I didn't question professors. I let folks take advantage of me. I allowed friendships to disintegrate because I wouldn't bring up things that bothered me until they had reached crisis level. I was a beautiful example of the passive person. In graduate school, I switched to the opposite extreme—aggressiveness; nobody was going to push me around. I was going to be tough. That didn't win me too many points, either.

It wasn't until after graduate school that I learned about assertiveness, and studied and acquired the skills involved. Now I'm a Ph.D. and a licensed counseling psychologist in my ninth year with a university counseling center. I'm a director and vice-president of Resource Associates, Inc., a consulting firm. I'm the mother of a 19-year-old son, with (not "at") whom I can talk. I can get up in front of 300 people and hold their attention. I can get the service I

167

desire in most stores, and I can deal with issues involving friends and colleagues. It has made such a difference in both my professional and personal life that I want to share it with you.

In this chapter, I'll describe the skills of positive communication, often called "assertive behavior." Assertive behavior is always based on mutual respect and on personal responsibility. I hope this chapter motivates you to examine your forms of interacting and to seek further training.

The importance of communications skills

In college and beyond, the skills of standing up for yourself effectively, of communicating your wants, needs, feelings, and ideas in a positive manner are extremely important. Concerned parents or teachers who look out for you may not be around when you need them, and mind readers are extremely rare. It's up to you to communicate your needs specifically, clearly, and with respect for yourself and the other person.

Stop and think a moment of the many occasions when you wished you had such skills! Perhaps you needed to talk to an advisor about getting into a course, or had to ask an instructor to explain an obscure point in a lecture. Maybe you and your roommates have never agreed upon living arrangements and responsibilities. The number of situations is endless and might include: resisting pressures from overly concerned parents, equitably sharing responsibilities on a committee, having your input heard and valued in classes, handling job interviews successfully, negotiating work requirements such as salary and hours. All these call for the skills of positive communication.

Some of you find it easy to stand up for yourselves, but many of you also find yourselves on the receiving end of negative results and reactions. For others of you, standing up for your rights is very difficult, and you go through life hoping someone else will figure out what you want, and do your standing up for you. The sad truth is, someone else rarely will.

Varieties of communication

Most of us picked up our communications skills in a rather disorganized fashion. We probably began by imitating parents, other family members, and our peers.

You might compare this to learning grammar exclusively from everyday conversations, without once consulting a grammar book.

Not standing up for yourself, or standing up in a poor way, tends to cause frustration and poor relationships with others. Generally, if we do our learning in the pick-it-up-as-you-go-along school, our communication of feelings, needs, and so on will tend to fall into one of four categories:

1. *Passive:* not speaking up, hinting, whining, poor-me routines.
2. *Aggressive:* speaking up in a put-down way, demanding, pressuring.
3. *Passive-aggressive:* speaking up in a confused way, saying one thing and doing another ("Sure, I'll be there on time," and showing up late).
4. *A mix of the above:* hinting sometimes, sending out mixed messages to others, and demanding at other times.

None of these attempts at communication is particularly well received by other people. The poor communicator is frequently disappointed, rejected, or even avoided.

Assertive behavior

The most effective and positive ways of standing up for yourself, and of communicating your needs and feelings properly are referred to as assertive behaviors. Assertiveness is clear, direct, respectful, responsible communication—verbal and nonverbal. It can be so much more effective than passive or passive-aggressive forms of communication because your chances of being heard and understood are greater, and the chances of the receiver of your communication drawing away, closing his or her ears to what you have to say, or coming back at you fighting are less. If others hear and understand you, and don't feel the need to protect themselves from you, your chances of getting an acceptable response are much greater.

One definition of assertiveness labels it as behavior that permits a person to stand up for his or her rights without denying others their rights. This definition is extremely important. If we simply stand up for our rights, we'll probably come across as aggressive. If we focus exclusively on the rights of the other person, we become passive. Attention to our own *and* others' rights is important in learning to be assertive.

And what are those rights? They include personal rights, such as the right to one's own feelings, and interpersonal rights, such as the right to ask others for what we want or need. To avoid denying others their rights, we need to be aware of, and consciously acknowledge, the rights of others. For example, although you have the right to ask a favor, other people have the right to tell you that they refuse to grant it.

Mutual respect and personal responsibility

To stand up assertively for your rights, two conditions must be present that are completely or partially missing from other forms of communication: mutual respect and personal responsibility.

Basically, these conditions can be expressed in the following manner: I respect myself and my right to my ideas, feelings, needs, wants, and values, and I respect you and your rights to the same. I take responsibility for myself. I don't require you to be responsible for me and for figuring out what I want; I'll figure it out for myself.

Passive, passive-aggressive, and aggressive behaviors tend to lack respect for the self and/or the other person, and all three tend to be irresponsible forms of behavior.

Examples of inappropriate behaviors

An example may help you distinguish the various behaviors. You are serving on a class committee, and one of the other students isn't doing her share of the work. You're becoming extremely frustrated and worried about the grade you may receive on the project if this other person doesn't come through. The *passive* approach might be to hint about the deadline, and leave it up to the other person to figure out that you're concerned. Using this approach, you show that you're not respecting your own feelings and needs enough to make them known, and that you're putting the major responsibility for figuring out what you mean on the other person.

The *passive-aggressive* approach might be to complain to another committee member. This shows a lack of respect for the person you should be addressing. Haven't you often said, "I wish he would respect me enough to come to me instead of talking to others about me?" This behavior is irresponsible because you probably hope that the person you complain to will take the responsibility of saying something to the individual at fault.

The *aggressive* approach might be to confront the individual in this manner: "You're messing it up for the rest of us. How can you be so inconsiderate? If you don't have your part ready by tomorrow, I'm telling the professor!" This attack ignores the other person's feelings entirely and possibly overlooks mitigating circumstances of which you may be unaware. Thus, it is disrespectful.

If these three forms of address are incorrect and inappropriate, what is the assertive, or proper, approach?

The assertive approach

The *assertive* approach respects the other person and does not attack her, yet still deals directly with the issues and is responsible enough to express feelings and wishes clearly (in specific words, not by implication or tone of voice).

Such a communication might sound like this: "Mary, I have a problem. Our project is due next week and I'm worried we won't have it ready on time. I had my part ready yesterday, the day we agreed on. I figure you probably have a heavy load and may have forgotten we agreed on that date. Still, I'm sort of frustrated and worried that we won't have a good project. Would you please make this a priority, and do your part so we can meet either tomorrow afternoon or noon the next day at the latest? I'd very, very much appreciate it."

The other person may feel embarrassed, but there's a good chance she won't feel as if you attacked her, and therefore won't be forced to take a defensive position. When people are attacked, they defend themselves either by "flight" or "fight." Using flight, they passively comply to another's wishes, but resentment builds inside them. Using fight, they openly throw back accusations or fight subversively (passive-aggressive) by getting the work done, but in a rather slip-shod fashion.

On the other hand, when you approach people in a respectful and open manner, chances are they'll hear you more clearly and respond in a more positive manner.

Formula for assertiveness

To make assertive communication your method for standing up for yourself, you may find the following formula helpful: $R\rightarrow$, $R\leftarrow$, S.

Respect the other person

$R\rightarrow$ reminds you to communicate respect for the other person. Incidentally, respect does not necessarily mean liking, admiring, or agreeing with that person. It simply acknowledges that the other person *is* a person with the same basic rights as you. In other words, you can dislike someone's behavior or disagree with her or him, and still offer basic human respect.

We communicate respect both in speech and in actions, in the words we choose to use, and in the nonverbal expressions that accompany the words. The verbal expression may be as simple as saying, "Excuse me," as you move through a crowd getting off an elevator, instead of pushing your way through silently. Your words may acknowledge that the other person has his or her own set of values and needs: "I realize you have established certain criteria for grades in this class . . ." is a good opener when you're about to discuss a possible grade change with a professor.

The verbal communication may even express empathy: "I realize you have a heavy load." It may offer the benefit of the doubt: "I'm sure it probably just slipped your mind." Respect for other people means giving them what we want to receive: courtesy, acknowledgement, and empathy.

Nonverbal communications of respect for others may be expressed in gestures, facial expressions, and tone of voice. Such communications may be more significant than words. Said in the wrong tone of voice, "I realize you have a heavy load" could have an opposite and sarcastic meaning. Attention to your nonverbal communications becomes essential to learning effective and positive methods of standing up for yourself.

Nonverbal expressions that communicate respect for others include a clear, relatively gentle and unhurried manner of speaking, eye contact when another person is talking, uncrossed arms to signal openness, and giving others appropriate physical space so they don't feel crowded or intimidated. Since many college campuses have international students, it's important to point out that cultural differences exist in nonverbal as well as verbal communications. Because of this, you should not take certain nonverbals as signs of disrespect when the individual expressing them is of a different cultural background. For example, Mediterranean, Latin American, and Middle Eastern people need much less space between themselves and others (as little as twelve inches) than their Northern European or North American counterparts (who require as much as three feet). Unless we're aware of differences like these, we could interpret such behavior as intimidating and disrespectful.

Respect yourself

R← reminds you to respect yourself and to accept personal responsibility for your feelings, wants, actions, and so on. A major way to accomplish this verbally is to use the first person singular pronoun: I, me, my—especially the "I." Say "I feel . . .," not "You make me feel . . ."; "I need more time," not "That's not a lot of time" (indirect, almost a hint), or "Give me more time" (a demand). Say "I don't want to . . .," not "Wellllll, maybe . . .," or "No! How could you ask me that?"

Nonverbal communication of self-respect also includes such things as eye contact and open body movements. Both imply that you believe what you say and have nothing to hide. Holding your head up instead of lowering it tends to communicate assurance rather than fear. Ending a spoken sentence with a softened, slightly lowered voice instead of an "up in the air" question mark shows that you have confidence in what you're saying.

Be specific

S stands for specificity, or being specific, which develops from personal responsibility and respect for the other person. Specificity means being responsible enough to figure out your views, feelings, and wants, and being able to communicate them as clearly as possible. It means avoiding labels or generalities about other people and their behavior. Instead of saying, "How can you be so inconsiderate?" when a smoker allows smoke to blow in your direction, you might try this: "I'm having a problem with the smoke from your cigarette. Would you please blow it in the other direction?"

Avoid labels such as "inconsiderate," "lazy," "poor attitude." Don't you feel attacked when others use these labels on you? Talk about the behaviors that lead you to think about those labels. Avoid generalities such as "love," "attention," and "respect." Instead, determine the specific behaviors you include in your definitions of those vague terms, and talk about those behaviors. For instance, if you don't like someone to keep looking at a magazine when you're talking to her, don't say, "You don't respect me." Instead, you might try saying, "I'm uncomfortable when I talk to someone and don't get eye contact. When we talk, I'd appreciate it if you'd put your magazine down. It would help a lot."

Choosing the proper response: an example

To see the formula at work, let's go through an example. Mark is a relatively conscientious student. His roommate John seems to be majoring in partying. John cuts classes and regularly borrows Mark's notes from the two classes they share. Although Mark has been rescuing John by giving him his notes whenever John asks (being the "good guy"), he is beginning to feel used. One important lesson from this example is that "rescuers become victims." If you do for others what they can and should do for themselves, they tend to demand more and more and value what they get less and less.

Mark's first mistake was not to make his position clear at the start. A suggestion I can't stress too strongly is: The more you take responsibility for yourself—know what you feel and what your priorities and wants are, and make them clearly known to others—the fewer problems you'll have down the road.

The first time John asked to borrow the notes, Mark could have said, "I know you missed class and need the material *(acknowledging John's plight: R→)*. But I don't usually lend my notes. I'll let you use them this time, but in the future, please don't ask. Find someone else or talk to the instructor" *("I" statements of a clear policy and Mark's wishes: R← and S)*.

If John pressures him, Mark may need to protect himself by tightening his communication and using what is sometimes referred to as a "broken record":

No matter what John says, Mark responds by repeating the major message: "I don't lend my notes." Here is an example:

JOHN: Ah, come on. I thought we'd be able to take care of each other in classes *(a guilt trip)*.

MARK *(resisting the guilt and focusing on the major issue):* I don't lend my notes out. This time I said OK, but from now on, no.

JOHN: Hey, what kind of buddy are you? I thought we could count on each other.

MARK: John *(using the other person's name may make him more attentive)*, I don't lend my notes. I hope you'll respect that, and not use it to judge whether or not I'm a good buddy.

At this point, John may start to slam out of the room in a huff.

MARK: Hey John, I'm sorry you've taken my not lending out notes that way. I hope later you'll accept my position.

Since Mark didn't take care of this issue at the outset, he's reaching a pretty frustrating point and probably establishing a negative pattern of interaction with John. He could slip into a passive approach easily, avoiding his room as much as possible so he can avoid John. Or, he could become passive-aggressive and let his frustration show in his voice, make sarcastic remarks, or even give John the wrong notes. Finally, he could explode in an aggressive outburst: "Don't you ever take your own crummy notes? I'm sick and tired of doing all your work for you. Find someone else to mooch off. And, by the way, I'm also sick and tired of ..." Here, all Mark's other little frustrations with John may come pouring out.

Any of these alternatives will result in added frustration on Mark's part, distancing between the two, or even fight or flight on John's part: a loud argument, sneak attacks, or stony silences. There's a good chance that both will be seeking new roommates at a time when reshuffling may be very difficult.

The assertive approach

The assertive approach, while not guaranteeing that Mark will get what he wants from John, at least opens the door for such a possibility. First, Mark needs to separate the issues he has with John—notes, noise, privacy, or whatever—and decide which issues he wants to deal with first. Dealing with individual issues is better than dumping a whole load of complaints on a person all at once. Mark should also find a time when he can talk to John alone. Complaints made in front of others tend to be disrespectful and cause the other person to be more defensive. Then he might say, "John, I know I've been lending you my notes for X and Y classes. *(By acknowledging his own part, Mark is showing respect for John: R→.)* But I'm beginning to feel used. I don't mind lending my notes if someone is sick, but I really don't like doing it on a regular basis *("I" statements and clarity of feelings and wishes: R← and S)*. I know I should have said something earlier *(again, R←, accepting responsibility that isn't John's).* I want to break that pattern. From now on, I'm not lending my notes, and I'm asking you not to ask me for them. Find someone else or talk with the instructor" *(more "I" statements and a clear statement of what he doesn't want and what he wants from John: R← and S).* If John pushes, Mark can resort to the "broken record" described earlier.

Learning effective communications skills

Since assertiveness, which encompasses standing up for yourself effectively and communicating in a positive manner, is a behavior pattern, we can learn these methods of interacting as skills. Learning communications skills is similar to learning to drive a car. First, you practice in "safe" places such as the driveway or empty parking lots. Later, as you feel more comfortable with your skills, you try driving on the streets, and, eventually, in five o'clock traffic. When you first learn to drive, such skills as braking smoothly feel unnatural and awkward. Later, after practicing, you reach a point where you don't even have to think about it.

The same is true with communications skills. First, you try simple skills in such places as a training group. When you first try these new communications, they may feel funny (uncrossing your arms, for example, if you're in the habit of keeping them crossed). Later, with practice, you find you can use these behaviors in the "real world." Still later, you'll find you don't have to think very much about them. At that point, they've become natural.

The best way to learn assertive behavior skills is through special training seminars. Most colleges and universities, through their counseling centers or continuing education programs, and many community organizations such as the YWCA and YMCA offer workshops, short courses, or seminars in assertiveness. Books listed at the end of this chapter may also be useful to you. Remember, though, that reading and learning aren't enough. Practice is the essential ingredient.

Suggested activities

1. Think about how you would explain to a friend that assertiveness is not the same as aggressiveness.

2. Indicate the type of communication in each of the following examples: assertive (AS), passive (P), passive-aggressive (PA), aggressive (AG).

_____ a. A mother indicates she would like her college student child to come home each weekend. The student replies: "Mom, I know you love me and want what's best for me. Right now, with studies and the friendships I'm trying to establish, what's best for me is to have most of my weekends here. I won't be coming home except at breaks, but I promise I'll write or call at least once a week. Thanks for understanding."

_____ b. You're asked to do a favor. Your reply: "Are you kidding? Hell, no!"

_____ c. You're a student and need to borrow a classmate's notes. You say to her: "I don't know what I'm going to do. I missed Dr. Carter's class last Friday and that test of his is next week. Oh, Lord, I know I'm going to do awful. I'll probably flunk."

_____ d. Someone pays you a compliment. You reply: "Thank you. I appreciate your noticing."

_____ e. You're upset with a friend who usually walks in late for meetings. He does it again. You say: "Oh, look. Sam's on time for a change!"

_____ f. You'd like to ask your roommate to play the stereo more softly. You say: "Mark, I don't have any problem with the fact that you enjoy the stereo loud. What I have a problem with is that, when I'm here and trying to study, the loud stereo breaks my concentration. When I'm out, do as you like. But, please, when I'm here, keep it lower. I'd appreciate it a lot."

Answers: a. AS b. AG c. P d. AS e. PA f. AS

3. Contact your college or university counseling center or continuing education department for information regarding workshops or seminars on assertive behavior.

4. Get together with friends or fellow students who are interested in developing these skills. Use the workbook *Assert Yourself* by Galassi and Galassi (see Suggested readings) as a guide for training.

Suggested readings

Butler, Pam. *Self Assertion for Women.* San Francisco: Canfield Press, 1976.

Emmons, M. L., and R. E. Alberti. *Your Perfect Right.* San Luis Obispo, Calif.: Impact Publishers, 1974.

Galassi, J., and M. Galassi. *Assert Yourself.* (workbook) New York: Human Sciences Press, 1977.

Jacubowski, R. and A. J. Lang. *The Assertive Option.* Champaign, Ill.: Research Press, 1978.

Anxiety Management

Kevin King, *Counseling Psychologist*
Counseling and Human Development Center
University of South Carolina

I became interested in anxiety management training back when I was in graduate school. At that time, I was put in charge of a large speech desensitization program designed to help people overcome speech anxiety. What no one knew then was that I myself suffered from speech anxiety. Actually, almost everyone does at some point in their lives. It's perfectly normal.

I was lucky, though. Being in charge of the speech desensitization program was like taking a crash course in learning how to manage anxiety. I came away from it with a great interest in developing my own management anxiety skills still further. And I wanted to be able to teach others how they could manage anxiety more effectively for themselves. In this chapter I try to do just that. It's just a beginning, but I hope you'll be interested in looking into it further.

Anxiety is a naturally occurring phenomenon. The only time we know for sure that people don't feel anxiety is when they're dead! So, to that extent, anxiety is a good thing to have. Yet most of us, as we grow and develop, don't really learn how to cope effectively with anxiety-producing situations, and the result is that the anxiety becomes so overwhelming that it can interfere seriously with our ability to perform as well as we could. The primary way to manage anxiety is to replace it with something that's incompatible with it. For me, the most incompatible thing to anxiety is relaxation. It's impossible to be tense and relaxed at the same time, and relaxation is a skill that we can learn just like any other skill.

You've learned how to be tense in most anxiety-producing situations; now

179

you need to learn to identify the warning signs or symptoms of anxiety. Then, instead of serving as evidence that anxiety is gripping you by the throat, such signals can alert you to use your relaxation skills to overcome the anxiety.

The signs or symptoms of anxiety are fairly easy to recognize and differ little from person to person. Basically, your rate of breathing will become more rapid and shallower; your heart rate will begin to speed up; and you'll probably notice some tension in the muscles at the back of your neck, shoulders, forehead, and perhaps even across the chest. You'll probably also notice that your hands and perhaps even your feet become cold and sweaty. There are likely to be disturbances in your gastrointestinal system, such as a "butterfly stomach" or diarrhea and frequent urination. You'll also notice that the secretions in your mouth begin to dry up, that your lips dry out, and that you may have trembling or shaky hands or knees. You may also notice that your voice quivers or even goes up an octave.

What happens when you're tense

A number of changes also occur psychologically during tension. You're more easily confused, your memory becomes confused, and your thinking becomes less flexible and much more self-critical. One of the things your body and mind are designed to do is defend you in times of threat or danger. Here's how that works: The mind, once aware of a threat (and that threat could be something as obvious as someone coming at you with a gun in hand, or it might be something like sitting down and taking an examination, speaking in front of a group of people, writing a paper, or studying for an exam), reacts in a defensive manner, and the anxiety you typically feel is part of that defensive reaction. In these situations, our adrenal glands produce adrenalin and a group of hormones called cortocoids. If the situation persists over a long period of time, you may also find it difficult to concentrate, and you may experience a general sense of fear or anxiety, insomnia, early waking, changes in eating habits, excessive worrying, general fatigue, and an urge to run away.

The urge to run away is one of the human body's responses to an anxiety source. In threatening situations, we have the urge to do one of two things: either to stand and fight or to run away. But many times both urges must be suppressed because they would be inappropriate for the situation. An example would be taking an examination; even though you might like to get up and run out of the room, it probably would not help your grade if you did so, and it's pretty difficult to fight with a piece of paper. So, we often find we must cope with a situation in a way that allows us to stay and face it and to do so using our potentials and skills to the maximum. This is where learning how to manage anxiety can help.

Managing your anxiety

There are two primary goals for learning how to manage anxiety effectively. The first is to *monitor yourself* so that you can be alert to any signs or symptoms of tension. The second goal is to *control that anxiety* using relaxation techniques and imagery, so you can eliminate the anxiety or, at least, bring it down to a manageable level. Keep in mind that you can never eliminate anxiety totally and it's not even desirable to do so. Your goal should be to manage that anxiety at a level that's helpful to your performance. For example, when an athlete goes out to perform, she probably won't do a very good job if she's so relaxed that she's just barely awake. On the other hand, if she's so keyed up that she can't contain herself, she probably won't do very well either. An athlete seeks an optimal level of tension. And that's your goal, too.

In any situation where you're trying to perform effectively or better, ask yourself what the appropriate level of tension is in that situation, and try to maintain or bring your level of anxiety up or down to that point. Relaxation is a skill that you can learn or perfect through practice.

In addition to being relaxed at the appropriate level, it's also necessary to provide yourself with a guide or model of behavior. For example, you might say, "I want to be more relaxed next time I take an examination," or more likely, "I won't be tense the next time I take an examination." It sounds good, but exactly what are you going to do differently? If you've practiced and rehearsed getting tense before, you're likely to behave in just the way you've always done. It becomes important, then, to identify the skills of relaxation or the skills of control so that you can see and feel yourself at an appropriate level of tension.

Imagining you're relaxed

This is where your imagery comes into play. Anything that you imagine in your own mind becomes a neuromuscular rehearsal. For example, if you imagine yourself walking down the sidewalk and tripping over each crack, you are much more likely to do so than if you see yourself walking calmly and smoothly along the sidewalk. The same is true of a performing situation. If you say to yourself, "Well, I've always done poorly there," or "I know I'll do poorly there," that's likely what you'll do because that's all that you've rehearsed. The way to get around those awkward performances of the past is to begin thinking and imagining yourself *being* and *feeling* exactly the way you would like to feel.

It's important to realize that anxiety is an internally cued response, and, therefore, it can be controlled through the use of imagery. You can simply imagine yourself back in a very tension-filled situation and literally feel the same signs of tension building again in your body, which is an excellent example of how that imagery controls your behavior in the present.

What I'd like you to do is to imagine right now the sequence of events or situations that led up to a particular tension-filled situation. To help you get a feeling for how comfortable or uncomfortable you are in that sequence of events, I'd like you to start yourself off at a very low level of tension. We'll call that level zero (0), although it's never actually 0. Then I'd like you to move through the sequence of events progressively until you reach the most uncomfortable part of that situation, and we'll label that as 100.

Example: taking an examination

To give you an example, let's take a situation that we'll call "taking an examination." You can imagine yourself on the first day of class, sitting there and listening to the instructor say, "In this course, we'll have four 1-hour examinations." You might assign a higher number to a situation that occurs during the week before the first hourly exam, when the instructor says, "Now, don't forget next week is our first 1-hour examination." The next situation might be several days before the exam, when you're sitting down to study in your room or the library. The next might be coming to some difficult material while you're studying. The next might be sitting down and studying the night before the examination. The next might be going to sleep the night before the examination. The next might be thinking about the exam that night. The next might be waking up the next morning and thinking about the exam. The next might be getting ready to come into school. The next might be walking to the building in which you're going to have your examination. The next might be seeing the doorway of the room where you're going to take the examination. The next might be walking into the examination room. The next might be sitting down at your desk. The next might be looking at other people talking about the examination and asking each other questions. The next might be seeing the instructor walk into the room with the tests. The next might be hearing the instructor say, "Put all your notes and books away." The next might be seeing the exams come down the aisle toward you. The next might be looking at the examination, and the last might be seeing that the first question is worth 25 points and not knowing the answer to that question.

Each of these particular situations can be lumped together into what we call "test anxiety," and yet each individual situation has its own unique level of tension. It's important that you know how differently you feel in each of these situations, and learn what the sequence of your anxiety symptoms or cues are so that you can use them as warning signs.

Levels of anxiety

Once you've identified your whole sequence, I want you to go back and to pick out two particular situations. One we'll arbitrarily call the 20-level, or low anxiety, scene and the other the 60-level, or high anxiety, scene. The distinction between the two is that in the 20-level scene you know that you're in an anxiety-producing situation but you don't feel unduly uncomfortable. In the 60-level scene, you're starting to feel much stronger signs of anxiety, but you still feel you're controlling the anxiety and it's not controlling you.

Once you've done that, I'd like you to think of a very relaxed scene, a time in your life when you were someplace where you were very calm, very relaxed, very much at ease. To help you with this, I'd like you to think also of how all five of your senses experience that situation. For example, you might be at the ocean, walking along in water up to your knees. As you walk along, you can feel the sand as it gives way beneath your feet. You can feel the coolness of the water on the lower parts of your legs. You can feel the warmth of the sun on the upper part of your body, and you might even feel the wind as it blows around you. You can smell the salt in the air and, if you were to lick your lips, you could actually taste it. You can hear the sound of the waves as they wash in and out and perhaps even hear some children playing in the distance. You can see the blue of the ocean, the blue and white of the sky, the white of the sand. And if you put all these together and close your eyes, you can actually feel yourself back there again. I'd like you to try and describe a situation like that for yourself now. It doesn't have to be at the ocean; it can be anywhere at all. But try to involve all five of your senses as you do.

Once you've developed your relaxation scene, you're ready to learn the skills of relaxation. I'm going to take you through an exercise now in which you're going to learn how to recognize the distinction between tension and relaxation. Begin the exercise by sitting or lying down in a very comfortable place. Remove any tight clothing, and perhaps your contact lenses or eyeglasses. Dim any bright lights and make sure you're not likely to be interrupted while you do this relaxation exercise. Once you have familiarized yourself with the complete exercise, have a friend read you the instructions while you follow them, or else record the instructions so you can play them back at your convenience.

The relaxation exercise

Now I'm going to ask you to count from one to five. As you do so, I want you to gradually close your eyes. One, two, three, four, five.

Take a nice deep breath, a really deep breath, and just feel your lungs expanding. Hold on to it, then let it out nice and slowly. And now, one more time, another nice deep breath, hold on to it, and let it out nice and slowly. That's fine.

Now we're going to work first on relaxing the hands and the forearms. The way to do this is first to extend your arms out from your body and make a fist with both hands. As you make this fist, notice the tension that builds in the muscles of the fingers, hands, wrists, and forearms. As you make that fist tighter and tighter and tighter and tighter, try to focus on where that tension is and how uncomfortable it feels. Now relax, let it go; just let the tension that was there a few seconds ago gradually fade away from those muscles—from the fingers, the hands, the wrists, and the fore-arms. Feel it letting go, giving way to relaxation, those nice, warm, sooth-ing feelings of relaxation.

Notice the difference. Notice how much more comfortable and relaxed those muscles feel now, compared to how they felt a few seconds ago. Once again, make a fist with both hands, making it tighter and tighter and tighter and tighter, feeling the tension building and building and building and building in the hands, the fingers, the wrists, the forearms. Notice where that tension is and how unpleasant it feels. Now relax, and just let it go. That's it, just let that tension go. Begin focusing on the difference as those nice, warm, soothing feelings of relaxation flow back into your mus-cles. Feel them become very long, very smooth, very comfortable, and very relaxed. Focus on how good that feels, how good it is to know that you're the one in control. Realize that you control your own relaxation, that you created that pleasant sensation of relaxation.

Now we're going to work on the muscles on the front of the upper arm called the biceps. The way to do that is to bend the arms at a 45° angle, make a fist and flex the biceps, flexing them tighter, tighter, tighter. And as you do so, feel the tension building and building and building, and focus on where it is and how uncomfortable it feels. Then relax, just let it go; let the arms drop back down and, as they do so, feel all the tension that was there fade away from those muscles. Feel the tension fading away and feel it being replaced by those nice, soothing feelings of relaxation, just becoming very comfortable and very relaxed. That's good.

Now let's do that once again. Bend the arms at the elbow, make a fist, and flex the biceps tighter and tighter and tighter and tighter, focusing on the tension—where it is and how uncomfortable it is—and relax. Just let your arms drop down, letting those muscles go, letting all that tension fade away, beginning to feel those muscles becoming heavy, very loose, and very relaxed. How good that relaxation feels!

And now we're going to work on the muscles on the back of the upper arm called the triceps. The way to do this is to lie down and put the back of your hands on the floor with your palms pointed at the ceiling and your arms extended at your sides, so that by pressing against the floor with the back of the hands, you'll feel the tension building in the triceps. Do that now and feel those muscles growing tighter and tighter and tighter and tighter; focus on where that tension is, how uncomfortable it is. Feel it building and building, and then relax, let it go, just let the tension go, just let it trail away from those muscles, feeling them becoming very long, very smooth, very comfortable, and very relaxed. How good the relaxation feels as it flows back into those muscles, massaging away any tension and replacing it with those good feelings of relaxation.

OK, let's do that once again, pushing down against the back of the hands, feeling the tension as it builds and builds and builds, focusing on how uncomfortable it feels. Now relax, let it go, just let it go. Let the arms fall into a nice comfortable position and, as they do so, feel them becoming very heavy, very limp, very relaxed; it's beginning to feel as if you couldn't even move them, they're just becoming very comfortable and very relaxed.

And now we're going to work on the muscles in the back of the neck. The way to do that is to gradually push with the back of your head against the floor and, as you do so, feel the tension build on the back of the neck. Feel those muscles growing tighter and tighter and tighter and tighter. Find where they are in your mind's eye, feel how uncomfortable they are. Then relax, let them go, let that tension go; feel the tension just fade away, feel those muscles become very long, very smooth, very comfortable, and very relaxed. Feel those nice, warm, soothing feelings of relaxation penetrate deep into the muscles, massaging away tension.

OK, now, let's do that once again, pushing back with the head, feeling those muscles growing tighter and tighter and tighter, focusing on where the tension is, how uncomfortable it feels. Relax, let the tension go, just let the head hang loose and, as it does so, feel the tension as it begins to fade away. Notice how much more comfortable the muscles are becoming as those good, soothing feelings of relaxation penetrate deeply into them, massaging away tension and replacing it with relaxation.

And now we're going to work on the muscles in the forehead. The way to do that is to raise your eyebrows up, trying to touch your eyebrows to your hairline. Raise them higher, higher, higher and feel the tension building in your forehead, focusing on where it is, how uncomfortable it feels. Then relax, just let the eyebrows slide back down the forehead and, as they do so, feel all that tension that was there a few minutes ago begin to fade away from the forehead; feel it fading away and being replaced with a nice, calm, tranquil wave of relaxation. Feel that relaxation spread across those muscles in the forehead. Feel how much more comfortable and relaxed they've become now. Very good.

OK, let's do that once again, raising the eyebrows up, feeling the tension building in the forehead, feeling those muscles becoming tighter and tighter, more and more uncomfortable, finding where the tension is, how uncomfortable it is, and relax.

Let it go, just feel the eyebrows slide slowly back down the forehead and, as they do so, feel the tension drain away from the forehead. Feel that nice, calm, tranquil wave of relaxation as it spreads back across the forehead, massaging away any tension, replacing it with relaxation.

And now we're going to work on the muscles around the eyes and the nose. The way to do that is to close your eyes as tightly as you can. Go ahead and close them as tightly as you can, closing them tighter, tighter, tighter, feeling where the tension is, feeling as if your eyebrows are going to come right down and touch your cheeks. Relax, let it go now, let the tension go, and notice how much more comfortable those muscles feel now, compared to how they felt just a few seconds ago, bringing back the relaxation, bringing it back, and replacing the tension with relaxation.

How much more comfortable those muscles feel now; feel them becoming very loose, very calm, and very relaxed. Let's do that once again, closing the eyes as tightly as you can, closing them tighter, tighter, tighter, focusing on the tension, noticing where it is and how uncomfortable it feels. Relax and let it go, just let that tension go, noticing that nice, calm wave of relaxation as it spreads down from the scalp, through the forehead, right on down to the eyes and the nose, washing away any tension, replacing it with those warm, soothing feelings of relaxation. Feel those muscles becoming very limp, very heavy, and very relaxed. How good those muscles feel and how good it is to know that you're in control of your relaxation. You're the one relaxing those muscles.

And now we're going to work on the muscles in the cheeks. The way to do that is to pull the corners of your mouth back toward your ears by making a big, ear-to-ear grin; just pull them back tighter, tighter, tighter, feel the tension that builds in the cheeks, where it is, how uncomfortable it feels, and then relax. Just let the tension go, let the cheeks fall back into place and, as they do so, feel that tension just drain away from the cheeks; feel that tension fading away, fading away, being replaced with relaxation, those good, soothing feelings of relaxation.

Now, let's do that once again: Pull back the corners of the mouth, feeling the tension that builds in the cheeks, feeling it building and building and building. Then relax, just let it go. That's good, just feel those nice, soothing feelings of relaxation flow right down the face, right through the cheeks, and as the relaxation penetrates the muscles, feel them becoming very loose, very limp, very relaxed.

And now we're going to work on the muscles in the jaw on the sides of the face. The way to do that is to put your teeth together and to bite down hard. As you do so, feel the tension that builds in the jaw and in the sides of the face. Feel those muscles growing tighter, tighter, tighter, focusing on where the tension is, how uncomfortable it feels; and now relax, let your jaw hang loose, and as it does so, feel the relaxation penetrate into those muscles. Just relax, let all that tension fade away from your jaw and the sides of the face, feel it fade away, feel those muscles becoming very long, very smooth, very relaxed. Now, let's do that again, putting the teeth together and biting down harder and harder, feeling those muscles in the jaw becoming tighter, tighter, tighter, and relax.

Let it go, let the jaw hang loose and, as it does so, feel that nice, calm, tranquil wave of relaxation flow down through the muscles of the jaw and the sides of the face, just washing away the tension, and replacing it with relaxation, those nice, soothing feelings of relaxation.

And now we're going to work on the muscles on the front of the throat. The way to do that is to put your tongue up against the roof of your mouth, push up with your tongue, and feel the muscles tightening on the front of your throat, feel them growing tighter, tighter, tighter. Focus on where you feel that tension, and feel how uncomfortable those muscles are, how tight and cramped they feel. Relax, let the tongue fall back into place and, as it does so, feel all that tightness and tension that was there just a few seconds ago begin to fade away, fade away, fade away from the tongue and the front of the throat; feel the muscles becoming very long, very smooth, very relaxed. How different they feel from the way they did a few seconds ago, how much more comfortable and relaxed you've made them!

Now, let's do that once again, pushing up against the roof of the mouth with the tongue, feeling the tension as it builds on the front of the throat, feeling those muscles growing tighter, tighter, tighter, growing more and more uncomfortable. Then relax, let them go, let the tongue fall back into place and feel that nice, calm, soothing wave of relaxation flow right down through your face, right on down through the front of the throat, massaging away any tension and replacing it with relaxation, those warm, tranquil feelings of relaxation.

And now we're going to work on the muscles of the shoulders. The way to do that is to shrug your shoulders up, trying to touch them to your ears, raising them higher and higher, higher, higher, touching the shoulders to the ears. Feel that tension in the front of the shoulders and the back of the shoulders and the sides of the neck. Relax now, just let the shoulders slide back down and, as they do so, feel the tension just fade away from all those muscles; feel the relaxation spreading through those muscles, massaging away any tension and replacing it with relaxation, those nice, soothing feelings of relaxation. Feel those muscles become very long, very smooth, very comfortable, and very relaxed, and notice the difference between the tension that was there before and the absence of that tension right now.

Let's do that once again: Shrug up the shoulders, feeling the tension that builds in the shoulders and the sides of the neck, feeling those muscles grow tighter, tighter, tighter, tighter, and notice where that tension is and how uncomfortable it feels. Then relax, let the shoulders slide back down, and, as they do so, feel that nice, soothing wave of relaxation as it penetrates deep into those muscles, massaging away any tension, and replacing it with relaxation, those nice, soothing feelings of relaxation; focus on how good those muscles feel, those good feelings that you create.

And now we're going to work on the muscles in the chest. The way to do that is to take a really deep breath and hold it, just hold that breath, and feel the tension as it spreads out across the chest. How uncomfortable it feels! Relax and exhale. That's good. Feel the tension fade as you exhale and feel it continue to fade away just a little bit more every time that you exhale; just continue to breathe very freely and very deeply, feeling that tension fading away further and further, taking you deeper and deeper into relaxation.

Now let's do that once again: Take another deep breath, holding it and feeling the tension that builds, and feeling the chest once again growing tighter and tighter. Exhale and relax. That's good. Feel that pressure fade away, and as you continue to breathe very freely, very deeply, feel those nice, soothing feelings of relaxation massage away any tension in the chest, and feel the chest muscles becoming very long, very smooth, very relaxed. How comfortable you're making them, and they're beginning to feel very heavy, very limp, very relaxed.

And now we're going to work on the muscles in the back. The way to do that is to make a gradual upward arch by pushing your stomach upward while keeping your shoulders and buttocks on the floor. As you do so, feel the tension that spreads across the small of the back, noticing how uncomfortable those muscles feel, how tight and tense they're becoming. Relax now, and just sink back down, sink down feeling all that tightness, all that tension just fading away from those muscles; feel them becoming very comfortable and very relaxed. Feel how much more comfortable they are now, compared to how they felt just a little while ago and how good that feels and how good it is to know that you can control it. You can create that relaxation.

Let's do that once again, now, creating that gradual upward arch and feeling the tension building and building and building. Relax; just sink back down and, as you do so, feel the tension fading away from the small of the back. Just imagine those muscles becoming very long, very smooth, very relaxed. Feel those good soothing feelings of relaxation penetrate deep into those muscles, massaging away any tension and replacing it with relaxation.

And now we're going to work on the stomach muscles. The way to do that is to pull in the stomach muscles, trying to pull them down toward the spine. As you do so, feel them become tighter, tighter, tighter, tighter. Then relax, let them go, and notice that, as you exhale, the stomach muscles relax further and further, taking you deeper and deeper into relaxation; feel the stomach muscles become more and more comfortable, more and more relaxed, focusing only on relaxation, those good, soothing feelings of relaxation.

Let's do that once again, pulling in the stomach muscles, feeling them grow tighter, tighter, tighter, tighter, more and more uncomfortable, and noticing where the tension is, how uncomfortable it is. Then relax, exhale and let all that tension go; as you continue breathing very freely, very deeply, feel that tension just evaporate from the stomach, feel it being replaced with those good, soothing feelings of relaxation. The tension just fades away as those muscles become very comfortable, very relaxed. How good that feels, and how good it is to know that *you're* the one who creates that relaxation. *You're the one in control of your own relaxation.*

And now we're going to work on the muscles in the thighs. The way to do that is to point your toes down toward the floor and, as you do so, feel the tension that builds in the thighs; feel the thighs grow tighter, tighter, tighter, tighter, and focus on where that tension is, how uncomfortable it is. Relax, let the legs fall back into a comfortable position, and, as they do so, feel all that tightness, all that tension just fade away from those muscles; just let that tension go, feel the muscles in the thighs become very long, very smooth, very comfortable, and very relaxed. Just feel the relaxation massaging away the tension, penetrating deeply into those muscles, making them very loose, very limp, very relaxed. How good that feels, and how good it is to know that *you* are in control, *you* relax those muscles, just letting them go, giving way to those pleasant feelings of relaxation.

Let's do that once again, pointing the toes down toward the floor, feeling the tension that builds once again in the thighs, feeling those muscles growing tighter, tighter, tighter, more and more uncomfortable. Then relax; let them go, just let all of that tension go, let it fade away and be replaced by those nice, warm, soothing feelings of relaxation. Feel the relaxation penetrate deeply into the muscles, feel them becoming very heavy, very limp, very relaxed.

And now we're going to work on the muscles in the calves. The way to do that is to gradually bend the toes back toward the head and, as you do so, feel the tension that builds in the calves, feel those muscles growing tighter, tighter, and tighter, and feel where the tension is. Then relax, let the tension go. How much more comfortable and relaxed those muscles feel now, compared to how they felt just a few seconds ago; feel that tension fading away, fading away, being replaced with those nice, soothing feelings of relaxation.

Let's do that once again, gradually bending the toes back toward the head, feeling the tension, finding where it is, feeling how uncomfortable it is. Then relax, let it go, let the tension go; feel it fading away from the calves, feel the legs and the feet becoming very heavy, very limp, very relaxed, feel those nice, soothing feelings of relaxation flowing throughout your entire body, feel it becoming very heavy, very relaxed. You're breathing very freely, very deeply, feeling your body sinking down deeper and deeper into relaxation. And you can feel the relaxation just wash away any tension as you feel yourself floating in those nice, soothing feelings of relaxation.

Now that you've learned how to relax yourself, you can practice this exercise once a day for a week or two. You'll find that you can relax yourself very quickly and very easily, and once you're able to do that, the next step is to learn how to apply that relaxation when and where you want to. You can learn how to use that deep muscle relaxation technique to create feelings of relaxation where you formerly had feelings of tension. You can begin to do this by imagining that 20-level anxiety scene that you identified earlier. As you imagine that anxiety scene, try and feel all of the feelings of discomfort that actually occurred when you were there. Remember that the two goals of anxiety management are, first, to monitor the feelings of anxiety and, second, to control the feelings. So, in imagining that 20-level scene, your goal is to find out exactly how your body and mind respond when you're in that situation.

After you understand your body signals or cues of anxiety during that 20-level scene, your next goal will be to imagine it once again after you've relaxed yourself, and then to stay relaxed while you imagine it for about twenty seconds. If you experience any discomfort while you imagine that 20-level scene for twenty seconds, repeat your visualization of the scene once again, and continue that process until you can imagine your 20-level scene for twenty seconds and not feel any discomfort. Once you can do that, imagine the 20-level scene again without discomfort for thirty seconds; if you feel any discomfort at this length of time, repeat the process until you can imagine it successfully without any tension or discomfort for thirty seconds. When you can do that, your next step is to imagine that 20-level scene for forty-five seconds, and when you can imagine it for forty-five seconds without feeling any discomfort, you can move on to imagining the 60-level scene, which you identified earlier.

The steps are the same: First, imagine the 60-level scene with tension, so you can be clear on your body's signs or cues of tension. Then imagine the 60-level scene for twenty seconds. Your goal is to imagine it without feeling any tension. When you can imagine it without any tension, move on to imagining the 60-level scene for thirty seconds, and when you can imagine it without any tension, move on to imagining it for forty-five seconds.

Once you can visualize that 60-level scene for forty-five seconds without any tension, your next step is to move on to what I call a "competency scene." That's where you imagine yourself going through that entire sequence of events, whether it's taking an examination or giving a speech or whatever it might be from start to finish. But, see yourself doing it the way you really want to do it. This is your positive, or competency, rehearsal. When you can complete that process from start to finish, seeing yourself thinking, feeling, speaking, moving exactly the way you want to—calmly, competently, and in a relaxed manner, you've achieved your goal. Once you can do that successfully, you may want to repeat the entire process with another situation. But the important thing to keep in mind now is that what were formerly anxiety symptoms for you have now become warning cues.

As soon as you're aware of the very first sign of tension, your goal will be to implement the relaxation process and that will be done by simply closing your eyes for a brief period of time, taking slow, deep breaths, reachieving that sense of relaxation that you can create, and perhaps even imagining yourself back in your relaxation scene once again. What you will probably notice is that you are now no longer threatened by being in situations that formerly caused you discomfort. You might be surprised when you find that your level of comfort is enormously greater than it used to be, and you'll find that relaxation now becomes a greater part of your total lifestyle, that you simply don't allow yourself to get out of control any longer because now you have skills that you can use anywhere, anytime. The skills are simply to learn to close your eyes briefly; take a slow, deep breath; and as you exhale, focus on your relaxation scene. The more you practice this technique, the more effective it will be for you.

Suggestions for further study

1. Recall your last troublesome experience. What were the anxiety cues you experienced, and in what sequence did they occur?
2. Determine what behaviors and thoughts you would have to go through in order to get through the event if it happened again.
3. Rehearse the sequence of events thoroughly in your mind so that there is no doubt about what you should do, no matter what happens in a troublesome situation.

Suggested readings

Benson, H. *The Mind/Body Effect*. New York: Simon and Schuster, 1979.

Benson, H., and M. Z. Klipper. *The Relaxation Response*. New York: W. Morrow, 1976.

Brown, B. *Supermind*. New York: Harper and Row, 1980.

Bry, A., and M. Bair. *Directing the Movies of Your Mind*. New York: Harper and Row, 1978.

Butler, P. *Talking to Yourself*. New York: Stein and Day, 1981.

Emmons, M. *The Inner Source.* San Luis Obispo, Calif.: Impact Publishers, 1978.

Ferguson, M. *The Aquarian Conspiracy.* Los Angeles: J. P. Tarcher, 1980.

Ford, N. D. *Natural Ways to Relieve Pain.* New York: Harian Press, 1980.

Glasser, W. *Positive Addiction.* New York: Harper and Row, 1976.

Green, E., and A. Green. *Beyond Biofeedback.* New York: Delta, 1977.

Jacobson, E. *Anxiety and Tension Control.* Philadelphia: J. B. Lippincott, 1964.

Kinser, N. S. *Stress and the American Woman.* New York: Ballantine Books, 1980.

Martin, R. A., and E. Y. Pollard. *Learning to Change.* New York: McGraw-Hill, 1980.

Ornstein, R. *Psychology of Consciousness.* New York: Harcourt, Brace, and Jovanovich, 1979.

Pelletier, K. *Mind As Healer/Mind As Slayer.* New York: Delta Books, 1977.

Shames, R., and C. Sterin. *Healing with Mind Power.* Emmaus, Pa.: Rodale Press, 1978.

Developing a Healthy Lifestyle

Randy Lamkin, *Coordinator of Student Health Promotion and Adjunct Assistant Professor of Health Education*
University of South Carolina

Linda Morphis, *Health Nurse Specialist*
Thomson Student Health Center
University of South Carolina

For Linda and me, educating and inspiring people to change their lives for the better is one of our most rewarding activities. Over the years we have both changed our lifestyles—in particular we've begun to take better care of our bodies by eating healthier food and exercising regularly.

I've always enjoyed being physically fit, and for the past five years I've been positively addicted to running. For several years I was a vegetarian, although now I'm a "moderate." I've experienced the benefits of changing my lifestyle and I know that all of us have the power to make our lives more rewarding.

I know how difficult the freshman year can be because at the end of mine, I flunked out of Georgia Tech. For the first time I really had to wake up to my responsibility for my own success. To me, life is a series of challenges that requires us to assume more and more of our personal power. Within each of us is a center of power and will that motivates us toward fulfillment and enhancement, toward competence and mastery. We grow as we're propelled forward by this central motive. At the same time, we're lulled backward into safe dependence and inertia. And each time, we ovecome the dependence and inertia and try something new, we risk, we learn, and

193

we grow. We become more powerful and whole persons. I feel that I've done this.

Linda worked for many years in a big-city hospital, where she became increasingly aware that many of the illnesses and deaths she saw were related to the way people lived, and that many were preventable. This awareness led her into a greater awareness of her own health, and she began trying to improve it. She changed her eating habits and gradually committed herself to regular exercise. One of the high points in her life was completing a 26.2-mile marathon run several years ago. The natural outgrowth of her experience has been a desire to help others become well and to support them in developing the skills necessary to live a healthier life. Her goal is to reach people before they become sick.

Linda and I both feel that we're all capable of positive change and that our potential for self-discovery and growth is virtually unlimited. We've written this chapter to help you become aware of this, too. By developing a healthy lifestyle, our bodies can become strong and our spirits can soar. It's an exhilarating thought!

David Carlson awoke with a start and looked at his clock. Darn! Overslept again! He vaguely remembered hearing the alarm ringing harshly in the quiet dorm room and realized he must have turned it off and gone back to sleep. "I've got to stop doing this," he mumbled irritably to himself. Staying up late studying, not sleeping well when he did fall asleep, and feeling as if he could hardly drag himself out of bed the next morning, had become a typical, unpleasant routine for David.

He hurriedly dressed and headed for the elevator, stopping only long enough to buy a Coke and a candy bar. The annoying thought of the ten extra pounds that had mysteriously appeared on his body since coming to school entered David's mind, but he pushed it aside. "I need all the energy I can get this morning," he thought as he left the vending machines.

A clear, crisp autumn morning greeted David as he walked across campus, but he was too intent on getting to class to notice. If he hadn't already taken all the cuts allowed in his English 101 class, he would definitely not be out yet. It was a morning he would rather forget. He felt rotten—not being able to sleep, lacking energy, feeling sluggish and fat—yet he didn't understand what was going on or, even worse, what to do about it.

David's story is a familiar one. If you identified with it, you're not alone. Unfortunately, too many college students accept feeling tired and sluggish as "normal." However, the good news is that it doesn't have to be that way. You can affect your health in a very positive way. You don't have to wake up each morning feeling tired and irritable. You can feel good every day. You can have abundant energy and a real zest for life. The things you do daily can have an important impact on your general well-being in the long run, as well as in the short run, while you're in college. Getting the proper exercise and choosing wholesome, nutritious foods can help you feel better and work better each day.

Before you set up roadblocks such as: I don't have time to exercise; running is boring; I can't eat properly between classes; the campus snack bar serves nothing but junk food—pay attention to some positive thoughts that have to do with taking better care of yourself. After all, you're an important person, and you deserve special treatment.

Many people who have gotten into the habit of running three times a week or more actually claim they are more productive after exercising than before. "I spend about ninety minutes stretching, running, showering, and dressing," says one professor. "By the time I get back to work, I feel recharged, and my mind actually seems to function better, and more sharply and clearly than before. I amaze myself with the amount of work I can accomplish in one such afternoon."

Or listen to a university student who found she *could* eat properly, even in the university cafeteria. "I don't starve myself ever," she says. "I choose salads from the salad bar, broiled rather than fried foods; I take advantage of all the fresh cooked vegetables they serve (sometimes I just load up on vegetables and skip the meat), and look for chicken or turkey or fish instead of beef."

These are not "health food nuts" or "exercise freaks" speaking, but rather typical individuals who realize that the habits they acquire at this point in their lives are likely to help—or haunt!—them for years to come.

What's your defense against growing into a lumpy, listless body? Or your excuse for not trying to grow out of one? The proper combination of diet and exercise *right now* can provide many of the right answers. The message is clear: Americans may literally be digging their graves with their teeth. The leading causes of death in our country—heart disease, cancer, stroke, and diabetes—are linked to the way we eat, either indirectly through obesity or directly through the types of food we put into our bodies. Millions of Americans are malnourished, not in the traditional sense, but in the form of overconsumption of highly processed "junk foods" that are loaded with sugar, salt, and fat.

Sugars found in their natural state (in fruits, vegetables, grains) are digested slowly and enter the bloodstream gradually, while refined sugar is rapidly absorbed. Some scientists believe this influx of high sugar levels in the blood creates imbalances in our system and may be related to the onset of diabetes or mood swings such as depression. Research also indicates that high salt intake contributes to elevated blood pressure, and there is strong evidence linking to heart disease the intake of foods high in saturated fat.

The average college student consumes approximately 126 pounds of sugar per year and two to five times more salt than is necessary for the body to function, and as much as 40 percent of daily calorie intake comes from fat.

There's no question that it's difficult to counteract these unhealthy eating habits. In our society, with processed convenience foods so readily available, it takes awareness and extra effort to choose foods that are wholesome and as unprocessed as possible. Becoming nutritionally aware includes realizing that the foods you eat actually do become you! It's a biological fact that cells in the body are developed and replaced as food is broken down and utilized. By eating well, you are treating your body with care and respect; you're arming yourself with basic tools that are physically essential for achieving your potential.

Your nutritional assessment

To help assess your nutritional habits, try the following self-scoring test.* It's important to recognize what habits already exist before beginning to make changes.

Circle point score if applicable to your diet.

Part I

1. I have one to two cups of milk or milk products (yogurt, cottage cheese, and so on) per day. — 1 point
2. I use low-fat or skim milk and/or milk products. — 1 point
3. I eat ice cream or ice milk no more than two times a week. — 1 point
4. I use solid, soft, whipped or liquid margarine in place of butter. — 1 point

TOTAL POINTS EARNED: _____

Part II

5. I do not eat meat, fish, poultry, or eggs more than once a day. — 1 point
6. I do not eat red meats (beef or pork) more than three times a week. — 1 point
7. I remove or ask that fat be trimmed from meat before cooking (also circle point if do not eat meat). — 1 point
8. I have no more than one to three fresh eggs per week, either in other foods or separately. — 1 point
9. I have meatless days and have such meat substitutes as legumes (beans, peas, and so on) and nuts. — 1 point
10. I usually broil, boil, bake, or roast meat, fish, or poultry (also circle point if do not eat these foods). — 1 point

TOTAL POINTS EARNED: _____

Part III

11. I have one serving of citrus fruit (such as oranges) each day. 1 point

---

*Prepared by Dr. Roger G. Sargent, Professor, College of Health, University of South Carolina. Used with permission.

12. I have at least two servings of dark green or deep yellow vegetables each day. — 1 point
13. I eat fresh fruits and vegetables when I can get them. — 1 point
14. I cook vegetables without fat (if I use margarine, it is added after cooking). — 1 point
15. I usually eat fresh fruit rather than pastries. — 1 point

TOTAL POINTS EARNED: _____

Part IV

16. I eat whole grain breads and cereals. — 1 point
17. Cereals that I prefer are usually high bran or high fiber. — 1 point
18. Cereals that I buy are low in the amount of sugar added. — 1 point
19. I prefer brown rice to common white enriched rice. — 1 point
20. I usually have four servings of whole grain products (cereals, breads, brown rice, and so on) per day. — 1 point

TOTAL POINTS EARNED: _____

Part V

21. I am within five to ten pounds of my ideal weight. — 1 point
22. I drink no more than 1½ ounces of alcohol per day. — 1 point
23. I do not add salt to food after preparation and prefer foods salted lightly or not at all. — 1 point
24. I usually avoid foods high in refined sugar and do not use sugar in coffee or tea. — 1 point
25. I normally eat breakfast and it usually consists of at least bread or cereal and fruit or fruit juice. — 1 point

TOTAL POINTS EARNED: _____

For your nutritional rating, place points earned in appropriate box:

	Excellent	*Good*	*Fair*	*Poor*	*Your score*
Part I	4	3	2	1	_____
Part II	5–6	4	3	2	_____
Part III	5	4	3	2	_____
Part IV	5	4	3	2	_____
Part V	5	4	3	2	_____

TOTAL POINTS EARNED: _____

Excellent	23–25
Good	19–22
Fair	14–18
Poor	9–14

If you scored less than "good" in your overall rating or on any part of the test, chances are you have room for improvement in the way you eat. A good way to begin is by choosing fewer processed foods.

Whole vs. processed foods

It's often difficult to tell the difference between whole, natural foods and refined, processed ones. A simple way to tell is by asking yourself how close the food is to the state in which it came from nature. The greater the number of additions, subtractions, or modifications, the less natural it is. The changes usually involve the addition of salt, sugar or other sweeteners, fats or oils, and the removal of fiber. Other changes might include a loss of vitamins and minerals, a reduction in flavor and taste, and the addition of preservatives, artificial coloring agents, and other chemicals.

When sugar and fats are added and the fiber removed, one obvious result is unwanted and unnecessary calories. The potato is a perfect example of what happens when processing takes place. The most natural way to prepare a potato is to bake it in the skin. This will give you 125 calories, plus fiber and vitamins, including a good amount of vitamin C. With a pat of low-fat margarine, the total calories is still only around 200.

Now, if you eat a serving of french fries instead of a baked potato, you get around 400 calories, a big decrease in vitamin C, and very little, if any, fiber.

Let's go further and say that instead of the fries, you eat potato chips. This means you will very likely eat a large amount before you feel satisfied, and you'll be getting around 500 calories, a whopping amount of salt, almost no vitamin C, and no fiber.

So, when you really think about the food you give your body, it makes sense to choose wholesome, natural foods rather than processed foods laced with chemicals and preservatives.

How to eat better

To further help individuals in their efforts to eat healthier, the U.S. Senate Select Committee on Nutrition and Human Needs has established dietary goals for Americans. The following list describes those goals:

1. *Increase complex carbohydrate consumption:* Of the foods you eat each day, the greatest number of calories (50 to 60 percent) should come from

fruits, vegetables, and whole grains. These foods are classified as complex carbohydrates (refined sugars are not included).

2. *Reduce intake of fat and foods high in fat:* This can mean cutting down the amount of red meat eaten (and that includes hamburgers), substitute more poultry and fish, and have meatless days several times a week. Fat is more concentrated in calories (1 gram of fat has nine calories, while 1 gram of carbohydrate or 1 gram of protein has four calories); therefore, foods that are high in fat content automatically have twice as many calories as low-fat foods.

3. *Reduce cholesterol intake to about 300 mg/day:* Go easy on meats (especially fatty red meats and pork), shellfish (shrimp, lobster), and eggs. Substitute skim or low-fat milk for whole milk. One egg has almost 300 mg of cholesterol and it may be wise to have no more than three eggs per week.

4. *Decrease consumption of sugar and foods high in sugar:* Limiting the intake of processed foods will go far toward reducing the amount of refined sugar in your diet. Approximately 80 percent of the sugar we eat is "hidden sugar." This means sugar has been added to the product and we may not be aware of it. Get into the label-reading habit. Ingredients are listed according to their percentage within the product. For instance, if sugar is listed first in the list of ingredients, that means the product has more sugar than anything else and should, therefore, be avoided.

5. *Reduce salt consumption by half or more:* Again, limiting processed foods, salty snack items (chips, salted nuts, and so on) and most of the "fast foods" so readily available, will go far in reducing salt intake. Experiment with other seasonings and spices (such as lemon, pepper, oregano), rather than using salt. Read labels. Look for the words *soda* and *sodium,* and the symbol "Na" on the labels (*sodium* bicarbonate, mono*sodium* glutamate, *sodium* benzoate, and so on).

But what if you live on campus and usually eat in the cafeteria or nearby places? With the foods they serve, it can be hard to eat sensibly. The following "healthful hints" are offered to those of you in this predicament:

- Keep fresh fruit available in your room for between-meal snacks.
- Nuts and dried fruits (raisins, figs, and so on) are also healthy snacks, but keep in mind their high calorie content.
- Drink fruit juice, skim milk, or water with meals rather than soda.
- Choose fresh fruits over pastries for dessert.
- Choose baked or broiled meats over fried, and select fish or poultry rather than red meats (beef and pork).
- Seek out restaurants that have salad bars.

In our fast-paced, overprocessed, convenience food-oriented society, eating well can definitely be a challenge. It may take effort in the beginning, but once you establish a sound pattern, choosing healthy foods becomes automatic.

Experiment, have fun, be creative—make an unbelievably good sandwich using whole grain bread, tofu and tahini spread, sprouts, and tomato, rather than a hotdog. (Your first adventure will be to discover what tofu, tahini, and sprouts are!) Have a luscious drink made with vanilla yogurt and fresh strawberries, rather than the chemical-laced, nonmilk "shakes" available at fast-food places.

Remember, eating whole, nutritious foods *can* make a positive difference in the way you feel. The choice is yours. Make it a wise one.

Let's get physical

We all want enough energy to do the things we like and need to do to be successful in college. Do you often feel a drop in your energy level in the early afternoon? Do you engage in some kind of vigorous exercise for twenty to thirty minutes at least three times a week (running, swimming, or brisk walking)?

Most of you who answered yes to the first question, probably answered no to the second one. As odd as it may seem, you usually get more energy back from exercise than you put into it. It's as if energy invested in exercise yields an energy "profit." A few minutes of exercise (instead of a junk food snack) may give you the extra energy you need. At the same time, by choosing exercise instead of a snack, you avoid the extra calories, and therefore the extra body weight, that you don't need.

The following are some basic questions that are frequently asked by students who want to begin a regular exercise program.

How do I get started?

The essential ingredients of a good beginning are (1) take it easy, and (2) have fun. Many people who don't continue to exercise after starting overexert themselves in the beginning. It's as if the motivation they've finally generated to overcome their lazy ways takes them too far, too fast, and they burn out. Maybe they've heard the phrase "No pain, no gain," and they believe that unless you suffer, exercise does no good. Muscle aches and twinges of joint pain are normal occurrences when you start. They should disappear in less than a week.

One way to know if you're overexerting while jogging or running is to take the "talking test." During exercise you should be able to carry on a conversation with someone exercising with you.

What if I don't have the time to exercise?

The less time you feel you have for exercise, the more exercise can help you! When you invest a small amount of time and energy into exercise, you make a profit. You get back more energy than you put in and you can use this energy to accomplish what you need to accomplish. The increased level of energy and alertness can help you be more efficient, and this saves time.

What's the best exercise?

The best exercise is one you do consistently. For most of us, that means it should be relatively inexpensive, convenient, and enjoyable (or at least not painful). It also should be steady, sustained, and vigorous activity.

The ideal exercise conditions the muscles and cardiovascular system and makes you physically fit, but is not overly strenuous. Your *target exercise zone* is between 60 and 80 percent of your maximum oxygen intake. Exercise below 60 and above 80 percent simply doesn't offer enough benefits for the effort expended. Your target exercise zone is approximately the same as 70 to 85 percent of your maximum heart rate. To compute your target heart rate (the heart rate you need to reach for the best conditioning benefits), simply subtract your age in years from 220. Your target heart rate zone is 70 to 85 percent of this number. For example, if you are 20 years old, your target is 140 to 170 beats per minute.

A good exercise session begins with five to ten minutes of stretching and warmup. Usually, twenty to thirty minutes of exercise in the target heart rate zone provides excellent benefits to the cardiovascular system. After exercising, there should be a five to ten minute cool-down period of less effort before you stop exercising.

Constant and rhythmic activities such as walking, jogging or running, swimming, aerobic dancing, racquetball, cycling, and cross-country skiing are best.

How do I know if I'm in the target zone?

To find out whether your heart rate is in the target zone, you simply count your pulse. To do this place your thumb on your chin and feel the carotid artery on the side of your neck. It's important to count your pulse as soon as you stop exercising because your heart rate slows down quickly. Count your heart beats for 10 seconds and multiply by 6.

You can stop exercising briefly to check your pulse to make sure your heart rate is in the target zone. If your rate is below 70 percent of maximum, you need to exercise more strenuously. If your heart rate is above 85 percent of maximum, you need to slow down. Soon you'll know whether you're in the target zone simply by physical sensations of heart rate, breathlessness, and so on, without continuously checking your pulse rate.

What are the benefits of exercise?

Exercise can make you feel fantastic! More specifically, regular target zone exercise can stimulate the following physiological changes:

1. Reduce resting heart rate
2. Reduce blood pressure
3. Increase heart size and cardiac work capacity
4. Increase heart-pumping efficiency
5. Increase oxygen-carrying ability of the blood
6. Increase respiratory efficiency
7. Reduce body weight and percent body fat
8. Suppress appetite
9. Burn up stored fat tissue
10. Prevent adult-onset diabetes

Many people don't realize that exercise also has important psychological benefits. Exercise promotes a feeling of well-being; it has a tranquilizing and muscle relaxing effect, prevents depression, promotes feelings of self-control, self-confidence, and improved body image, and promotes sound sleep.

Regular vigorous activity may just be the overlooked answer to many physical and emotional problems. The first step is the hardest. After that, the rewards of being a physically fit and active person greatly outweigh the initial effort.

Conclusion

One of the most exciting challenges of being in college is the freedom to create your own personal lifestyle. It's a new experience and a new beginning. As a college student, you have more power and responsibility than ever before, and using your power to help yourself become healthier offers great rewards.

Your health, both physical and emotional, has a great deal to do with your success as a student; and lifestyle habits, the things you do on a day-to-day basis, have everything to do with being, and staying, healthy.

By choosing a lifestyle that includes wholesome nutritious foods and vigorous physical activity, you take a giant step toward health, well-being, and success.

You can be vigorously alive, feel great, and be alert and prepared. You can have sufficient energy, not only for meeting the daily demands of classroom assignments, but also for the fun, social events, and personal relationships that enhance college life.

The coming years can very well be the perfect time for establishing lifestyle patterns that can positively affect the quality, and perhaps the quantity, of your life.

Suggested activities

1. Keep a record of everything you eat or drink for one week. Make a note of how you felt, where you were, what activities you were doing, and how hungry you were. At the end of the week, review your diary and look for patterns: Are you eating a lot between meals? Are you eating foods high in refined sugar and fat? Are you eating when you aren't very hungry? Are you eating for recreation (when you're bored or anxious or when you watch TV, for example)?

2. With several of your classmates, identify campus or community resources that can assist you in the following areas: nutrition and weight control, exercise and physical fitness (including aerobics classes, jogging groups or clubs), and wellness or health promotion. Report your findings to the class.

3. Organize a Fun-Run for everyone enrolled in the freshman seminar classes at your college.

4. Plan a nonmeat covered dish meal. Have each student bring a dish to share with the class.

Suggested readings

Ardell, Donald. *High Level Wellness.* Emmaus, Pa.: Rodale Press, 1977.

Cooper, Kenneth. *The New Aerobics.* New York: M. Evans and Co., 1970.

Farquar, John. *The American Way of Life Need Not Be Hazardous to Your Health.* New York: W. W. Norton, 1975.

Ferguson, James. *Habits Not Diets.* Palo Alto, Calif.: Bull Publishing, 1976.

Fixx, James. *The Complete Book of Running.* New York: Random House, 1977.

Lappe, Frances. *Diet For a Small Planet.* New York: Ballantine Books, 1977.

What You Should Know about Alcohol and Other Drugs

Michael Shaver, *Director,*
Campus Alcohol Project
University of South Carolina

I was still living at home when I started college, and the changes that occurred there were something I recall quite clearly. Many of the old restrictions my parents had placed on my time and my working schedule seemed to disappear, and I began to realize how much freedom I suddenly had, and how much of my success at college was up to me. Very slowly it dawned on me that perhaps I was being seen as an adult, and I found that realization to be both exciting and alarming. I resolved, however, to accept the challenge of responsibility, and set out to master it.

Unfortunately, I didn't do so well at handling responsibility. In fact, I learned more about the abuse of freedom than about its constructive use. This was very clearly reflected in my grades. I really made a mess of it.

My sophomore year began two years later, but I returned to college with a great deal more maturity and understanding of what I wanted to get out of it.

After graduating with a degree in experimental psychology, I began to work in alcohol and drug abuse, counseling with individuals and families who had these problems. Many of the patients I worked with were young, and I invariably found that, while the immediate problems were with substance abuse, emotional prob-

205

lems always underlay the abuse. Essentially, each person found that whatever was making him or her unhappy in life was most easily dealt with by getting drunk or high, and each went through an important period of life staying high or drunk, and not learning how to do anything about the problems he or she was having. Many had no skills in dealing with other people, many were not able to hold jobs, and going back through the learning process was very difficult.

In working with these individuals, I learned much about the development of alcohol and drug problems, and learning that helped me develop some of the ideas about prevention that are expressed here. Many of the thoughts aren't original, but applying them to the problems of abuse prevention can be very helpful. The field of prevention has grown both in this way, and through learning from those who have experienced alcoholism and drug addiction.

Moving from treatment into prevention has been a growth and learning experience for me, and one I continue to enjoy enormously. Working with students is one of the most rewarding efforts I've ever undertaken. It's a challenge, to be sure, but one I hope to continue meeting for some time.

College has traditionally been a time for experimenting and testing one's limits. Many students come to college with little or no experience in living on their own and making their own decisions, and suddenly here they are with literally hundreds of new options. It's a unique and exciting experience, often challenging and fun, but at times it can be confusing.

One option that's going to require some decision-making skills is the use of alcohol or other drugs. This chapter will provide you with objective, factual information about these substances in the belief that whatever choice you make, it should be based on facts. Both drugs and alcohol have the potential to provide benefits and to cause problems. The difference lies in how they are used and why.

By now, you've probably heard many scary stories and warnings about what alcohol and other drugs can do to you, and you're also probably tired of hearing them. Sometimes the facts about the use and abuse of alcohol and drugs can be frightening, but the real issue at this point is that you probably would rather *not* be told what to do all of the time. It's very normal to feel that way. As an adult, you'll need to start making some of your own decisions, but this doesn't mean you should ignore reality. What will be most helpful to you right now are facts on which to base your decisions.

The college campus has come a long way from the era of the sixties. Many good things came from that period: programs such as this one, and the general feeling by college administrators that students should be treated more like the adults they are. On the negative side, colleges have gone through a very slow transition from the heavy use of "street" drugs such as LSD and PCP, and have turned back to the heavy use of alcohol. While marijuana and amphetamine-type drugs have not entirely disappeared, their widespread use has declined considerably.

The primary drug of abuse among today's new college and high school students is alcohol. The latest research shows that the age at which people first begin drinking is now 16 or less. This is quite a drop from the reports in 1974, which showed that the usual age for a first drink was 18 to 20. These figures show rather clearly that people are beginning to drink much earlier, so that by the time they reach college, their drinking habits may be firmly established.

Alcohol is being rediscovered for several reasons. The first is that it's legal, and it's a lot easier to go to the convenience store and buy a six-pack than to try to make a contact and pay $25 to $30 an ounce for marijuana or an equally high price for other drugs. Another reason is that, since people don't view alcohol as a drug, they treat its use differently. Many people often feel that heavy drinking is "just a part of going to college," and often let studies slide. The message is clear to them: Drinking is something everyone does in college, and it's completely OK.

Why do people drink? Why do they use drugs? When you ask these questions, you generally get an answer like, "I don't know" or "I never really gave it much thought" or "Because they want to, I guess." I'm sure I've answered that question one of those ways before, but my involvement in the field of alcohol and drug abuse treatment has given me a chance to look at some of the real reasons. One of the most striking things I found was that people generally *don't* give much thought to their drinking habits or drug use behavior. It's my hope, therefore, that this chapter will provoke some thinking on these questions, as we look at some of the actual reasons people decide to drink or use drugs, and the benefits and difficulties they often encounter as a result.

"Everyone else is doing it": the social aspect of use and abuse

"Everyone else is doing it" is the answer you most often hear, but let's look at what it can mean before deciding if it's a good or a bad answer. By now, some adult who is significant in your life has probably told you that you need to begin to think for youself, and that it doesn't matter what other people are doing. (As I recall, the classic parental example is, "If your friends jump out of a window, are you going to do that, too?") The problem is that becoming responsible and thinking independently are not things that simply happen to you one day, although it might be nice if they did.

Peer influence affects us all, regardless of age, sex, or national origin. An added complication is your arrival at square one of a four-year experience that's exciting but not always something you feel ready to take on alone.

We all need friends to talk to, to play and have fun with, and in general to share our college experience. Getting to know people often means getting involved with things that they're doing, which may include drinking or drug use. Being highly social animals, our urge to belong or "fit in" is very strong, and there are some good reasons for this. It's normal to begin to move away from the strong influence of your parents during your teen years and to begin to identify more strongly with your peers. In some cases this means that a form of rebellion may take place at home. Two common outcomes often result from this event: You may begin to rebel against your parents' control, and you begin, along with your peers, to sample all the things freedom has to offer you.

If drinking is part of your peer group's activity, it becomes one of the things you share with them. If drinking is kept in perspective in your group and not given an undue amount of importance, then it's simply a part of your shared activity. It can, however, become too important to the dynamics of belonging to your group, and if this happens, trouble can result. For some individuals, drinking becomes their only form of gaining recognition and approval within the group. Instead of finding out that they're "a good drinker" or "can really hold their liquor," they might find out that drinking is beginning to interfere with other more important aspects of their college experience.

Fortunately, many people find this out in time and moderate their drinking, putting it in its proper perspective. Others find out the hard way that heavy drinking is not something that will get them the recognition and friendship they need.

It's important to realize that the vast majority of students make the decision about whether or not they will drink *before* they get to college, but still must decide *how* and *when* they will drink. These two important decisions relate closely to the way you'll structure your social and academic life at college. Poorly made decisions can have serious consequences; sensibly made ones can lead to a rewarding and well-balanced learning experience, socially as well as academically. Let's take a look at some of the differences.

When should I drink?

Almost anyone will tell you that people generally drink or use drugs for relaxation or to enjoy a social event. Whether or not this happens depends on when it's done, and deciding when is the best time may not be as hard as you think. One key to making this decision is to ask yourself: "If I decide to go out drinking or to get high, what effect is that going to have on my goals for being here at college?" This may seem ridiculous to you at first. After all, if you go out drinking with friends tonight, are you really going to ruin your chances for a career as a brain surgeon? Of course not. The way to properly use this question is to ask it on a daily basis. That way, you may be more likely to decide that studying for that mid-term you have tomorrow is more important than partying tonight. You shouldn't neglect your social life. It's a very important and beneficial part of your college experience, but you have to keep it in perspective. Studying is also a rather important thing you can learn to accomplish with some gentle self-discipline.

Another aspect of "when" in college is choosing between weekends and weekdays. It's easier to enjoy a party when you don't have some guilt nagging at you about what you should be studying, and Friday and Saturday are usually times when this isn't as much of a concern. To be realistic, I'm sure you won't always decide to study rather than socialize, but keeping this question in mind can be helpful to you in developing work/leisure habits that will help you get where you want to go in college.

Feelings

"When" may be starting to look like a more important question to you now, so let's look at another part of the question. It goes, "When I feel ..." People get into all sorts of situations in college that may provoke all sorts of feelings. At different times, you may experience a range of feelings from fear and sadness to satisfaction, pleasure, and even euphoria (and everything in between), all in one semester. This is quite normal for students, especially for new freshmen taking in the novel experience of college. Within this range you could find some unpleasant feelings (one that comes immediately to mind is sadness), and when you don't feel the way you want to feel, the most human thing to do is to take some kind of action that will help you feel better.

It's normal to feel sad sometimes, and that in itself is no need for panic or worry. But sometimes you can feel "stuck," and changing that feeling seems impossible. One way to change the way you feel, of course, is by using alcohol or other drugs. Relaxing with friends and having a couple of drinks is one way to feel better. Going to a party and having some fun is another. The problem can be that you might begin to rely on alcohol and drugs instead of looking for other, more useful ways to deal with problems and meet your needs.

Other solutions

The way you really learn to handle situations is by trying new things that offer successful solutions to your problems. For example, sometimes professors say things in class that don't quite get through to you, and you know that if you could just understand this one point better, the whole course could come together for you. In a situation like this, the best thing to do is go to the professor and talk about it, but many people don't feel free to do this. The choice you have to make is whether to stumble through on your own, or take the risk of trying something new, and make an appointment to discuss things with this intimidating person. (There's also the fear of appearing stupid because you don't understand something.)

What will you do? For some, the choice is easy. For others, very hard. What you will find 99 times out of 100 is that this professor will talk to you, help you understand to the best of her ability, and you'll feel much better for the experience. Once you try a new behavior, you'll feel better about trying it the next time because one success gives you the confidence to go for another.

When people rely on alcohol or other drugs to get them through difficult times, they avoid risking new behaviors and don't acquire the social, academic, or interpersonal skills that will help them succeed. With the possible exception of actual physical addiction, this is probably the most serious alcohol/drug abuse problem a person can develop. The ups and downs of life are how we learn, and avoiding these can lead to more serious problems. Another important thing to keep in mind about the learning you do in college, is that you develop many strong habits and behavioral patterns that will stay with you for the rest of your life.

A model of learning

Learning occurs in most people in a cyclical sort of way. Figure 15–1 is a very simplified but accurate representation of the learning cycle:

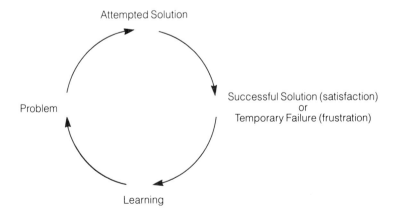

Figure 15–1 The learning cycle

Whether you solve the problem the first time around or not, you still learn something about it in your attempt, so learning is always part of the cycle. Even if you're unsuccessful, you can go around the circle again with another possible solution, and this time possibly succeed. The point is that if you try, through new behaviors, to solve the problem, eventually you will. However, you'll always learn something *every* time you try.

The cycle incorporating the use of alcohol or other drugs (Figure 15–2) looks somewhat different:

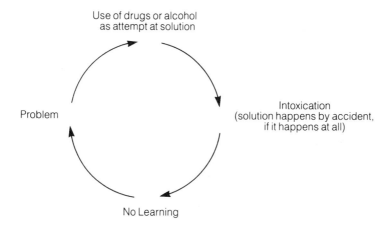

Figure 15–2   Learning cycle incorporating alcohol or drugs

As you can see, the difference is that most of the time no learning takes place, other than what you learn about being drunk or high.

If people get drunk or high every time they need to deal with a new situation, such as talking to their professors, they might muddle through it by luck, but more likely they'll decide not to go through with it. Getting drunk or high doesn't give a person any information about how to handle a meeting, or how to succeed in a class. All the person usually gets out of it is a drunk or a high.

If you try to succeed, you'll learn to feel good about yourself and your abilities. If you get drunk every time a problem comes up, you'll find yourself with a lot of problems hanging around waiting to be solved. Learning to deal with problems by building your skills and self-confidence is a life-long process that's only just beginning for most students, but with continued effort you can succeed. Each success will build on itself to help you find the next one.

How should I drink?

At first, this may appear to be the wrong question. Many people feel that the proper question is "Why?", but we're talking about *how* people use alcohol and not just their reasons for doing so. People drink in all sorts of ways, and learning the proper way can mean the difference between a pleasant interlude and a harrowing nightmare.

The majority of drinking occurs in a social setting with other people. Used in the most responsible way, alcohol can enhance and add to the enjoyment of social events.

Most everyone agrees that the world can be very stressful at times, and cause you to become tense, anxious, or upset. College is certainly no exception, and often it can be more stressful than a career. What makes a social event most enjoyable is being able to relax with other people and to talk, laugh, and share good feelings to help ease the effects of tension. Alcohol does several things in your body that help you relax rather quickly.

Alcohol relaxes you

When you take a drink and the alcohol enters your stomach, it is absorbed directly into the bloodstream through the stomach wall and the small intestine. As soon as it's in the bloodstream, it begins to circulate within the system and goes almost immediately to the brain, where the first area affected is the frontal lobe. This part of the brain governs, among other things, your judgment, inhibitions, and self-control.

Alcohol slightly reduces or depresses the function of this area, so that initially you have slightly less self-control and inhibition than you normally do, and you feel relaxed. As a result, you can think and act with less concern than usual over the consequences of your behavior.

Physically speaking, this translates into a feeling of relaxation and well-being. It also means that you become more talkative and sociable, since you are more relaxed. This is the effect that most people drink for. Unfortunately, many people seem to feel that if one is good, two is better, and four is surely better than two. Actually, to maintain this relaxed, comfortable feeling requires less than one drink per hour. This means one beer, one mixed drink, or one 5-ounce glass of wine, since they all contain the same amount of alcohol. The human body can only "process out" 1 to 1¼ ounces of alcohol per hour, so you can maintain the level that feels good by limiting your drinking to the amount your body can process per hour.

Alcohol and food

A second social use of alcohol comes from our highly developed and discriminating sense of taste. When you're tense, your senses don't work as well. You don't take the time to pay attention to the subtle differences in the tastes and smells of things when you're busily concentrating on your daily tasks.

Drinking wine with a meal often helps you enjoy these things by relaxing you first, and then by enhancing the flavors of your food. When you take the time to savor a wine, and pay attention to what it can do to the taste of food, you realize the reason people order some wines and turn others down at a restaurant. If you drink this way, you're very likely to enjoy it. If you drink too much, your senses will become dulled instead of sharpened.

As part of your own education about alcohol, you may want to contact someone who knows about wines, and try tasting various wines with different kinds of foods. The effect the right wine can have on food can be striking! The idea is not to become intoxicated, but to relax and learn to appreciate subtle taste differences. You'll find that the experience can be very pleasant. This isn't true only with wine; many people enjoy beer with food also.

A time to drink

Another way people consume alcoholic beverages is to limit their consumption to certain times. For students, this often means weekends. Depending on the event or activity you choose, your drinking may range from having a few beers with friends to spending the entire week drunk.

You'll find that the only real reason many parties at college take place is so people can drink. These parties go by a number of names—keggers, beer busts, PJ parties—and in many cases students come to these events for the sole purpose of "blowing it out" and getting as drunk as possible. People have parties to be with others in a social setting, but often they appear to feel that the only way to enjoy a social event is to get "wasted." This seems to be in keeping with the "if one is good, two is better" sort of logic.

If you're accustomed to binges of heavy drinking, you may feel ill at ease in a social setting. On the other hand, evidence indicates that by restricting these events to weekends only, you might at least limit some of the problems you could develop if you drank during the week.

How you drink is generally determined by what you want to get out of the situation. If you want to be sociable and relaxed, one drink an hour may help you do that. Try to keep in mind that a valuable aspect of college is the wide variety of experiences it offers. Through personal experience and conversations with other people, I have found that the times people remember as best were the ones where drinking was only part of the reason for being there. The real emphasis was on being with a good group of people and enjoying good music and food in an atmosphere where they could relax and talk.

Much of the excessive drinking that goes on in college is apparently a result of thinking that others expect it. Try spending time instead finding out what really makes a good party good!

Responsible drinking

Responsible drinking is a somewhat new concept in education, and it's based on the assumption that alcohol is not going to disappear from our culture. Therefore, it makes sense to give people the facts about drinking in an unbiased and straightforward way so they can make informed decisions about its use or nonuse. To see how this approach developed, it's necessary to look briefly at the history of alcohol education.

Scare tactics

Many approaches have been tried in substance abuse education, none of them extremely successfully. One of the first methods was the use of "scare tactics," where people were subjected to various lectures on the evils of use, and told horrible stories about lives destroyed by addiction. At my school, this was the job of the school nurse, an iron-jawed matron who seemed to relish the task of "putting the fear" into fifth graders. While some of her stories obviously were factual, these classes served, at least temporarily, to scare the pants off students. They also served to arouse a great deal of curiosity about this "forbidden fruit." When these tactics were presented to more mature and sophisticated high school students, they were simply ignored.

From the gruesome to the horrible

The next educational efforts came from the area of law enforcement. To a large degree, these consisted of films of accidents and injuries that had occurred due to drinking and driving. As a scare tactic, the films were effective, since they ranged from gruesome to horrible. They were completely factual, but they often were so horrible that people chose to block them out and ignore their obvious messages.

The permissive era

The next developments in substance abuse education were an outgrowth of the demand in the 1960s for greater freedom of choice at a younger age. During this period, many educators began to feel there was little use in attempting to educate students about drugs or alcohol. The drinking age was lowered in many states to 18 for the use of beer and wine, and everyone seemed to agree that this was logical, since 18-year-olds were being drafted to fight in Vietnam. Unfortunately, this turned out to be a poor decision, since one of the most apparent results was a dramatic increase in traffic deaths among 18 to 20 year olds.

All of these ideas were developed with the very best of intentions and genuine concern, but they discounted a couple of realities: People traditionally demand to make their own decisions about things that affect them, and you can get into a lot of trouble using or abusing things that you don't know much about.

Finally, responsible drinking

The model of responsible drinking has evolved from these experiences in education. It emphasizes the presentation of clear and factual information about alcohol and drugs and their effects. It covers all useful issues, including legal statutes, effects of substances on the mind and body, and the results of addiction, and also takes into account a great deal of information about how alcohol can be used (and enjoyed) in a way that does not create problems for people. More than just a model for education, it gives very clear notions of positive and negative effects, talks about the social issues involving drinking, and helps people dismiss false notions or myths about use.

The biggest difference in this model is that it doesn't assume that something bad is going to happen simply because you may decide, at some point, to try drinking. As thinking creatures, we respond to fear in a negative and often angry way, and this colors our thinking about the subject matter. On the other hand, people often respond to a good clear presentation of factual material by thinking about it, which is the key to responsible drinking: *thinking about what you're doing*.

Many campus programs are built around this model, and its reception by students, who seem to appreciate being treated as rational adults, capable of making choices, rather than as children who must be frightened into submission, has been excellent. By educating people in this way, we have a better chance as a culture to develop agreements about what responsible use means, since to some it means not drinking at all, and to others it may mean heavy use only on weekends. It's easier to develop these agreements in an atmosphere of information and choice, and as the notion of teaching responsible use becomes more widespread, we should become more consistent in our attitudes and behaviors as they relate to drinking.

Drinking, drugs, and driving

When people take drugs or drink, and then try to drive a car, they are usually not aware of the dangers they create for themselves and others because they fail to realize the effects these substances have on them. So, I'd like to briefly look at this with you.

One of the very first things alcohol affects is the ability to make sound judgments. It also affects your level of inhibition. Most people know what a judgment is, but some are not familiar with what an inhibition is, so I'll explain it the way someone explained it to me: Inhibitions are what keep your clothes on in public. This means that you have the ability to take your clothes off anywhere you wish. You know how to undo buttons and unzip zippers, and so on. But most people don't do that because they realize that this isn't acceptable behavior in public, and can even lead to arrest.

Without going into value judgments on the legal aspects of nudity, let's just say that an inhibition is like a little voice in your head telling you what to do and not do, based on what you have learned. Alcohol reduces the effect this little voice has on your behavior, which is where we get the image of the drunk dancing with a lampshade on his or her head—something the little voice would have told them was not a good idea, had it been fully functioning.

After the first few drinks, your judgment is affected, and with each additional drink other things begin to happen: Your balance goes haywire, and you may slur your words when you try to talk. Your reaction time becomes much slower than normal, and vision and coordination become poorer. Add these effects to your lower inhibitions and you may begin doing things like dancing with a lampshade on your head and, in general, looking like a real mess.

Now, with your judgment impaired, you can hardly be objective about your condition. On top of that, it's time to go home. This is why so many people go to their cars and feel they're perfectly able to drive home.

The fact is, at a blood-alcohol level of 0.10, you are seven times more likely to have an accident than if you were sober. When you're drunk, you simply cannot make good decisions because your judgment is "drunk" and your brain is not fully functional. The skills necessary for good driving are also affected: coordination, depth perception, reaction time, judgment, and inhibition.

The facts are alarming: In a recent year, 50,000 people were killed on the road, and 50 percent of these accidents were caused by a driver who had been drinking. There is much less evidence on drugs and driving because drugs are not always tested for, but evidence indicates that the use of drugs can impair a driver's abilities just as much as drinking can. The tragedy is that this 50 percent was preventable. There's one sure way to make certain you don't find yourself in this situation, and it's really very simple: *If You Plan To Drink, Plan Not To Drive.* Or, *If You Plan To Drive, Plan Not To Drink.* This allows you to use your good judgment while it's still good—before you drink.

Figure 15–3 gives you a good idea of what level of drinking is safe for you, based on your body weight, how many drinks you've had, and how long you take to drink them. Going by these limits could save you more than your license.

As a driver who may sometimes drink, you should also know about a law every state now has, called the Implied Consent Law. This means that by accepting a driver's license, you agree that you will take a breathalyzer test, if requested, by an officer who has reason to ask you to do so. If you refuse to do this, you will be forced to give up your license for a period of time (usually 90 days), and when you go to court you may still be charged with driving under the influence.

I should also mention the other expenses related to a DUI or DWI charge. If

KNOW YOUR LIMITS

CHART FOR RESPONSIBLE PEOPLE WHO MAY SOMETIMES DRIVE AFTER DRINKING!

APPROXIMATE BLOOD ALCOHOL PERCENTAGE

Drinks	Body Weight in Pounds								Influenced
	100	120	140	160	180	200	220	240	Influenced
1	.04	.03	.03	.02	.02	.02	.02	.02	Rarely
2	.08	.06	.05	.05	.04	.04	.03	.03	
3	.11	.09	.08	.07	.06	.06	.05	.05	
4	.15	.12	.11	.09	.08	.08	.07	.06	
5	.19	.16	.13	.12	.11	.09	.09	.08	Possibly
6	.23	.19	.16	.14	.13	.11	.10	.09	
7	.26	.22	.19	.16	.15	.13	.12	.11	
8	.30	.25	.21	.19	.17	.15	.14	.13	Definitely
9	.34	.28	.24	.21	.19	.17	.15	.14	
10	.38	.31	.27	.23	.21	.19	.17	.16	

Subtract .01% for each 40 minutes of drinking
One drink is 1 oz. of 100 proof liquor, 12 oz. of beer, or 4 oz. of table wine.

SUREST POLICY IS . . . DON'T DRIVE AFTER DRINKING!

Figure 15–3   Effects of alcohol in the bloodstream

you lose your right to drive, that's pretty hard to deal with. If you work, this creates other problems. Many states also require you to attend a training program (if you are charged with DUI) at your own expense, in addition to any fines assessed in court.

Next comes insurance. If you're so charged, your insurance rates can go up to three or even five times their normal rate, and can stay up there for as long as three years. Aside from the extreme danger to yourself and others that driving drunk creates, it can be a very expensive charge even if you don't serve a jail term, which is also a possibility.

Getting back to what I mentioned earlier, it's much safer to plan ahead. If you're going out with the intention of drinking, designate a driver who will not get drunk and will get everyone home (it doesn't always have to be the same person). If you find that you are too drunk to drive, stay where you are. Most everyone has floor space where you can sleep. If you can't stay, call a cab or a friend, and get them to take you home. Almost anything you do is better than drunk driving, for you and everyone else on the road. One more thing: Listen to your friends. If they tell you that you're too drunk to drive, believe them.

Addictions

In order to cover all bases, we need to address a subject that no one really likes to think about: the addiction that can develop to alcohol and other drugs (that's right, alcohol is a drug and is classified as a central nervous system depressant, similar in effect to the tranquilizer Valium). While the incidence of full-blown addiction occurs in only a minority of students while they're in college, it does happen to about 5 percent of the population. Keep in mind, also, that people develop habits in college that stay with them for years after. If you develop habits of heavy drinking and/or drug use, they could seriously affect your later life.

Some of the myths people have about addiction lead them to believe that it can't or won't happen to them. One of the biggest is that addiction tendencies are inherited from parents. While there is some evidence that this might happen, the fact remains that many individuals develop addictions with no family history. Another myth is that if you drink only beer, you can't become an alcoholic. This is completely false, since a twelve-ounce beer has just as much alcohol as a mixed drink or a glass of wine. We also seem to have some false notions with regard to our images of alcoholics and drug addicts, whom we view as middle-aged derelicts living in the streets, or young, ethnic group junkies living in New York City. These images, strongly reinforced by TV and movies, are simply not reality. The average American alcoholic is not easy to identify, since most are employed, married, have families, and generally function normally in society. Most of the clients I saw in my experience in alcohol and drug abuse rehabilitation were white males from middle-class family backgrounds. These people become much more like our stereotypes when their addiction causes them to lose their jobs, separate from their families, and get kicked out of the house into the street. At this point, they begin to look more like addicts, but their problems existed long before they reached this point. Generally, no hard evidence exists to support the existence of the "addictive personality," since the problems of addiction touch all races and socioeconomic levels.

Another problem with addiction is that people feel that once the addicting substance is taken away, the problem is solved. The fact is that people become addicted not only to a substance, but also to the experience, or the high that they feel. During rehabilitation, they have to adjust not only to the physical absence of their drug, but also to the fact that they must learn to do other things that replace the drug experience. Many clients have told me that they really didn't know what they were getting into when they began using drugs or alcohol (and often both).

Addiction can be medically dangerous, and anyone who feels he or she may have an addiction problem should seek professional help.

Certain behaviors can indicate the presence of a possible problem: (1) Drinking when there's a good reason to stay sober; (2) getting into fights or being thrown out of places because of drinking; (3) getting into trouble with the law because of drinking; (4) having accidents and being injured because of drinking; (5) drinking alone, and/or needing a drink in the morning; (6) having shaking hands the morning after; (7) not being able to remember what happened the night before; (8) being told by a doctor that drinking is affecting your health.

Many of these things can happen to anyone once, and maybe even twice, but if they begin to be a regular thing, you're probably looking at a serious problem in the making.

When you're really overwhelmed

At times, even the most well-adjusted person may have difficulties dealing with the hectic life of a student, and may benefit from the help others have to offer. This is a highly responsible way of taking care of yourself by making use of the many resources on your campus. Here is where you might begin to look for other help.

- *Friends and Fellow Students.* Friends can be a helpful resource. Talking to someone like yourself, who is going through the same things as you, can be a rewarding experience. You'll probably find out that most people feel the way you do, and you can solve problems together.
- *Hall Advisors and Residence Directors.* If you live in a residence hall, check in with your hall advisor or the residence hall director. These are usually upperclassmen or women who have probably been through many of the same experiences you are having. Often, they receive training in helping skills, and can put you in touch with other resources on campus.
- *Professors or Academic Advisors.* These advisors can help you sort out the many new challenges of college. While they're more inclined to work with your academic problems than your personal ones, often the line between these two is a very fine one.
- *The Counseling Center or Chaplain's Office.* People here can also be of assistance. These professionals in counseling and therapy offer a wide variety of services to students with problems. Don't be put off by titles; they're helpers not only by profession, but also by choice.

You don't need to feel alone on a campus full of people. Others are either experiencing the same things as you or they've already gone through them. You may have to reach out a little, but that's a valuable thing to know how to do. By looking for help with your problems, you help yourself in several ways: You learn how to ask for help and how to use the resources around you, and you just may find the solution to your problem.

Alcohol: facts vs. myths

1. People do things when they are drunk that they would never do when sober. True or False?
2. About what percentage of adults in America drinks alcoholic beverages?
   a. 95 percent   b. 70 percent   c. 50 percent   d. 33 percent
3. Alcohol is a stimulant. True or False?
4. Fifteen percent of all people killed in drunk driving accidents are in their teens. True or False?
5. How many alcoholics are estimated to be in the United States?
   a. 500,000   b. 5–6 million   c. 9–10 million   d. 15 million

6. Most people can judge when they are too drunk to drive. True or False?
7. In most states, the blood-alcohol level at which you are legally drunk is:
   a. 0.05   b. 0.10   c. 0.12   d. 0.15
8. Americans spend as much on alcohol as they do on education. True or False?
9. Best estimates indicate that _____ percent of all highway fatalities are alcohol related.
   a. 80 percent   b. 25 percent   c. 50 percent   d. 60 percent
10. Black coffee, "walking," or cold showers will sober a drunk up faster. True or False?
11. A large person will sober up more quickly than a small person. True or False?
12. Alcohol is an aphrodisiac. True or False?
13. Which has the greatest amount of alcohol in it:
    a. one drink mixed with 80-proof liquor   b. one 4-ounce glass of 12 percent wine   c. one 12-ounce beer   d. all have the same amount
14. A person may overdose on alcohol just as with other drugs. True or False?
15. Certain behaviors can serve as "warnings" to tell a person that he or she may have a drinking problem. True or False? If true, name some:

1. _____	6. _____	11. _____
2. _____	7. _____	12. _____
3. _____	8. _____	13. _____
4. _____	9. _____	14. _____
5. _____	10. _____	15. _____

Quiz answers

1. True. Inhibitions are lowered by drinking, giving us "permission" to do things we might be too shy or smart to do when sober.
2. b. 70 percent
3. False. Many feel it's a stimulant because it lowers inhibitions, and because it relaxes or loosens us up.
4. False. The figure is approximately 60 percent.
5. c. 9–10 million. These are alcoholics, not just heavy drinkers. (This is roughly three times the population of the state of South Carolina.)
6. False. Most people are horrible judges of this. As the brain becomes more affected by drinking, we are less able to judge our level of debilitation.
7. b. 0.10. You can, however, be arrested and charged with DUI with a blood-alcohol level as low as 0.05 if the officer sees that you cannot function properly.
8. False. They spend about twice as much on drinking.
9. c. 50 percent. This is approximately 25,000 people per year.

10.	False.	All you get is a wide-awake drunk. The body processes 1 to 1¼ oz of alcohol out of your body per hour. Time is the only thing that will sober you up.
11.	False.	We all sober up at the same rate. A large person may need to drink more than a small one to get the same level of intoxication, however.
12.	False.	It lowers our inhibitions and makes us more willing to take risks and do things we might not otherwise do, but it also lowers sensitivity and at legally drunk levels can often adversely affect performance.
13.	d.	All have the same amount of real alcohol in them, 1 to 1½ oz.
14.	True.	When you pass out (not blackout), the body is going to sleep so that no more alcohol can be put into it.
15.	True.	

1. Drinking when there is a good reason not to, or getting drunk when there is a good reason not to
2. Having accidents or injuring yourself because of drinking
3. Missing classes or appointments because of drinking
4. Getting into fights because of drinking
5. Being asked to leave a bar or party because of drinking
6. Blackouts: When you can't remember what happened when you were drinking, even though you continued to function during that time
7. Getting into trouble with the law because of drinking
8. Needing a drink to "get you going" in the morning
9. Using money for drinking that should have been used for something else
10. Having "shaky" hands the next morning
11. Being told by a doctor that drinking is affecting your health
12. Feeling the effects of drinking in class or on the job

Suggested activities

1. Ask your friends why they drink or use drugs. Then ask yourself.
2. Find out what student organizations exist on your campus that deal with alcohol and drug abuse, and find out what they do.
3. Pay attention to how much promotion goes on at your campus by companies that sell alcoholic beverages. If possible, talk to a local distributor and find out how they work on campuses and why.
4. Try organizing a survey (5–10 questions), and ask other students about their attitudes and habits concerning drinking and drug use.

5. Ask an authority figure, such as a university administrator, what rules he or she would make for your campus about drinking and drug use? You might talk to some other students about this, and then compare them to your own school's policies.

6. Talk about how you would handle someone who was drunk and insisted on driving his or her car. If you've ever done this, you might want to share your experience.

7. Try to locate someone who is knowledgable about wines, and find out how one chooses wine to go with foods. If possible, find out if there are places you can go to participate in wine-tasting activities (or organize your own).

8. Try planning a "responsible party" with other students. What foods would you serve, in what kind of place would you hold it, how many people would you ask, how would you handle any drinking there, and during what holidays or other times would it be good to have a party?

9. Organize a debate or discussion on what the legal age for drinking should be. This is a very current subject in many states, and there are many pros and cons.

Suggested readings

Alberti, R. E., and M. L. Emmons. *Your Perfect Right*. San Luis Obispo, Calif: Impact Publishers, 1974.

Berne, Eric, M.D. *Games Alcoholics Play*. New York: Ballantine Books, 1971.

Blexrud, Jan. *A Toast to Sober Spirits and Joyous Juices*. Minneapolis: Comp Care Publications, 1976.

Brecher, Edward, ed. *Licit and Illicit Drugs*. New York: Little, Brown, 1972.

Fort, Joel, M.D. *The Addicted Society*. New York: Grove Press, 1982.

———. *The Pleasure Seekers*. New York: Grove Press, 1969.

Glasser, William, M.D. *Positive Addictions*. New York: Harper and Row, 1976.

Jacobson, Hacker, and Atkins, *The Booze Merchants*. Washington: Center for Science in the Public Interest, 1983.

Lingemen, Richard. *Drugs from A to Z*. New York: McGraw-Hill, 1969.

Mecca, Andrew, M.D. *Alcohol in America; A Modern Perspective*. Belvedere, Calif.: California Health Research Foundation, 1980.

Outerbridge, David. *The Hangover Handbook*. New York: Harmony Books, 1981.

Peele, Stanton. *How Much is Too Much*. Englewood Cliffs, N.J.: Prentice-Hall, 1981.

———. *Love and Addiction*. New York: Signet Books, 1975.

Ray, Oakley. *Drugs, Society and Human Behavior*. Toronto: C. V. Mosby, 1978.

Selye, Hans, M.D. *Stress without Distress*. New York: Signet Books, 1974.

Tart, Charles. *Altered States of Consciousness*. Garden City, New York: Doubleday, 1969.

Weil, Andrew. *The Natural Mind*. Boston: Houghton Mifflin, 1972.

Beyond Academics: Activities

Thomas C. Shandley, *Director of Student Activities*
and Mark G. Shanley, *Director of Student Development*
University of South Carolina

Although Mark and I were primarily involved in different activities as undergraduates, both of us feel our lives were changed by our extracurricular involvement.

During my first year at college I was involved in no campus activities and studied just enough to get by. To me, college meant attending class and thinking about high school. Then I became involved in my residence hall's government and in the college activities board. What a difference between the four years of drudgery I could see looming ahead and the challenging growth-producing four years that college actually became!

I learned the frustrations of being a leader. I learned of the need to divide my time wisely among study, work, and recreation. And I actually earned better grades than when I'd been a green freshman. When it came time for me to make decisions about my career, I felt confident and ready for anything. I chose to become an educator, and since earning my master's degree in higher education administration, I've worked in student activities administration.

Mark joined a social fraternity as a freshman and found that his involvement with it became the most important factor in his persistence to do well in college and in the establishment of his career. Fraternity brothers tutored him through difficult freshman classes and fraternity-sponsored activities helped him develop and polish valuable interpersonal and social skills. Finally, at the urging of fraternity members, he took on a succession of chapter and cam-

225

pus leadership roles that led eventually to his decision to become a college administrator.

Things could have turned out very differently for us. We may not have continued in college or we might now be in different careers. We would certainly have missed out on the opportunity to grow and develop with the wide and varied groups of individuals we each were involved with. We hope that this chapter will stimulate you to get involved in some of the many activities at your school. We know you'll find the experience rewarding.

Your college experience can be so much more than what you learn within the walls of a classroom. Many of your concerns about college may have rested with questions such as "How well will I do with freshman English?" "Will I make the grade?" These are legitimate concerns that all freshmen probably have in common with each other.

But there is so much more. I was fortunate enough to have a mother who encouraged me to "get involved" on campus and to become a well-rounded student. She was the placement director for a college and, as the individual charged with helping students turn their degree into a career, knew the value of involvement in campus activities. Little did I know that I would make a career out of providing such experiences for other students!

What is a student activity and what is its purpose in higher education? Student activities can generally be described as anything involving a group of two or more students who form an organization or participate in an activity or an organization that can effect social, moral, or political change. What this definition comes down to is any activity from producing a student newspaper to learning how to whitewater canoe, to joining a sorority, to attending a play, to promoting a concert. The opportunities on any campus usually stretch as far as you allow your collective imagination to flow.

Thus, your life as a student can be so much more than a continuation of the discussion of what your professor teaches in the classroom. College allows you an opportunity to expose yourself to a variety of intellectual, political, social, and moral commitments that nicely supplement what you will learn within the classroom.

The history of student activities

Some people have always felt that a student's moral and social development should be left to the home and that life at college should concentrate on the basics of the academic experience. However, since early in the history of higher education, cocurricular activities have emerged as an integral part of student life. As you have undoubtedly observed, your social, political, and moral beliefs are challenged daily in the atmosphere created by students gathering together.

The first established effort by students to organize an activity began in the 1800s in England, when students at Cambridge and Oxford universities formed debate teams. This activity spread throughout England and eventually spread to Harvard in the United States. During the early 1900s, the strong foundation provided by the Young Men's Christian Association, which has a long-established reputation of commitment to the moral and spiritual development of young people, is credited with providing the impetus for many of the organized activities that exist on college campuses today.

Essentially, as students began to flock to the college campus—as they began to share classes, dorm rooms, meals, and after-hours—their common interests began to organize. The objectives of the university or college in providing an education for the student began to encompass opportunities for students to develop not only intellectually, but culturally, ethically, physically, and socially as well.

As a result, the following set of general goals for cocurricular activities has emerged:

1. To help create a stimulating, creative, and enjoyable campus environment that supplements academic offerings.
2. To provide opportunities for students to establish a laboratory or practical base for learning experiences.
3. To provide opportunities for students to participate in personal and interpersonal experiences that aid in psychological and social growth.
4. To provide a setting and programs for increasing the interaction and understanding among the many different ethnic groups on campus.

Student organizations began to form as an offspring of academic offerings or as a reaction to collective interests among students. The drama clubs, marketing clubs, debate societies, and fraternal organizations emerged with faculty serving as advisors. The "Greeks" (fraternities and sororities) were formed out of a common interest in mutual friendship, scholarship, and service to the university and community. Eventually, colleges began to establish formal settings for this interaction to occur, and today, almost every college or university has what is commonly referred to as a student center or union. The student center or "campus living room" can be anything from a place to hang out, pick up your mail, or grab a soda, to a center providing a rich variety of cultural, social, and aesthetic entertainment. By the 1930s many of the student activities that exist today were established on our college campuses.

With the social and political turmoil of the 1960s, the interests of the college student changed as well. Many students were frustrated with their lack of control over or input in the events that controlled their lives, and the facilities and funds to support student activities became a vehicle for the expression of these frustrations. The campus was a hotbed of expression through the student newspaper, rallies, and debates. Student power became more significant in governing the university, and the role that student organizations such as the student government and student newspaper played was critical.

Eventually, over time, students and administrators, realizing the importance and popularity of these "out-of-the classroom" experiences, instituted what is commonly called a "student activities fee" to fund such programs and organizations. Usually controlled and administered by students, this fee is used to maintain and support the entire student activities program from initial funding to the payment of full-time advisors at some institutions. As a result, student activities are a vital and contributive participant in the present collegiate experience.

The variety of student activities

Regardless of the size of the institution, most colleges and universities have made some kind of commitment to student activities, although the variety and scope of programs vary considerably.

As a student, you may become involved in activities on any of three levels: one-to-one, small-group, and large-group. An example of a one-to-one activity may involve competing in a billiards tournament in the student center. For those interested in athletics, competing in an intramural tennis or wrestling tournament is a one-to-one example. Singular involvement may also simply be attending a film or lecture on campus.

Small-group activities can be anything from participating in a theatrical performance to joining a student organization to participating on a softball team to writing for the college newspaper. Finally, involvement in a large campus group is another option. These groups are usually highly visible and hold a dominant position on the campus. Such organizations include the student government, student program board, a large fraternity or sorority, or the campus choir.

Despite the level of involvement you choose, dozens of opportunities exist for you to become a part of a student activity, whatever the size of your campus. Go to your student union or center to find out more about involvement or participation in any cocurricular activity. Let's explore in more detail some of the major areas you may be interested in.

Intramural and recreational sports

Typically designed for students who enjoy competing in athletic events but who may not be varsity or scholarship athletes, intramurals can play a large role in campus life. Whether it involves an individual or team sport and is co-rec, all-male, or all-female, the opportunity is there for you. The type of program, depending on the size and emphasis of your institution, can be anything from the traditional football, basketball, and softball leagues to co-rec water polo, horseshoes, 5'10" and under basketball, or a 6.2-mile run. Though the events are certainly competitive, enthusiasm and willingness to learn are as important as ability in intramurals. Another rather new trend in this area is the sport club, an activity available at some colleges. These can range from a backpacking club formed by a group of students who have a common interest to a flying and sport parachuting club for those a bit more daring. Involvement in a sport club not only provides an opportunity to get to know people who have similar interests, but also—because instructional clinics are often provided—a chance to develop a lifelong skill as well.

Student organizations

On any campus, the first and largest component of student activities is the network that makes up student organizations. It's very simple to start a student group with only ten students. Their focus usually falls within the broad boundaries of social, religious, academic, political, or service organizations.

A brief listing of typical student organizations might include:

- Karate Club
- Sailing Club
- Bowling League
- Greek Letter Social Fraternities
- Association of Iranian Students
- Hong Kong Student Association
- Student Newspaper

- Amnesty International
- College Republicans
- Association of Afro-American Students
- P.E. Majors Club
- Student Christian Fellowship
- Finance Club
- Graduate Womens Association
- Student Bar Association
- Chess Club

Social organizations traditionally have been the area of most interest to students because they involve such groups as the student program board and social fraternities and sororities. For students seeking others who share the same religious beliefs and interests, the comfort of a religious organization can be very rewarding. In recent years, academic-related student organizations have received the most attention from students. For instance, if you're a business major interested in pursuing a career in marketing, there may be a marketing club that not only invites guest speakers from the industry but is a social outlet as well. An engineering club might hold social activities as well as conduct design competitions outside the classroom. Many faculty participate on a regular basis in such organizations, and students find them to be valuable sources for employment contacts. Several years ago, I asked the campus marketing club to develop a building usage survey for the student center. This project provided vital information for us about the students who used the building, and was a good practical experience for the members as well.

Student union

Some of the largest and most significant student organizations are in the student union and student media areas. In almost every college center or union, there is an organization charged with providing a well-rounded set of programs for the campus community. This group usually consists of committees that plan lectures, cultural events, films, concerts, short courses, and travel programs. Other programs have included videotape, dance, and outdoor recreation committees as well. Funded by the student activities fee and run by the students, these organizations plan, produce, and evaluate all of these program areas. Obviously, many student volunteers are needed to run such a group.

The kinds of things that you receive in return for your involvement include a firsthand experience in preparing and administering a budget, in creating the publicity techniques needed to promote an event, and in developing the leadership skills necessary to activate and motivate volunteers and the organizational skills needed to pull off an event. In working with a variety of people in a variety of settings, you learn about your ability to get along with, as well as lead, others. If you're a journalism major, you can gain experience in drafting news releases for upcoming events. As a business major, you can gain experience in marketing, financial planning, or revenue projection. Perhaps best of all, you have the opportunity to learn outside of your principal focus of study.

Student media

One of the most visible and critical areas of student activities is student media. Comprising the student newspaper, yearbook, and often a radio station, student media organizations cover campus events as well as provide entertainment. Educational and vocational opportunities for students are endless. A typical reporter for a student newspaper must have the ability to gather information and produce a story, as well as develop the personal skills necessary to interview. Students with an interest in photography can find an outlet for this expression through the newspaper or yearbook. Many students also gain valuable sales experience as advertising representatives for the newspaper or yearbook. This may provide some income as well. Of course, for those who want to become editors, not only are the preceding skills necessary, but the leadership qualities needed to run a large, complex organization are critical. Because of the impact a newspaper can have on the campus, the editor is under the watchful eye of everyone from the college president to the average student.

For those interested in broadcast media, working in the radio station can be fun as well as educational. Whether you are a disc jockey, news reporter, or program director, you'll find the responsibilities are significant and the work rewarding. If you have the technical knowledge and/or interest, you can always find an outlet for your interest at the station, where the equipment is always in need of maintenance and supervision.

Of all the experiences available to you in cocurricular activities outside the classroom, those in student media may well provide the best practical work experiences of all.

Fraternities and sororities: myths and realities

Each year, thousands of college freshmen across the country confront the question of whether or not to pledge a social fraternity or sorority. For some of you, the question is a casual one as you assess the wide variety of social and recreational opportunities available at most colleges and universities. For others the question assumes extreme proportions in the panic to identify and be accepted by the "right" group. A third group of students consider fraternities and sororities as elitist groups of social snobs to be avoided at all costs.

College fraternities and sororities are student organizations based on friendship and social interaction. They are recognized or registered by the colleges and universities where they exist, and operate within the general guidelines of other campus organizations. Beyond these basic guidelines, fraternities and sororities place more specific and demanding requirements on themselves and typically develop separate governing bodies to coordinate their activities and functions. Most importantly, they belong to a larger national organization that unifies and integrates the local campus fraternity or sorority into the larger framework of a common history, purpose, tradition, and system of values and ideals. The national fraternity or sorority provides a lifelong membership and identity that binds members and chapters from all parts of the country.

The college fraternity movement began in 1776 at the College of William and Mary with the founding of Phi Beta Kappa. Established initially as a literary and debating society, Phi Beta Kappa and the other early Greek letter societies arose in response to the disciplinary standards that narrowly restricted student life in the colonial colleges. These fraternities were organized, often secretly, to assert the rights of free speech, assembly, and independent decision. As they were initially secret societies, fraternities developed secret oaths, rituals, codes of laws, handshakes (grips), initiation ceremonies, and mottos in Greek or Latin to establish their unique goals and aspirations. These characteristics still apply to most fraternities and sororities today.

A fundamental strength of fraternities and sororities arose from the need of students to belong to some form of community and to fill an emotional and social vacuum left by the academic curriculum and the often intimidating and impersonal campus environment. Greek life offered an opportunity to bring together small groups of students and to develop a more manageable and cohesive "family" atmosphere than was possible in college dormitories.

National fraternities and sororities

Early chapters of individual fraternities and sororities that expanded to nearby college campuses typically were loosely united through a common name and principles only. The beginning of a more formal structure occurred when a particular chapter was designated to maintain the important documents and records of the fraternity or sorority. "Conventions" of chapter delegates were held to establish policy and administrative practices for the collective chapters and to elect central officers for the fraternity or sorority.

As the number of chapters on different campuses increased and expanded geographically, regional territories and officers were established. Finally, "national" offices and administrative staffs were created to coordinate the membership and activities, such as maintaining membership records, supervising the financial operations of the undergraduate chapter, arranging national conventions and regional leadership conferences, and otherwise administering the operations of these complex organizations.

Membership

Fraternity or sorority membership is both an opportunity and a responsibility. The opportunities are numerous: You may live in the fraternity or sorority house (if available) and enjoy the benefits of communal living with a group of good friends; you can participate in a variety of social and recreational activities ranging from formal dances to mixers with other chapters to playing on an intramural team; and you can meet and develop close and lasting friendships with other chapter members. Membership also provides opportunities for personal and social development, and the ability to learn and practice valuable interpersonal and leadership skills.

Fraternal living can complement the formal classroom experience. It provides you with a means of personal identification and helps you avoid the feeling of being lost in the vastness of the typical college or university setting.

Finally, membership provides an opportunity to get actively involved in a dynamic organization. By voicing your opinion in chapter meetings, participating in rush or social activities, or assuming a leadership role, you can exercise the opportunity to affect the course and direction of your chapter. Also, serving as an officer in the chapter or heading a committee to plan and complete a project provides you with an opportunity to learn and to work with and through other people in an organized setting. Managing and delegating responsibility are important skills in a society that is increasingly dominated by formal groups and organizations.

Membership is an opportunity, but it's also a responsibility; it requires your time, energy, and enthusiasm; it involves active caring for other members and the chapter as a whole; and it requires your financial support.

Two other points should be made about membership in a fraternity or sorority. Research has shown that participation in extracurricular activities, especially membership in social fraternities and sororities, is significantly related to staying in college. And experience has shown that the leadership, interpersonal, and organizational skills developed by fraternities and sororities have been highly evaluated by employment recruiters.

Finances

Membership in a fraternity or sorority involves a significant financial commitment and responsibility. Each chapter establishes its own budget to cover the costs of running the house, providing social activities and other functions, and meeting its obligations to the national fraternity or sorority. Based on this budget, the chapter then identifies the income needed to cover its expenditures and establishes dues requirements for members accordingly. Dues vary widely from chapter to chapter and from campus to campus, but a general fee of $200 to $500 per year (not including room and board) might be expected.

The cost of fraternity or sorority membership including room and board (where members live in the chapter house) is competitive with residence hall living and, in some cases, is even less expensive. Fraternity and sorority dues can be viewed as advance contributions to future social and recreational opportunities systematically provided by the chapter. Dues should be considered in perspective to the costs for similar activities that you would otherwise directly assume if you weren't a member. In most cases, the collective contributions of many members make possible a variety of activities that a student could not individually afford.

When considering fraternity or sorority membership, you should clearly identify the financial responsibilities involved and consider how you will be able to meet those responsibilities for *all four years* of typical undergraduate membership. You must evaluate these costs with other financial commitments and determine if you want to or can afford to make fraternity or sorority membership a priority.

If you choose to explore fraternity or sorority membership, be sure to look at all the available groups before you decide to join. Look beyond the size, facilities, and image of each group and find out what the members are like. Look for a group of people you enjoy being with and whom you like and respect. Remember, once you make the choice, your fellow brothers or sisters will become a significant influence on the rest of your college career and beyond. You'll become a lifelong member of a national Greek organization and will continue to have opportunities for ongoing involvement.*

The value of student activities

What is it about planned activities outside of the classroom that makes your college or university commit thousands of dollars to them? Perhaps the following story, based on a true experience, will provide some of the answers. Larry was a student at a large state institution, majoring in media arts. He enjoyed his chosen field and worked fairly hard in the classroom. Yet he felt that wasn't quite enough, and began to look for additional experiences. As a sophomore, he joined the student union and became involved in the concert and the film committees. He liked the chance to have a say in the kinds of programs that were brought to campus, and made several new friends as well. While working on the film committee, he was given the opportunity to contact agencies for the major film companies to order the semester's films. He enjoyed the responsibility and prestige associated with his job and was proud of the work he was doing. He had studied film in the classroom and enjoyed attending films, but this gave him a chance to see the industry from the inside as well. He did a good job and, after a year in the union, was selected to chair the film committee. Now, not only did he find himself responsible for an entire film program involving a large budget and number of films, but he also had the responsibility of leading some twenty other students. He attended several leadership workshops on time management, delegation, communication, and motivation provided by the student activities center and soon began to learn how to guide the activities of the committee.

As he became heavily involved in the organization, Larry found that the course work within his major took on a whole new meaning. He found that he could apply some of the theory to actual practice in his job. After graduation, through the experiences and contacts he made while serving as a member of the student union, Larry was offered a job as a sales agent with a major film distributor and today is doing quite well.

I received a letter from Larry a year ago and among his comments were:

I really believe that being in the union as chairman of Cinematic Arts helped me prepare for the "real thing." I am constantly working under

---

*A very special acknowledgement is made to Jack L. Anson, outgoing Executive Director of the National Interfraternity Conference, who provided invaluable direction and resource materials about fraternities and sororities.

pressure and having to meet deadlines. If I hadn't had to deal with them in school, it would be a lot harder now.

In addition to providing valuable practical experience, as it did for Larry, involvement in student activities is valuable for many other reasons as well:

1. To provide programs of an educational, recreational or moral value.
2. To help you get to know other students with similar interests.
3. To involve you in an organization that allows you to grow intellectually, physically, spiritually, or socially.
4. To develop your personal ability to lead others. This includes being able to elicit responses or actions from others, working with others, and having others depend on you for direction and motivation.
5. To involve you in a valuable, practical experience. This may directly supplement your academic major or provide you with a whole new set of learning experiences.
6. To produce the lifelong value of volunteerism or service to others that often happens with your involvement in student organizations.
7. To develop lifelong leisure skills. This often happens in sport clubs, where a student becomes interested in an activity such as flying and continues to enjoy it long after graduation.
8. Perhaps most importantly, to provide a place and situation for simply having fun. Student activities can be a wonderful release from the pressures of studies.

Many people believe that a student's most important teacher is another student. Whether that's true or not, we all know the influence our peers have had on us throughout our lives. Thus, your relationships developed with close friends and peers can be of primary value to you in your overall development as a student.

The value to the institution

Although a great deal of this discussion about student activities has stressed the value to the individual student, the college or university certainly benefits from these programs as well. A full schedule of cocurricular activities imbues a campus with the stimulating, vibrant atmosphere distinctive of higher education. To an institution of higher learning, this atmosphere can provide:

1. An attractive, well-rounded educational experience for students and prospective students.
2. A learning experience complementary to the curriculum offered.

3. An avenue to encourage meaningful interaction between students, faculty, and staff. For the faculty and staff, involvement with student programs as members or advisors is another method of interacting with students on an informal basis.

4. An opportunity for students to become well-rounded in their educational, moral, and social development. Numerous studies on student retention show that students who are active in campus life find their experience to be much more meaningful and are more likely to remain in school than the student who doesn't participate.

5. An attractive student for prospective employers. A college recruiter is often not just interested in the educational or technical skills of a candidate, but in the leadership and community service qualities as well. Employed graduates are much more supportive of the education they received and of the institution than unemployed students. I have several visits a year from major companies recruiting on campus who ask for the names of the top student leaders.

6. As alumni offices have recognized, students active in cocurricular activities tend to be more supportive of alumni activities after graduation. This often means more financial support for the university.

The impact of cocurricular education

Your opportunities to learn and grow certainly reach beyond the walls of the classroom. Whether your interests are skydiving, ceramics, marketing, or student government, you can pursue that interest, develop additional skills, and meet other people, all within the student activities part of your collegiate experience.

Campus life is radically different today than it may have been for your parents. Receiving a degree is no guarantee of a job or a secure future. Because a college degree is now the norm rather than the exception, employers are looking at the other features that may set you apart from that large population of college grads. These features include your major, grade point, service to community, and job experience. And they also include your participation in cocurricular activities. Those activities that were fun and rewarding, and that provided you with the opportunity to develop your leadership, communication, budget, and personal skills, may well give you the slight advantage you need in getting a job.

Higher learning certainly includes the study of Western civilization, English literature, and advanced calculus. But it also includes development of the ability to understand an individual from another culture, appreciate the performing or visual arts, learn the value of service to others, and expand on other such skills that will be with you for life. The learning laboratory that participation in student activities can become is an opportunity that should play a vital role in your overall college education.

I encourage you to stop by your student activities office on campus and check out what is available to you. It's never too early to get involved and I think you'll find that many student organizations are eager to have freshman members. Your college experience is what you make of it. Take advantage of what you've got!

Suggested activities

1. Find out about upcoming events on campus. Determine one or two that are of interest to you; seek out a participant and find out how you can become involved.
2. Consider starting your own organization if there isn't one already for your particular hobby or interest.
3. Find out whether you can get academic credit for your involvement with student activities.
4. Arrange a panel discussion with members from each of the Greek coordinating councils on your campus (Interfraternity Council, Panhellenic Association, and Pan Hellenic Council).

Suggested readings

Anson, Jack L. "Fraternity Life in the 70's." *College Today* (Georgia–Florida ed.), 1976–1977 (Media Direction, 550 Monroe Place, N.E., Atlanta, Ga. 30324).

Astin, Alexander W. *Preventing Students from Dropping Out.* San Francisco: Jossey-Bass, 1975.

Robinson, John. *Baird's Manual of American College Fraternities.* 18th ed. Menasha, Wisc.: College Press, 1968.

Rudolph, Frederick. *The American College and University, First Edition.* New York: Random House, 1982.

Schreck, Thomas C. *Fraternity for the Year 2000.* Indianapolis: American College Fraternity Bicentennial Commission, 1976.

On Becoming a Leader

Dennis Pruitt, *Vice President and Dean of Student Affairs*
University of South Carolina

*As a student athlete in college, I had some opportunities to experi-
ence good leadership roles as captain of both intercollegiate basketball and baseball teams. But I was to discover in my junior year
that the experiences gained through participation in intercollegiate
athletics were at times shallow, and often were sheltering. Luckily
(and I mean by pure chance), in my junior year I became a class
senator for our student government association. In my senior year, I
was president of that same student organization. That leadership
experience was a catalyst for my personal and professional development that exceeded every experience I had previously had, including
my years as an athlete. President John Kennedy once said, "Leadership and learning are indispensable to each other." During the
past ten years I have studied leadership feverishly, conducted leadership retreats at almost 200 colleges and universities, spoken at
over 100 conventions, and delivered enough class lectures, club
speeches, and private pep talks to melt down my vocal cords and
change the pitch of my voice. My conclusion: Students can enrich
their extent of knowledge, their level of skills, and their personality
development extensively by assuming leadership roles in college
clubs or organizations. Kennedy said it. And I said it. Why don't
you discover it? Read on!*

Leadership and learning

Ever since I had my first leadership position in elementary school (I was a class fire marshall) I've had an urge to learn more about life by serving others. Through the first thirty years of my life, I've served in numerous leadership positions—from class senator to SGA president. From Sunday school teacher to chairperson for a regional March of Dimes Telerama. From vice-president of my college alumni association to chairman of the board of directors of a professional association. Based on these experiences, I've made some general observations about leadership and learning.

First, it took a lot of time, energy, and effort to perform each leadership role. But while I gave a lot, I got an awful lot back in return. There are incredible rewards for participating in an organization.

Second, I've observed that most college students today are just like I was. They face four leadership dilemmas: (1) once you join a club or organization, you somehow develop a secret desire to assume a leadership role; (2) you don't know why you want to have a leadership role—in fact, you're confused because you don't really understand how having a leadership position in a student organization can possibly complement your classroom studies; (3) you don't think, even in your wildest imagination, that you're qualified—and you don't think you can commit the necessary time and energy to develop yourself into an effective leader; and (4) even if you wanted to pursue and obtain a leadership opportunity, you don't have the foggiest idea how to go about it. Well, sit back, relax, and read on. This chapter will stimulate your thinking about these and other questions so that your leadership anxiety will be reduced to a tolerable level and will allow you to seek and obtain the college leadership role of your choice.

Your secret desire to be a leader

From the earliest days of childhood, most of you can remember your parents suggesting that you, their dear little child, might one day grow up to be president of the United States. We are programmed to be leaders from our earliest childhood days. Each of us yearns for the attention, admiration, and sense of self-achievement that is bestowed on the leaders of our society. Now that you're in college, there will be a certain informal pressure to become a member of some club or organization. And once you've been a member of your organization for a short period, don't be surprised if you develop an urge to contribute to the quality of your group by serving in a leadership capacity.

Generally, students don't talk to other members of their organization about their desires to obtain leadership positions. We're much too humble to take the "please nominate me" approach. Rather, we prefer to be drafted by our friends because they believe we are the most logical and well-qualified person for the leadership position. So what happens is that students often find themselves secretly desiring a leadership position but not receiving a nomination. In fact, many members of the club believe that you're not even interested in the leadership position. If you are, whether it is as parliamentarian or president, *go ahead and let your friends know*. Early in the game the secret is to let the word out, in a tactful and humble manner. Otherwise, you may find yourself being passed over time and time again for some other candidate who is "more available or more willing." If nothing else, just assume that in all probability you'll want a leadership position at some point during your organizational life, and start planning for it the day you're initiated into your organization.

Justifying the time for leadership

One reason students won't acknowledge their secret desire to assume a leadership position is the dilemma they face of justifying to themselves and to their parents the time and energy they'll take away from academic studies to fulfill their leadership responsibility. Good point! Perhaps by discussing your purpose in attending college, I can enlighten you as to how well this cocurricular experience will complement your classroom studies.

Students attend college for various reasons. You may be seeking to increase your earning power, to be trained for a better job, or to simply enjoy the social activities. Perhaps you don't really have a good reason for attending college, but you've always assumed that "it's the thing to do."

So why are you *really* in college? Believe it or not, I discovered the *real* reasons for attending college while attending a rock concert. After the concert, a famous rock star was having the customary interviews. A reporter asked what ingredients were needed to be successful in the entertainment industry. The rock star replied candidly and without hesitation: "There are three reasons for my success. First, as I was growing up I found out everything I could about the music and entertainment industry. Second, I have skill in using the knowledge I have acquired. I can play over twenty musical instruments. I have written dozens of songs. In other words, folks, I can apply the knowledge I have acquired to accomplish tasks. Third, and most important, I am one heck of a nice guy! Everyone, everywhere likes me!"

If you think about it, those are the exact reasons you're attending college. You are here to pursue knowledge, to develop skills in applying the knowledge you acquire, and to develop your personality. No one would argue that these needs are fulfilled by the experience you have in your academic classrooms. But I (and many other individuals who are "products of the cocurricular leadership experiences") would suggest that you can enrich your knowledge and skill level as well as further develop your personality if you will take the risk and make the commitment to become a good student leader.

Benefits of the leadership experience

Few individuals would argue that students are advantaged, or enriched, by engaging in a college leadership experience. But to list all the potential benefits would fill a book. Each student learns and benefits from the experience in a number of different ways. But most students realize certain common work and life skills from having been a student leader.

Student leaders are exposed to a variety of workplace skills, including (but of course not limited to) the following topical areas: motivational techniques; conflict resolution skills; communication skills; administering praise and criticism; facilitating an effective meeting; accepting and delegating responsibility; utilizing various leadership styles; committee management; decision-making techniques; problem-solving methods; project/program management; planning and organizing skills; volunteer recruitment techniques, and so on and so on and so on! This is an impressive list of workplace skill topics, but an even more impressive list of benefits exists for a student's personal development.

Your college days are such a fast-paced transitional period that you probably won't take the time to discover and develop your life skills. Students in leadership positions have the opportunity and the resources to develop many life skills. For instance, time management becomes more essential to the student who has assumed extra responsibilities, so the student leader becomes a time management expert. Students learn financial management, interpersonal communications skills, how to deal with power (your own as well as that of others), and how to deal with success and failure.

Further, as a student leader you'll find that you learn resiliency skills, how to deal with shyness, and how to cope with stress. Student leaders generally realize and exhibit a very high degree of self-esteem. They are keenly aware of their personal strengths and limitations. Student leaders are a unique breed; they are more likely to be dependable, active, persistent, responsible, and much more achievement-oriented than students who don't assume leadership positions. Student leaders almost always tend to be more socially oriented and more popular—just two more good reasons for you to seek a leadership position in your college organization. Isn't it obvious that the payoffs and benefits far exceed the risk and the time commitment? You decide!

The big payoff

The biggest payoff of being a student leader is that you'll learn the tools of program management, the organization of an activity, program, or project. Program management has four components, but each one is an extremely complex process. First, one must *select* the activity for the participants or the audience. Second, the event or activity must be properly *promoted*. Third, the person in charge must *produce* the activity (actually *have* a dance, or a concert, or a fund-raiser event). Last, the person in charge must *evaluate* the event to determine its success. Program management (the selection, promotion, production, and evaluation of an activity) appears on the surface to be a simple process, but experts spend years developing proper skills for it. Student leaders get a head start on their fellow students who will be joining them in the work force because they are actually developing and practicing techniques for program management, day in and day out, while in college. What a payoff!

The other major payoff is learning to take risks within the comforts of a somewhat protected environment. Colleges and universities set up rules and procedures to protect the student leader from too much risk, but you'll have an advisor who will encourage you to push yourself to the limits to accept new challenges. The mentor relationship established with your advisor, and the freedom to operate with your peers within the protective climate of the university will foster your creativity. In a society where creativity is stifled, you'll find that yours is rewarded and that your skills for generating ideas and solutions are increased. Learning to take risks and using creative approaches to resolve problems are other good justifications for spending your nonacademic time in a leadership role. If you have a part-time job, ask your supervisor how important these skills are. That will help confirm your interest and desire in pursuing a leadership position in your organization.

I'd love to, but I'm not qualified and I can't commit the time

If the truth be known, virtually no student leader is "adequately prepared" to assume his or her *first* or *second* or subsequent leadership position.

Just imagine going into a Statistics 500 class and taking the final examination—*on the first day of class!* Could you pass it? Few of us could. Could you even understand the questions? Probably not! Entering into a leadership experience, you really don't know what you're supposed to do, either. Or how to do it. Just like the Statistics 500 class, you have to go through the experience of "going to class" in order to gain enough knowledge and skills to be effective and feel confident. So don't hesitate to enter into a leadership role because you don't know the ins and outs of leadership. It's a phenomenon that affected me and one that will affect you and every other individual who undertakes a *new* experience.

Think about this dilemma that you and your friends will face in college. You tend to avoid things you don't do well and things that are discomforting to you. But the real truth is, if you don't do something well, that's all the more motivation to become accomplished at it. So even though the fear of assuming a leadership position may leave you feeling inadequate, uncomfortable, or under stress—don't worry. It's quite normal. It's the same anxiety you have when you walk into that difficult class for the first time. And, you can ease your anxiety by pondering the following questions *before* you assume a leadership position:

1. Whom should I talk with to discuss the particular responsibilities of a leadership position?

2. How will a leadership role complement my formal academic studies? Can I obtain a balance between the time required for my academic study and my leadership position? How will a leadership role better prepare me with life and work skills?

3. What can I do for an organization in my capacity as a leader? What can my organization do for me?

4. What type of organization will provide me with the best leadership opportunities? What would my main responsibilities be as a leader in a club or organization?

5. What would I like the most about being a student leader?

6. How can I determine my leadership style and the areas of my leadership style that need improvement?

7. What traits or characteristics are important for good leadership? To what extent do I have these traits? Can I learn new skills that will help me compensate for deficient traits?

8. What techniques will I use to handle my successes and failures? Can my self-esteem handle the emotional letdown of nonelection or nonappointment?

9. If I assume a leadership position, will I become a victim of the "hazards of student leadership" (scattering my talents and time too thin, disregarding grades, becoming egotistical, loving power more than people, and so on)? What can I do to maintain a proper perspective on my leadership position?

10. Is there a resource person or persons on campus who can help me gain more knowledge about myself, my organization, campus activities, and the role of campus leaders at this college?

11. What do *I* really want from my leadership experience?

12. What kinds of leadership training seminars or classes are available from my school, church, or the company where I have a part-time job?

Now about the time factor. We all have discretionary time, time we can spend as we wish. You can choose to use yours in whatever ways benefit you the most. Most student leaders find that productivity is a function of time. The more things that need to be done, the more things get done. If you're completely overburdened, a real problem exists. However, when you're faced with boredom or inactivity (probably the worst form of work), nothing is harder or more time consuming than trying to figure out a way not to be bored. Program your time and it will all fit together into a nicely packaged semester of adventures. OK, we've got you. Now how do you go about becoming a student leader?

How to obtain a leadership position

If there were a formula for obtaining a leadership position, I would gladly provide it. But because there is no formula, the process for obtaining the position becomes even more adventurous. Some hints may help you through. First, get involved in the club or organization early in your college career. Most colleges have social, honorary, music, media, academic, governance, programming, and athletic organizations, among others. Once involved, be involved! Accept responsibilities for even minor assignments such as hanging posters, sitting at a voting booth, or arranging the cleanup committee (we call it "dirt work") for a major activity. Work up to the major task assignments when you feel comfortable with your leadership skills. As you do these tasks, learn all you can about programming management and working with people. Try leadership techniques you've seen other model leaders use. Don't be afraid to take risks and don't even be afraid to fail. Never hesitate to ask for the advice of those who are older, wiser, and more experienced than you (try your advisor first). Often, their insights can prevent an embarrassing flop.

Basically you must *want* a leadership position and only you can determine how to get it. But always remember, you don't have to be the president, or even the vice-president, to have a satisfactory experience.

I'll never be able to adequately express how valuable my leadership experiences were to me. But I'd like to close with this thought: Your college years will be some of the best years of your life. The thousands of experiences you have in college will provide you with positive experiences and memories for the rest of your life. My challenge to you is this: Give something *back* to your college and to your organization. Do something for them through a leadership role, so that you'll leave a legacy just as one was left to you. It's a great adventure. Go make some memories!

Suggested activities

1. Review some of the literature in the suggested reading list. Many colleges have a leadership library in their campus activities offices or counseling center.
2. Ask the president of your club or organization if you can chair the next meeting to experience the thrill and art of leadership.
3. Seek out a project or program assignment that will allow you to assume a leadership role (the assignment could be at work, at church, at school, or even in a family setting).
4. Ask your campus activities advisor which persons are "model" leaders. Observe them in their leadership role, then spend some time talking with them about their leadership experience and their techniques.
5. Schedule an appointment with one of the professional staff members in the campus (or student) activities office to discuss possible leadership roles in the student center, student government, or a club or organization. Residence hall professionals are also good resource people.
6. Try to arrange an internship with a very active office on campus (may we suggest the college development office, the president's office, or the admissions office) or with the manager of a community business or volunteer agency so you can observe a supervisor actually managing a project, activity, or department.
7. Enroll in a class that focuses on the various aspects of leadership or organizational management (a business course in organizational behavior or human resource management, an ROTC leadership course, a public administration course, and so on).
8. Seek a position with a volunteer association in the community or a school so that you can learn to be a good follower.
9. Ask some close and trusted friends, or a professor whom you know well, to assess your leadership style and abilities. Listen closely to suggestions they give you and consider responding to their insights. Ask a campus activities advisor to help you set up an experience to develop your skills.
10. Seek permission to write a term paper about leadership in an appropriate class. (Your subject may be very specific: Leadership Styles, Leader Characteristics; The Art of Delegation; Managing and Motivating Volunteers; and so on).
11. Read a biography about one of the great leaders of our society.
12. Ask your college president, or the chief executive officer of the major business in your town (such as a bank) to present a lecture to your club on "My Personal Leadership Style—What Works For Me."

Suggested readings

Introductory level literature on leadership

Koehler, J. W., K. W. E. Anatol, and R. L. Applebaum. *Organizational Communications*. New York: Holt, Rinehart and Winston, 1976.

Lawson, L. J., Leslie Griffin, and Franklyn Donant. *Leadership Is Everbody's Business*. San Luis Obispo, Calif.: Impact Publishers, 1976.

Young Men's Christian Associations. *Y.M.C.A. Training Volunteer Leaders*. New York: Y.M.C.A., 1974.

Intermediate level literature on leadership

Henning, M., and A. Jardin. *The Managerial Woman*. New York: Simon and Schuster, 1976.

Hersey, P. G., and K. H. Blanchard. *Management of Organizational Behavior—Utilizing Human Resources*. Englewood Cliffs, N.J.: Prentice-Hall, 1977.

Leadership and Social Change, Lassey, W. R., and R. R. Fernandez, eds. La-Jolla, Calif.: University Associates, 1976.

Lawson, L. F., J. Lawson, and R. A. Donant. *Lead On! The Complete Handbook for Group Leaders*. San Luis Obispo, Calif.: Impact Publishers, 1982.

McGregor, D. *The Human Side of Enterprise*. New York: McGraw-Hill, 1960.

O'Connell, Brian. *Effective Leadership in Voluntary Organizations*. Chicago: Follett Publishing, 1976.

Wilson, Marlene. *The Effective Management of Volunteer Programs*. Boulder, Col.: Volunteer Management Assoc., 1978.

Advanced level literature on leadership

Blake, R. R., and J. S. Moutan. *The New Managerial Grid*. Houston: Gulf Publishing, 1978.

Jennings, Eugene E. *An Anatomy of Leadership—Princes, Heroes, and Supermen*. New York: McGraw-Hill, 1972.

Kutz, D., and R. L. Kahn. *The Social Psychology of Organizations*. New York: Wiley and Sons, 1978.

University Associates. *The Annual Handbooks for Group Facilitators, 1972–1983*. San Diego, Calif.: University Associates.

Magazines or journals

Leadership. Published by the American Society of Association Executives, 1575 Eye Street N.W., Washington, D.C.

Student Leadership Development Series. One article per issue in *Programming Magazine*, Published by NACA, Box 11489, Columbia, South Carolina.

Part Four

NEW BEGINNINGS: NONTRADITIONAL LIFE ON CAMPUS

Community and Technical Colleges: New Environments for New Learning Needs

Judy C. Brown, *Professor of English and Chairman of Developmental Studies*
Clayton Junior College

During my high school years, the question for me had not been whether to go to college, but where to go. I spent a lot of time writing off for information about schools in every romantic-sounding place I had ever heard of: Hawaii, California, Florida, even Canada and France. I wrote to the "Big Ten" and the "Seven Sisters" and most of their cousins. Eventually I had a shelf full of beautiful catalogs, but no idea at all of where I should go to college.

In my senior year, I began to get serious—and considerably more practical. Most of my friends were going to the University of Tennessee at Knoxville, about twenty miles from my home. They, and my parents, clearly expected that I would go there as well, that I would leap from a high school graduating class of 200 to a college freshman class of over 2000. In fact, I was terrified at the thought.

I was so scared of those numbers and so unsure of finding my own place in all that crowd that my parents finally agreed (at some sacrifice to themselves) to send me to Maryville College, a small, private college, even smaller than my high school, where I could learn to live on my own in more secure surroundings. It was with great relief that I said good-bye to my university-bound friends and

251

*headed for my pleasant, tree-shaded campus where cars were pro-
hibited and all the students could get in the chapel at one time.*

*After two years at that school, I was ready and eager to transfer
to the same university that had seemed so formidable to me at first.
There I made good grades and good friends, learned that large
numbers don't have to mean faceless anonymity, and graduated
with sufficient enthusiasm and confidence to go on to graduate
school. Maybe I would have done as well if I had gone to the university at first, but I doubt it. I think those first two years were the
most important of my academic life.*

*When I finished my graduate work and sought my first profes-
sional job, that early experience probably influenced me to look
closely at two-year colleges. I realized that there are both challenges
and pleasures in helping students who are just starting their college
careers to take full advantage of all that college offers them. While
two-year colleges are not the only places where good college beginnings can take place, they often have many of the qualities that
made my first two years so helpful and rewarding to me. My years
at Clayton Junior College have confirmed that observation over and
over.*

When I started college in 1960, I couldn't have gone to Clayton Junior College—it
didn't exist. In fact, in the more than twenty years since my first college days,
the two-year colleges have enjoyed remarkable growth. Whatever they may be
called—junior colleges, community colleges, technical colleges, or just colleges—
there are now well over a thousand of them, serving tens of thousands of students.
In many states, networks of public and private two-year colleges have joined
four-year "senior" colleges to make a college education available to practically
everyone who wants it and can benefit from it.

In spite of the numbers of students who choose to begin college in two-year
schools, and even in spite of the excellent reputations that many of these schools
enjoy, occasionally those of us who work at two-year colleges encounter questions about the quality of our schools. Most of the time we're delighted by these
questions because they give us an opportunity to boast: about the quality of our
faculty, the strength of our academic programs, and the opportunities for students to learn and grow. How much a student learns ultimately depends on the
student more than on any other factor, but many two-year schools have created
learning environments that are equal to or even superior to those of four-year
schools. You'll soon discover that your educational experiences will be exciting
and demanding, and that you'll be proud of the successes you earn.

In order to be successful at a two-year college, you'll need to know all the things that any college student should know (many of which are discussed in other chapters of this book). But you also need to be aware of some opportunities for learning and some decisions about your education that are not exactly the same as those faced by students enrolled in most four-year schools. This chapter will try to give you a perspective that will help you see how that information applies to you in a two-year college experience.

Starting off with reasons

You and your classmates probably have a wide variety of reasons for enrolling in a two-year college. Cost and convenient location are frequently important factors. The availability of interesting programs of study or the school's overall good reputation can also influence your choice. Maybe your family or friends or school counselors have helped you make your decision. Whatever your own personal reasons are, looking at these general reasons can help focus your thinking about how this choice may affect you immediately and in the future.

Cost and location: the money cousins

Is a two-year college cheaper than a four-year college? The answer to that is a definite "maybe." Some two-year schools can be less costly to attend than some four-year schools (and some can be as costly or more costly). Tuition at two-year schools may tend to be somewhat lower than at four-year schools, and many two-year schools make special efforts to keep costs for textbooks, materials, lab fees, meals taken on campus, and other needs as low as possible. Often, however, the most important cost-saving feature of a two-year school is location. Students who attend the two-year college may live nearby or within easy commuting distance and may, therefore, be able to live with parents or other relatives and save the cost of separate lodgings. Living with your family can be considerably less costly than living in campus residences or in an apartment of your own.

The cost savings may be reduced, however, if you must maintain a car to get to and from school or if your family insists that you contribute to your own upkeep. If you thought of cost as a primary factor in selecting a two-year college, perhaps you should work out a budget sheet to figure out the real costs of your college education. In Chapter 9 of this book, there's a sample cost sheet. When you fill it in, be sure to be both honest and realistic. Also remember that even if you're living with your parents, you are an adult and should make money decisions accordingly. Costs of health care or insurance, savings, contributions, gifts, and memberships are part of most adults' budgets. Have you allowed for them in yours?

Managing your money wisely can be very important to your college career and, ultimately, can affect your entire future. For example, let's imagine the situation of a college student who has a job and is earning a reasonable salary while going to school. Let's say that right now she's living at home, isn't being required to help pay for food and lodging, and has modest college expenses. In this situation she may be tempted to take on debts for a new car, vacations, or charge accounts, all of which she can afford on her current salary. When this student does leave home, what will happen? She may find that she can't support herself *and* pay her debts *and* afford to continue her college education. She may also come to feel that attending school is a drain on her time and an intrusion on her lifestyle. More than a few students "stop out" of college under these circumstances; some never return. Hopefully, this will not happen to you, but if it should, you'll discover that two-year schools are particularly sensitive to students who have had to "stop out" of school. The school will probably try as much as possible to help you get started again, but it can't replace the lost time. Careful financial planning and goal setting can help you avoid the problem in the first place.

Programs: degrees or not degrees?

Chapters 7 and 8 discuss the selection of a major and related concerns. Students at two-year colleges usually have a wide choice of majors and may have some special options not generally available at four-year colleges. Most two-year colleges offer two basic kinds of programs: transfer and career. Each has its own advantages, depending on what your goals and needs are.

Transfer programs. Think of these programs as the first two years of a baccalaureate or bachelor's degree. The two-year transfer programs offer general education courses in humanities, social sciences, natural sciences, mathematics, and, often, physical education. The English, history, biology, and physical education courses that you take at a two-year college are very much like those you would take in your first two years at a four-year college. Often schools refer to these courses as "core" courses, and usually they can be transferred to four-year schools. These core courses plus major area courses lead to an associate degree.

Selecting a major (and an associate degree program) is very important to the two-year college student. This is often the same area in which the student plans to earn a bachelor's degree later on. However, the two-year college major and the associate degree may be flexible enough to allow a student to explore a field without making an absolute commitment to major in that field at a transfer institution. For example, a student who majors in economics at a two-year school will likely take four or five economics courses—more than would be usual for an economics major in the first two years at a four-year school. If he then discovers that he doesn't want to make economics his lifework, he can still earn his associate degree in economics but can choose another major—perhaps business management or history, or psychology—at his four-year school, and will still be able to transfer most or all of his course work. Exploring some majors may involve slightly more risk, but generally the opportunity to "try out" a field is a real plus for the student who isn't absolutely sure of what he or she wants to do (and occasionally for the one who seems to be very sure!).

Career programs. Not all students who attend two-year colleges plan to transfer. Some are interested in two-year career programs that will help them find employment immediately after they complete their training. Some four-year schools offer such programs and award associate degrees to students who complete them, but most two-year career programs are offered by two-year colleges. Programs such as electronics, data processing, nursing, dental hygiene, secretarial studies, medical laboratory technology, and a host of others fall into this category.

Because these programs are designed to prepare students for specific kinds of jobs, much of the course work is designed to teach exactly what the student needs to know to be able to repair avionics equipment, or manage a business office, or practice as a dental hygienist. Most have laboratories that give students the chance to learn by doing and to practice what they have learned. Field experiences allow students to experience the kind of workplace where they will eventually have jobs.

A career program is an excellent choice for the student who is sure of a career goal. It may also be a good option for students who have an interest in a specific field of work and would like to get a bachelor's degree in that field but cannot afford to spend four straight years in college. Most career programs do not have as many hours of general education courses as transfer programs, but they do have some. Thus, students who decide on a career program and later want to go on for a bachelor's degree will find that most of their general education courses and, perhaps, some of their career courses will transfer. A few schools are now developing what are called "2 + 2" career programs. In this arrangement, a two-year program is designed to mesh with a bachelor's program. These programs are not common, although more are being added every year. Your registrar or counseling office can tell you whether there are any such cooperative programs between your school and a four-year college.

Certificate programs. A two-year school may also offer job training that requires less than two years to complete. These experiences lead to certificates rather than to associate degrees. A student who is interested in being employed as soon as possible may choose one of these certificate programs. The course work in such programs is designed to develop specific job skills. There are few or no general education courses. Students in these programs may find that much of their course work will not transfer to another school or be applicable toward a higher level college program. However, some certificate programs are designed to duplicate the first year of a two-year career program. In my own school, the one-year certificate in electronics requires the same technical courses as the first year of the associate degree electronics program, making it easy for a student to continue later on. On the other hand, the one-year licensed practical nurse program is not the same as the first year of the registered nurse program. Therefore, a student who earns a certificate and becomes a licensed practical nurse might have to start all over again in order to become a registered nurse at some later date.

Options. The real point in considering program options is to remember that the more understanding you have of your own goals and needs, and the more knowledge you have about the options available to you, the better your decisions are likely to be. The faculty and staff at your school are very interested in helping you make wise decisions, but, in most cases, you must take the initiative and ask for their help early in your college career—when you need it most and when it can do you the most good.

Transferring after completing an associate degree

If you are planning to continue your college education after you finish an associate degree, you should be thinking about that transfer from the day you first enroll. You need to have a copy of the current college catalog from the school to which you will transfer. As you select your college courses, compare the course descriptions in your institution's catalog to those in the transfer institution's catalog. Also, be sure you take into account the differences in credit hour values. Take, for example, these two catalog descriptions from two different institutions:

English 101—A course in writing; subjects include the paragraph, the short essay, and the report. Students will analyze their own and other writers' work. 5 hours.

English 111—Principles of rhetoric, organization, expansion, and evaluation of writing; composition of essays. Analysis of written work. 5 hours.

These two courses would probably be very similar and would likely be transferable *if* (and it's a big if) both schools use the same term length: semester or quarter. If, however, English 101 carries five semester hours of credit, and English 111 carries five quarter hours of credit, the transfer is no longer a simple matter. Although the courses cover similar material, one is considerably longer than the other and has more "contact hours" (time the student is in class). Therefore, five quarter hours is equal only to 3.33 semester hours of credit by usual formulas of calculation. To change semester hours to quarter hour equivalents, multiply semester hours by 1.5 (some schools use 1.33). To change quarter hours to semester hour equivalents, divide by 1.5 (or 1.33).

Another transfer matter can involve required courses. Sometimes the school to which you are transferring may require courses not required or offered at the school you plan to attend later. Transfer between private and public institutions accounts for most of these differences. For example, schools that are affiliated with a religious denomination may require religion, Bible, or church history of all students. Sometimes these courses will transfer to other schools; sometimes they will not. If you have any questions about transferring your courses for full credit, you should call, write, or visit the registrar or admissions office at the school that you plan to attend. In fact, this contact is a good idea even if you don't anticipate any problems. The admissions staff may be able to offer advice that will make your transfer even easier.

Transfer before completing a degree

If you enroll in a two-year college, must you finish your associate degree before you transfer to a four-year school? In most cases the answer is no, but a qualified "no." That is, *when* you transfer may be a matter of *what program* you're in. Some institutions refuse to accept transfer students who have completed fewer than a specified number of credit hours. Occasionally, these transfer requirements apply only to specific programs within an institution. You might be able to transfer from your school to a state university at almost any point in your program, but you might not be accepted into the business management program at that institution unless you have forty-five hours (or some specific number of hours) of credit to transfer. You might also be required to have completed certain courses before you can be accepted as a transfer student. If you plan to transfer, it's very important that you be aware of such regulations so that you're less likely to be inconvenienced by them. Your college probably has a counselor or advisor who is familiar with transfer procedures. This person can help you weigh your choices and, if you decide to transfer, make the change smoothly.

Do working and studying go together?

Many students are discovering that working and studying *must* go together; without one, they wouldn't be able to afford the other. If you're one of these people who work at least part-time, you're in good company. At some two-year colleges, 80 percent or more of the students have jobs. For this reason you may find that your college officials have done a lot of thinking and planning to help make life more agreeable for you.

If you're working as much as twenty hours per week, it's a good bet that you need to take a reduced schedule of classes and arrange those classes around your work hours. Many, perhaps most, two-year colleges offer classes from as early as 7:00 A.M. to as late as 11:00 P.M.. Usually the school will offer both day and evening courses for some of the most popular majors and required general education courses. If your work limits the time that you can schedule your classes, it's very important that you plan carefully on what classes you will take and when you will take them. If you're an evening student and a course that you need for graduation is offered at night only one time per year, you need to be sure that you'll be ready to take it at that time. That is, you should plan to complete any prerequisites before that course is offered. This kind of planning ahead means that you are more likely to meet your timetable for graduation without a hitch.

Even if you're a very conscientious student and are accustomed to taking responsibility for yourself, it may be difficult to do this planning and decision making without some help. Your school has counselors or faculty advisors who will be glad to talk with you about your schedule or the courses you should take. When you go to see your advisor, be sure that you take a copy of your work schedule as well as any other information that may affect your time or course selection. With this information, your advisor will be able to give you accurate, helpful advice.

Another element to consider in dealing with your work is its possible educational value. You may not find a job that exactly matches your career goals, but you may find one that has some elements in common with the career you want. A prepharmacy major might find that being a clerk in a drug store, while not directly involved with preparing prescriptions, gives a good view of the work situation of a pharmacist. Sometimes it may even be wise to allow the possibility of getting experience to outweigh salary in selecting a particular job. The experience you get working as an orderly or aide in a hospital may be very valuable to you as a respiratory therapy major, so much so that you would select that job over one where you might make more money, for example, as a construction laborer.

Working and going to school can be a difficult juggling act, and sometimes you may need to be in two places at once. When your boss wants you to help with inventory on the same evening your accounting professor has scheduled a special study session to help students get ready for a big test, what do you do? First of all, don't panic. Second, don't overlook the chance that your current employer may be very interested in your educational development, and may be willing to work with you in arranging alternate work schedules when your school schedule creates problems. Some employers may even pay part of your school expenses. Not all employers are this agreeable or forward-looking, but if yours doesn't now do this sort of thing for students, perhaps no one has ever asked, or perhaps you could sell the idea to him or her.

Another way in which work may serve you is through cooperative ("co-op") work-learning situations. If your school has a co-op office, you may be able to use its resources to help you find a job within your field. Various arrangements between a student and an employer can be worked out, but the basis of co-op is that a student works either part-time or full-time for pay and, usually, for college credit. When the student graduates, he may take a job with his co-op firm if one is available, but he's usually not obliged to do so.

The really important concern of the college student who is also an employee is to do as much as possible to see that work helps, or at least doesn't hinder, educational goals. If working creates problems for you, don't despair, but do ask for help. Chapter 9 contains information on the financial assistance that may be available to you; check it out. And even if you don't qualify for aid, you can talk to a counselor who will help you balance your alternatives and make the best choice from among them.

What if you need academic help?

When you first settled on a two-year college, maybe you were relieved that it had admission policies that were "open" or not very restrictive. If your high school average in academic subjects wasn't so great, or your SAT or ACT scores were less than thrilling, or you've been out of high school a long time and have gotten rusty in some academic areas, an open admissions policy allows the school to offer you a fresh chance at an education. In order for the chance to be a real one, a school that admits students who have had some problems in the past usually takes very seriously its responsibility to help them be successful. It may provide special review courses to help students develop or brush up on their academic skills, or it may provide tutoring or special learning laboratories to supplement a student's course work. Sometimes a school requires students to participate in these activities; sometimes it just advises them that help is available. Whatever the case, the student is the one who must decide to take full advantage of these services.

Occasionally, students are resentful that they are picked out as needing academic help. They would prefer to be allowed to enroll in whatever courses they want and take their chances. Unfortunately, for many students this "chance" wouldn't be much of a chance at all. Without some academic assistance, many students would be overwhelmed by the demands of their courses and might never be the successes that, with help, they could become. Schools, after all, are in the business of helping students become winners, and they are willing to do what is necessary to see that all students have an equal chance at success.

Personal growth in the two-year college

The very act of choosing to attend college, and of choosing a two-year college in particular, presents some very special opportunities for personal development. For most people, the previously described concerns of money, major programs, work, and academic help are the most significant matters in attending college. But some other matters must not be ignored. Chapters 10–17 offer some helpful information about personal development, but there are some unique features of life in a two-year college that we should consider here.

How to find friends in two years or less

Two years is not a very long time by most standards. In terms of people, this time frame means that you may have a limited time to develop friendships among the people who are in school with you. Often, you'll share a few quarters or semesters together and then they, or you, will move on—to jobs or to other colleges. If some of your friends enrolled in college at the same time you did, you can probably count on those friendships to continue and to help you make other contacts. But even if you don't know many other people at school, you can do a lot to keep from being lonely. In fact, a two-year college is a great place to widen your circle of friends and acquaintances, if you only have a bit of courage.

During the first days of any class, try to take the same seat for each class meeting. This will help the other students (and the teacher) recognize you. Pay attention to your classmates, to those who seem to be well prepared and who ask intelligent questions. Just as soon as the class has settled into a routine, take the initiative to approach one of these people. Compliment her work, or follow up on a line of thought that the class inspired. Usually your interest will be warmly welcomed. Perhaps an opportunity to study together will arise soon. If you're already in a class with one or more friends, offer a casual invitation to a new person to join all of you for coffee or to look over the class notes.

Since you'll be in a class with people of all ages and different backgrounds, use the opportunity to meet some of the people who have had experiences very different from yours. The college environment seems to encourage flexibility and openness in personal relationships. You may discover that real friendships grow out of this exciting diversity.

Teachers can be friends, too

The two-year colleges often have the right to be especially proud of their faculties. At many four-year colleges or universities, research is as important as or even more important than what a faculty member does in the classroom; but in two-year colleges, the emphasis is on superior teaching. Two-year college faculty members do research and writing, but their main job is teaching students; usually they sought out a two-year college position for that very reason. Faculty members at two-year colleges are often willing to develop a personal interest in their students that can be very encouraging and helpful. These personal relationships with faculty members can help students feel more comfortable with college and more self-confident. They may allow students to find role models and to develop a clearer sense of ways that professionals in certain fields look at the world. For these reasons, students should do as much as possible to help develop good relationships with their teachers. One strategy is to ask the teacher for help in going beyond the text assignment, to research an interesting side issue, or to explore an idea in greater depth. Another is to ask for clarification of a lecture point. Any contact with the teacher should be genuine, purposeful, and directly related to the course. No instructor welcomes a student who simply takes up office time to chatter pointlessly, but practically all will take an interest in serious students or will respect and help students who are honestly confused.

Other help and where to find it

Every two-year college has resources to help a student learn and be successful. All schools have libraries or learning resource centers. Most also offer learning labs, tutors, advising and counseling centers, and other forms of help to supplement formal classes and to allow students to explore personal interests.

Clubs and organizations offer two-year college students good opportunities for personal development. A student who is willing and able to devote some time and energy to membership in an organized activity will usually establish an additional circle of friends and may discover new ideas as well. Among the strongest extracurricular groups on a two-year campus are usually those that are identified with a career field—student nurses' club, business majors' club, electronics club, and so on. At some schools, sports organizations are also active. Many schools don't participate in intercollegiate sports, but intramural competition can be great fun for the participants. You might determine which groups on your campus seem to be strong, continuing groups, and try to choose one of them that interests you. Alternatively, you might pick a group that seems to need new blood and invest your time in it. The rewards in new friends and new experiences can be great either way.

If clubs and organizations don't seem to offer what you need, there are still lectures, movies, and musical or dramatic performances on campus almost every week—free or at very low cost. Of course, it's impossible to find time to go to everything, but if you get into the habit of checking the campus newspaper or announcements board and putting interesting events on your schedule, you're likely to get to at least some of them. These are also good places to meet people, and your participation will help you feel more involved in the life of the campus.

Sometimes it isn't entertainment that you need so much as someone to share a problem or to lend a sympathetic ear. College students have problems with their families, their personal relationships, and their jobs as well as with their classes. The counseling center can help with some of these problems and can find other assistance if the problem is one they aren't equipped to handle. There's no charge for their services, and they always maintain confidentiality. No matter how complicated or embarrassing your problem is, take heart; they've probably heard worse! In any case, they're helpers, not judges.

Beyond the two-year college

"Two-year college" is really just a name. It certainly doesn't mean that everyone does what he or she wants to do in exactly two years and then packs up and leaves. Students who have a lot of demands on their time apart from school may find that they'll take more than two years to graduate or complete their programs. A few students may carry heavy course loads, attend every term including the summer, and graduate in less than two years. Still others may attend for a while, "stop out" for a while, and return. Their work may be spread over several years.

What all these students have in common with you is that you've all found that the two-year school provides you with the chance to earn a good education. Whether the next step is transfer to another college, a job, or some other option, you have invested time, money, and yourself in a period of learning, changing, and growing. The experience won't be the same for everyone, but for most people it's an experience marked by both pleasure and pride.

Suggested activities

1. Write down your own reasons for choosing a two-year college. Share your reasons with your classmates and make a combined list. Can you think of other reasons that did not appear on any of the original lists but that might be factors that would influence choice of a college?

2. How much does transportation really cost you (car payment, maintenance, public transportation, and so on)? Can you think of any ways to reduce this cost and still get where you need to go? Are there any other ways you can think of to reduce the cost of living and going to school?

3. Look at a copy of the catalog from a four-year college. (Your counseling office will probably have a large collection of these, or you can order one directly from the school). Find your major in the catalog (or any major if you are undecided) and compare the first two years at the four-year school with the program at your school. Are there differences that would affect transfer? How could you deal with these differences?

4. Select a two-year career program at your school and interview a faculty member who teaches in that area. Find out what the job opportunities are, the duties, the salary, and so on. Write a letter to a friend or relative recommending that that person choose or reject this career field. Be sure to give reasons for your recommendation.

5. Many students who had poor high school records or entrance test scores may do very well when they go to college. List some possible reasons for this change. Do any of these reasons apply to your situation? Did any of them influence your decision to attend college?

6. Using your major (or any major) as a starting point, list the jobs that you might be qualified for right now that would give you helpful skills

or knowledge related to the job you ultimately want to have. Check the classified ads of your local paper to see if any of these jobs is being advertised.

7. Does your college catalog have a section listing the faculty and their college degrees? If so, mark the names of those who hold associate degrees. Try to interview one of these faculty members to find out his or her reasons for attending a two-year school. Ask this person to tell you what he or she liked or disliked about the two-year college.

8. Using your college catalog, information from the counseling center, campus newspapers, and so on, make a list of the free or low-cost resources for learning and personal development available on your campus.

Suggested readings

Barron's Guide to the Two-Year Colleges. 2 vols. Woodbury, N.Y.: Barron's Educational Series, 1981.

Cass, James, and Max Birnbaum. *Comparative Guide to American Colleges.* New York: Harper and Row, 1983.

Chernow, Fred B., and Carol Chernow. *Careers for the Community College Graduate.* New York: Arco Publishing, 1981.

The College Blue Book. New York: Macmillan, 1983.

Cross, K. Patricia. *Beyond the Open Door: New Students to Higher Education.* San Francisco: Jossey-Bass, 1971.

Gleazer, Edmund J., Jr. *This Is the Community College.* Boston: Houghton Mifflin Company, 1968.

Gray, Eileen. *Everywoman's Guide to College.* Millbrae, Calif.: Les Femmes, 1975.

Irish, Richard K. *Go Hire Yourself an Employer.* New York: Anchor Press/ Doubleday, 1978.

Lederer, Murial. *The Guide to Career Education.* New York: Quadrangle/ The New York Times Book Co., 1974.

Mitchell, Joyce Slayton. *Stopout! Working Ways to Learn.* New York: Avon, 1978.

See also college catalogs from a wide variety of institutions. Write to the admissions offices of the colleges; usually, a catalog is sent free of charge to anyone who requests it.

The Minority Student on Campus

Francine G. McNairy, *Dean of Academic Support Services and Assistant to the Academic Vice President Clarion University of Pennsylvania*

Editors' note: We asked Fran McNairy to write this chapter because of her special insight into the problems facing minority students who choose to seek higher education on campuses where they remain minorities, just as in the world at large.

Dr. McNairy is a professor, administrator, and counselor who has counseled scores of students at Clarion University of Pennsylvania. Hence, when she writes about the special challenges minority students face, she employs as her model the classic trials of the black student on a predominantly white campus. All minority students will benefit from the advice Dr. McNairy offers, but this essay will also benefit those in the majority as well. If you're a minority student, read this chapter with special care. If you're not, read it just as carefully, for you'll not only discover some important facts about your minority friends and neighbors; you just might unearth some valuable insights about yourself.

When I think about my freshman year at a predominantly white university, these are the things I remember. " 'Negro' students who graduate from your high school tend not to do well at this university; therefore, we encourage you to attend a summer precollege program," said a representative from the university. (I did.) "You'll do well here if you never take a math course," stated my advisor during the freshman orientation program. (I never did take a math

265

course and I paid for it!) No one would sit next to me in Psychology 80. There were 300 students in that gigantic lecture hall!

One day, by accident, I wandered into the commuter cafeteria, and there they were, black people! I was so glad to see them that I think I ran toward them. The group was composed of primarily upperclassmen, with two graduate students. "Hey, what's your aim in life?" hollered Jack, one of the graduate students, to me as I approached the group. I opened my mouth to respond, but I don't think anything coherent came out.

Can you imagine how I felt when they told me that we were in a university with over 20,000 students and that maybe, just maybe, there were a total of 50 black undergraduate and graduate students? Later I found out that 15 of the 50 black students were freshmen!

As the semester progressed, I spent a considerable amount of time in the cafeteria and became better adjusted to the university. That corner in the cafeteria was my home away from home. Those black students were my family and support system. They reprimanded me for cutting class, and applauded me for my achievements. There were no black faculty, as far as I knew.

Interaction with white students was fairly minimal. They appeared not to know what to say to me, and vice versa. Communication with white faculty members was a little different. They had the information; therefore, I did talk to them. My grades were not that fantastic, though, and it wasn't until my junior year that I became a serious student.

Now I'm a professional social worker with a Ph.D. in communication and an associate professor in my second decade at a college where I'm the Coordinator of Academic Development and Retention.

I've written this chapter so that all students might better understand the concerns and problems that minority students face every day at predominantly white colleges or universities. These concerns and problems have a long tradition and history. Their resolution will not occur overnight; however, I hope this chapter will contribute toward their solution.

Higher education is a challenge to anyone. But if you happen to be black and plan to attend a predominantly white college, you need to be prepared to meet the additional demands you will face. Over the years, blacks have waged a prolonged struggle for access to knowledge and credentials through education. That only 50 percent of black students who enter college graduate is tragic, especially when black communities throughout the United States are suffering from a severe brain drain of its most talented and trained members.*

More than 72 percent of all black students in higher education in the United States are enrolled in traditionally white colleges. (Braddock, 1981) Nevertheless, the predominantly black institutions, most of which are in the South, have continued to be the major supplier of black four-year college graduates. They awarded 69 percent of all bachelor's degrees received by blacks. (Middleton, 1979)

Such statements explicitly describe a state of urgency for black students who attend predominantly white colleges and have implications for other minority groups as well. This chapter is designed to inform black students of the realities of higher education. It represents a synthesis of ideas from other black educators, black students, and published research. It is equally important to understand the prolonged struggle that has been waged by black people to gain access to knowledge, education, and credentials.

The history of blacks in education

Prior to 1619, blacks came to America as explorers, servants, and slaves. They were part of the first settlement in what now is known as South Carolina. By 1624, every colony except Georgia had black citizens—free men, artisans, and slaves. The slave trade was extensive throughout the North and South. Contrary to popular notion, blacks continuously fought against slavery, many times petitioning colonial leaders for freedom. Soon after the Revolutionary War, New England abolished slavery. (Compton, 1980)

Retention of black students during the years of slavery was not a problem, since it was illegal for blacks to be educated in most colonies, particularly in the South. In the 1700s the South Carolina legislature ruled that anyone found educating slaves would be fined 100 pounds. In Georgia, the financial penalty for teaching a slave was 50 percent greater than if one willfully castrated or cut off the limb of a slave. (Higginbotham, 1978)

While southern colonies intensified their restrictions, other colonies enacted different legal codes to govern, protect, control, or restrict the education of slaves. In 1704, a catechism school for "Negroes" was established by Elias Neau. (Bergman, 1969)

---

*"Half of All Black College Students Never Graduate." *Gary Crusader* vol. 20, no. 30, December 26, 1981, pp. 1–2.

But although the earliest laws of this country prohibited blacks from receiving an education, many blacks managed to learn anyway. John Russwarm received a college degree at Bowdoin, the first black to graduate from college, in 1826. (Bennett, 1962) Because blacks were denied entry to colleges, black colleges were established in the 1800s, beginning with Lincoln University in Pennsylvania and Wilberforce University of Ohio.

American public education was on the rise in the 1800s, but education for blacks became less available. After 1831, the southern state legislatures outlawed education for blacks. The South feared that education would make slaves aware of a better world than their own. (Compton, p. 251) In the North and South, free black children were the victims of segregated schools, while black property owners paid taxes to support schools their children could not attend. Thus, the concept of separate but equal was introduced. It was the norm, however, for black schools to be less "equal," to have less adequate resources than white schools. In 1896, the United States Supreme Court, in *Plessy* vs. *Ferguson,* declared the doctrine of "separate but equal," stating there was no discrimination as long as the separate facilities were equal. This decision remained unchallenged until 1954, when the United States Supreme Court, in *Brown* vs. *Board of Education,* ruled that racial segregation in public schools was unconstitutional. (Bremner, 1970)

The 1960s witnessed measurable improvements for blacks, resulting in (1) the economic boycott in Montgomery, Alabama, which demonstrated that such an action was an effective method of significantly reducing segregation in the marketplace, (2) the end of segregation in such public facilities as lunch counters, (3) the end of segregation in interstate transportation, (4) the admission of more black students into previously segregated colleges and universities, and (5) the development of the Black Student Movement in higher education. (Karenga, 1980) The leadership included such individuals as Martin Luther King, Jr., Malcolm X, and Angela Davis. Key organizations supporting civil rights efforts for blacks, such as the Southern Christian Leadership Conference, Congress of Racial Equality, National Association for the Advancement of Colored People, and the Black Panther Party, helped raise the consciousness of black youth and opened the doors for further educational opportunities in higher education.

The decade of the 1960s was an era of progress and saw the development of black political, economic, and educational institutions. As those institutions weakened or were dismantled in the 1970s and 1980s, many of the gains were lost, while the rate of black students on white campuses increased significantly. (Braddock, p. 403)

Black student, white campus: the realities

Since the civil rights movement began, black students and faculty members have weighed the advantages and disadvantages of receiving a college education at a predominantly white college. The advantages often include access to more academic and multicultural resources and a broad social network leading to employment and/or graduate and professional schools. On the minus side, the high dropout level of black students negates the gains, and may be traced to the absence of a social life, differing faculty expectations, racism, and the attitudes of many black freshmen.

Social life

In a poll conducted by the *Black Collegian,* black students on predominantly white campuses agreed almost unanimously that the social climate on campus did not complement their interests and experiences.

Many colleges or universities are located in rural areas. If the campus is miles away from the nearest urban center, social life for blacks is indeed restricted, and might require that they develop appropriate social resources to meet their own needs. Most colleges have committees, composed of students and faculty, that provide recreational, cultural, and social programs for the campus. While some committees attempt to sponsor multicultural programs, black-oriented programs are seldom a priority. Where black programs are offered, you will usually find one or more of the following: a high percentage of minority students, many of whom volunteer for the student activity committee; a well-organized black student organization or cultural center; a college-sponsored human relations committee that has funds to provide some components of the black experience within its programs.

Faculty expectations

While the quality of social life has considerable impact on the adjustment to college, academic performance is still the major criterion for success on campus. College is a challenge for most freshmen. If faculty and freshmen share their expectations of each other and believe they can learn from one another, the adjustment period is easier. But if the faculty member has a set of expectations that does not complement those of a student, there will be conflict and the student may suffer.

Jewell Taylor Gibbs identifies the kind of problems black students might experience at predominantly white colleges or universities. These problems might also apply to other minorities in similar situations. She expresses concern that black students and white faculty members often have expectations about one another that may be incompatible.

One such expectation by faculty has been that black students will be assimilated into the university community without substantial alteration of academic structures or programs. (Gibbs, p. 463) Gibbs points out that, although some black students are admitted into college as "high risk" students, the academic support services available to help strengthen their basic skills has proved inadequate. Many black students, on the other hand, believe the college will be flexible in responding to their needs. Therefore, when their needs are not immediately addressed, they may become frustrated and, in some instances, hostile. The point is, if your needs aren't recognized, you must take responsibility for identifying those resources on campus that can help you function better, and utilize them to help you. Such resources include your academic advisor, the financial aid office, academic support center, counseling center, library, your college dean, and other key administrators.

The first faculty expectation is accentuated by the second: black students are expected to compete academically with white students, who generally have superior high school preparation. In fact, many faculty members don't assess individual student skills. On the other hand, many black students expect college courses to be a continuation of high school work and are often confused by the qualitative and quantitative differences in courses and study assignments. (Gibbs, p. 464)

Imagine that you're enrolled in Spanish 101: College Elementary Spanish. The range of skills among students in that class can vary from no previous high school Spanish to one or two years of high school Spanish. Some students may have learned extensive vocabulary skills, while others were taught in a conversational style. Yet, the instructor establishes a pace and level of performance that might exceed some students' backgrounds, and his or her teaching methods will seldom change to accommodate those who have had no exposure to the language. The instructor will expect all to keep up with the assignments and attain the performance level established by the instructor. No matter the course, you will be expected to keep up, despite your high school preparation.

Therefore, it's important that you recognize your own expectations of college, and simultaneously, the college's expectations of you. If they are compatible, it will be easier for you to meet them. If a difference exists, you must identify that difference and take steps immediately to close the gap.

Face it: racism does exist

While good study habits and strong basic skills are necessary for success in college, another component is equally important. That component is confidence in yourself. You must believe that you can succeed. This is not as simple as it sounds. Your degree of self-confidence is measured by how the environment responds to your efforts. Gurin and Epps state:

The confidence the black students felt about basic abilities and the likelihood that their talents and efforts would be rewarded greatly influenced how hard they tried, what they tried for, and how effective they were. (Gurin et al., 1975)

The high dropout rate of black students in white colleges might be related in part to their perception that, regardless of how hard they try, they will never receive good grades. In fact, in the *Black Collegian* poll, one student stated:

Another problem is that black students have a hard time making high grades. Professors seem to think that black students are average students and a "C" is the highest grade we can receive. (Lemieux, 1978)

Thus, many black students believe that a conspiracy of white professors and administrators exists against them. If we look at the history of higher education, this belief can be substantiated in part. One scholar, Maurice Taylor, reports that college textbooks and other reading materials often portray negative images of blacks. (Taylor, 1978)

Bear in mind, however, that although some faculty members and administrators may be racists, such an explanation for the poor performance of black students is hardly adequate. It's important that blacks garner all of their self-confidence and work with a conviction that they can succeed. Maurice Taylor articulates this message:

Despite documented evidence and belief in an academic conspiracy which is designed to sabotage their educational achievement, black students need to shore up confidence in their abilities to achieve, and believe less than that may only perpetuate failure. (Taylor, 1978)

Admission to college does not guarantee success

Many blacks reading this book are the first in their families to graduate from high school or enroll in college. Such accomplishments, while indeed outstanding, are not considered during exams and final grading. It's easy to become involved in the excitement of registering for courses, meeting new people, having more free time, and not being under the direct influence of parents. However, given the history of blacks in higher education, and the social, academic, and psychological realities you face at white colleges, it's important that you understand the indicators of success as defined by the college.

The college measures success by three indicators: A and B grades, the dean's list, and a grade point average (GPA) of 3.0 or better. Consequently, any student who aspires to success must obtain these indicators. Aspiring for C's and D's will not make you successful.

Why bother?

The realities for black students in white colleges might shock you and could cause blacks to ask: Why bother? The answer is simple. Because of the 1954 Supreme Court decision, blacks now have options they lacked before. While the success rate of black graduates from predominantly white colleges may be gloomy, scores of blacks have succeeded and have established a healthy precedent for those who follow. Space does not permit a complete listing, but among these distinguished men and women are Thomas Bradley, Mayor of Los Angeles; Shirley Chisholm, U.S. Congresswoman; A. Leon Higginbotham, Jr., Judge, United States Court of Appeals for the Third Circuit; Paul Robeson, scholar, musician, athlete, political activist, and actor; Alvin Poussaint, psychiatrist and scholar; and Carter G. Woodson, journalist and editor.

Thousands of blacks have graduated from white colleges and universities, some famous and some not so famous. Their names might not appear in the history books, but they, too, have strengthened the black community.

How black students can thrive at white colleges

The following recommendations are based on two assumptions.

- *Assumption #1:* Education is a learning process, not merely a union card for obtaining a job. If you learn how to learn, you can obtain any kind of knowledge you desire on any subject. No one can take away your ability to learn, provided you develop a sound process.
- *Assumption #2:* Education is an active process. Most students, black and white, are, for twelve years, passive receptacles of information; yet real education involves your taking an active role in the process. You're not a computer that spits back data that was programmed into it. You're a thinking human being who can receive information, weigh its credibility, determine its applicability and utility, and, ultimately, identify other information that is conflicting or relevant to it.

With these assumptions in mind, I'd like to share two concerns with black readers. The first is that education presents a series of dilemmas for the young, inner city black. Glasgow argues that education offers students three alternatives. The first is to adopt the philosophy of the educational system, thereby rejecting the values, customs, beliefs, and philosophies of the black community. The second is to reject educational systems totally and focus on the black community, since it is known and familiar. The third option is a compromise: to deliberately select the positive aspects from both the black community and the educational system. (Glasgow, 1981)

The recommendations in this chapter support the third option. Significant philosophies, values, customs, information, and behavior must be identified, learned, and experienced by black youth. Blacks do not have to give up their identities while attending a white college. Instead, by learning the fundamental, valuable aspects of education, a black student may emerge with a stronger identity and self-concept.

The second concern results from the first. It's very easy for black achievers to be convinced they're significantly different from the underachieving black person. According to Glasgow, black achievers are encouraged to believe that their exceptional individual capacity alone led to their success and that they need not identify too closely with the plight of the underachiever. (Glasgow, p. 154) However, black students should be aware that, while their acceptance into college *is* an achievement, it's not the be-all and end-all. While they might have worked hard, many equally capable blacks of the same age may never have achieved as much simply because the doors of opportunity were locked in their faces.

A black student's enrollment in college should result in a geometric progression for the black community. If two people help two people, and the pattern continues, the black community eventually will have the skills and technology required to overcome all the barriers to full equality. This does not presuppose that everyone should go to college. It does, however, advocate that black people should have the opportunity to choose!

Therefore, the recommendations for black student success at a white college are: establish measurable goals; develop a clear sense of self-awareness; identify and appropriately utilize black administrators, faculty, and student resources; develop critical thinking skills; and get involved in campus activities.

Establish measurable goals

A goal is an objective or end that one strives to obtain. It is measurable if you can assess progress and accomplishment after reaching it. Goals are short-range if you plan to achieve them in the immediate future. Long-range goals require considerably more planning and time to accomplish. Such goals usually encompass a year, five years, or a lifetime of planning and implementation. Goals provide direction and purpose. They should be realistic, yet challenging. Most importantly, they should be relevant and meaningful to the goal setter.

You might establish a short-range goal on a daily or weekly basis. Such a pattern helps maintain a feeling of productivity and accomplishment. An example is to schedule study hours on a regular basis to complement the courses you're taking. On that basis, a three-credit course should receive a minimum of three hours' study, perhaps three times a week.

Another short-range goal might be to achieve excellent grades. A's are indicators of excellence, C's are examples of mediocrity. Like other students, blacks must not view themselves as descendants of a mediocre people. Their heritage, like those of so many other races and nationalities, is rooted in pride and determination.

Long-range goals require substantial thought and planning. Without working on short-range goals, however, it's practically impossible to achieve the long-range ones, such as career plans. Consider what you want to do with the next four, ten, or twenty years of your life. If you're black, dare to pursue careers that are nontraditional for black people, yet critical to the development of the black community.

Develop a clear sense of self-awareness

Learning is an active process, and you are ultimately responsible for your own education. New information, values, and opinions will pass your way daily. It's important that you learn to evaluate them and apply them to what you already know. Because what you learn becomes a part of you, blacks should be encouraged to read as much African and Afro-American history as they can. History encompasses the political, economic, social, and psychological dynamics of a people. If you have no understanding of your own history, it may be impossible for you to comprehend your current situation, not to mention your future.

Expose yourself to black scholars in literature, psychology, economics, business, political science, the arts, sociology, and the natural sciences, and be prepared to discuss this knowledge in any setting. Much of this information will not be in your college texts, but it will be in your college library and you'll have to work at finding it.

Utilize other blacks on campus

Your first year in college is critical because, among other things, it establishes a pattern for your future education. Needless to say, comprehensive knowledge of "where to turn" is a requisite for graduation. For black students, special resources represent the bloodline to success in college: black faculty, administrators, and achievement-oriented black students. Such persons have a wealth of knowledge and skills that, when shared with you, can facilitate your learning processes. Seek these individuals out.

Black faculty and administrators have been where you want to go. Besides being experts in their academic fields, they know about financial aid, study habits, the limited social life for blacks, and racism. Whatever you may think, the collective knowledge of black academicians is too valuable for you to ignore. Learn from them and communicate with them.

Other black students who are serious about learning, especially upperclassmen, can be another helpful source. Since they're a part of your generation, they'll be open and candid with you. The important lesson is to study with, learn from, and emulate those who are serious about their futures.

I certainly don't advocate that blacks segregate themselves from the majority community. Realistically, white administrators, faculty, and students also have valuable knowledge and resources from which blacks can benefit. But black people must be resources for one another if the success rate of black graduates from white colleges is to improve significantly. As Dr. Ron Karenga so aptly put it:

We don't need any more street corner philosophers. We don't need any more individualists who contribute in their own way. Individuals had 450 years to get their own way together and it hasn't worked yet. It's about time we had a collective effort and moved on that. (Halisi et al., 1967)

Develop critical thinking skills

Education is a process, not a fact, so never permit yourself to accept information on face value. Learn to ask questions and to think through information logically. Critical thinking rejects emotional reactions. Critical thinking involves a rational approach, which includes identifying a problem or situation, generating possible solutions, weighing pros and cons, choosing the most appropriate solution, evaluating the outcome, and living with the consequences. (See Chapter 6.)

College exposes students to a variety of theories, statistics, values, and other information. While it's important that you know such things, it's equally important that you learn to examine the credibility and utility of course material or informally shared information. Rote memory might get you through some multiple choice exams, but it won't help you learn to analyze or apply information. More importantly, your ability to thrive in college and beyond depends heavily on your ability to evaluate information correctly. What you see might not be what you get!

Sound critical thinking offers several advantages. First, you will be armed to present your own ideas instead of echoing the opinions of others. Second, those ideas will be rooted in serious and thorough groundwork. Finally, you'll be assertively prepared to address issues and concerns that confront you either in the classroom, in administrative offices, or in extracurricular activities.

Get involved in campus activities

Pursuing a college degree involves more than attending classes, taking exams, and earning grades. College provides an opportunity to obtain a social or interpersonal degree as well as an academic one. You'll enroll in classes to obtain grades and, ultimately, the bachelor's degree. But simultaneously, you can develop or strengthen leadership and organizational skills by participating in extracurricular activities that could complement your career interests, political positions, social priorities, and cultural concerns.

The importance of earning this second "degree" is that, by doing so, you'll gain actual experience in developing policies and programs that have an impact on the college community. Such experiences often supplement skills in fiscal management, budget development, program planning and evaluation, community organization, political organization, and public speaking. Campus involvement will help you keep abreast of current ideas that affect not only your college, but higher education in general. (See Chapters 16 and 17.)

Quite frankly, the only way to ensure minority input into curriculum, cultural programs, policy decisions, and other significant factors in the college is for minority students, faculty, and administrators to be involved collectively. Gurin and Epps found that college experiences contribute considerably to the academic performance of black college students. They described the "committed achiever" as the most successful type of black student. The committed achiever has more contact with faculty outside the classroom, belongs to more campus groups, holds more leadership positions on the campus, and participates more often in at least some black organizations. (Gurin and Epps, p. 366)

For a well-rounded college experience, you should determine the variety of extracurricular activities available. Determine which organizations meet your needs and interests. Develop those skills that lend themselves to future employment possibilities. And if you're black, Hispanic, or of some other minority group, seek those ties that contribute to the collective organization of your community.

These recommendations are designed to help you as you proceed through your freshman year. Naturally, there is no substitute for hard work and commitment, and no miracle cures to push you through your four years. Only perseverance, thoroughness, and discipline will move you toward success. Be assured, however, that if you follow these recommendations, you'll have a more fulfilling academic year.

A final word to black students who are reading this chapter: You are already a survivor in that you have enrolled in college. You have the intellect and ability to succeed at this stage of your life. You join other black students who, as a collective unit, have the potential to change the immobility of the masses of black people. Take note of your historical past, examine the realities of the present, and prepare yourselves to shape the future. You have the equipment to conquer and surpass the educational opportunities your ancestors obtained for you. The author shares these words with you as you proudly walk forward.

Equipment

Figure it out for yourself, my lad
    You've all that the greatest of men have had,
Two arms, two hands, two legs, two eyes,
    And a brain to use if you would be wise,
With this equipment they all began,
    So start from the top and say, "I can."

Courage must come from the soul within,
    The man must furnish the will to win,
So figure it out for yourself, my lad,
    You were born with all that the great have had.
With your equipment they all began,
    Get hold of yourself and say: "I can." (Clark, 1939)

ANONYMOUS

Suggested activities

1. Discuss the implications of the high dropout rate of blacks from predominantly white colleges.
2. Discuss the critical skills needed to build a stronger black community, as defined by blacks in various disciplines or professions, such as sociology, political science, public administration, business, and education.
3. Examine your reason(s) for attending college. Establish short-range and long-range goals for your college career. Develop a plan of action for meeting your goals. Develop an evaluative mechanism to measure your accomplishments.
4. Identify and interview all faculty members and administrators of your minority group. Determine their areas of expertise and what resources they have that might enable you to thrive in college.
5. Identify minority graduates from your institution who have been successful in their chosen careers.
6. Identify minority upperclassmen who are "committed achievers" and interview them to determine how they have been successful students.
7. Identify key committees/organizations that have an impact on the minority experience. Become actively involved in at least one of them.

Suggested readings

Baldwin, James. *Nobody Knows My Name.* New York: Dell Publishing, 1961.

Biko, Steve. *Black Consciousness in South Africa.* Edited by Millard Arnold. New York: Random House, 1979.

Carmichael, Stokely, and Charles V. Hamilton. *Black Power—The Policies of Liberation in America.* New York: Vintage Books, 1967.

Douglass, Frederick. *Narrative of the Life of Frederick Douglass, An American Slave, Written by Himself.* Edited by Benjamin Quarles. Cambridge, Mass.: Harvard University Press, 1960.

DuBois, W. D. Burghardt. *The Souls of Black Folk.* New York: Fawcett Publications, 1961.

Grant, Joanne, ed. *Black Protest—History, Documents, and Analyses 1619 to the Present.* Greenwich, Conn.: Fawcett Publications, 1974.

Haley, Alex, and Malcolm X. *The Autobiography of Malcolm X*. New York: Grove Press, 1976.

Higginbotham, A. Leon, Jr. *In the Matter of Color and the American Process—The Colonial Period*. New York: Oxford University Press, 1978.

King, Martin Luther, Jr. *Stride Toward Freedom—The Montgomery Story*. New York: Harper and Brothers, 1958.

————. *Why We Can't Wait*. New York: New American Library of World Literature, 1964.

Nkrumah, Kwame. *Africa Must Unite*. Uniontown, Ohio: International Publishing Corp., 1970.

Nkrumah, Kwame. *Neo-Colonialism: The Last Stage of Imperialism*. Uniontown, Ohio: International Publishing Corp., 1965.

Robeson, Paul. *Paul Robeson Speaks: Writings, Speeches, Interviews, 1919–1974*. Edited by Philip Foner. New York: Brunner-Mazel, 1978.

Woodson, Carter G. *African Background Outlines: Or, Handbook for the Study of the Negro*. Negro University Press, 1936. Reprint. Greenwood, 1968.

Wright, Richard *Native Son*. New York: Harper and Row, 1940.

Notes

Bennett, L., Jr. *Before the Mayflower: A History of the Negro in America, 1619–1962*. Chicago: Johnson Publishing, 1962, p. 343.

Bergman, P. M. *The Chronological History of the Negro in America*. New York: Harper and Row, 1969, pp. 24, 64.

Braddock, Jamills Henry II. "Desegregation and Black Student Attrition." *Urban Education* 15, no. 4 (January 1981): 403–418.

Bremner, R. H. ed. *Children and Youth in America: A Documentary History*, vol. 1. Cambridge, Mass.: Harvard University Press, 1970, pp. 513–539.

Clark, Glenn. "One of Dr. Carver's Favorite Poems," in *The Man Who Talks with the Flowers: The Life Story of Dr. George Washington Carver*. St. Paul: Macalister Park Publishing, 1939, p. 38.

Compton, Beulah Roberts. *Introduction of Social Welfare and Social Work*. Homewood, Ill.: Dorsey, 1980, p. 190.

Gibbs, Jewel Taylor. "Black Students/White University: Different Expectations." *Personnel and Guidance Journal*, vol. 51 (March 1973): 463–469.

Glasgow, Douglas G. *The Black Underclass—Poverty, Unemployment, and Entrapment of Ghetto Youth*. New York: Vintage Books, 1981, p. 63.

Gurin, Patricia, and Epps, Edgar. *Black Consciousness, Identity and Achievement*. New York: John Wiley, 1975, p. 366.

Halisi, Clyde and Mtume, James eds. *The Quotable Karenga*. Los Angeles: US Organization, 1967, p. 15.

Higginbotham, A. Leon, Jr. *In the Matter of Color—Race and the American Legal Process—the Colonial Period*. New York: Oxford University Press, 1978, pp. 198–258.

Karenga, M. R. "Black History from Civil Rights to Human Rights," *The Black Collegian* 10, no. 4. (February/March 1980): 10–16.

Lemieux, Melba, "Black Students on White College Campuses," *Black Collegian* 8, no. 4 (March/April 1978): 16.

Middleton, Lorenzo. "Enrollment of Blacks Doubled Since 1970." *Chronicle of Higher Education* 17 (January 29, 1979): 2.

Taylor, Maurice C., "Academic Performance of Blacks on White Campuses." *Integrated Education* 16 (September/October 1978): 29.

The Disabled Student on Campus

Brenda Cooper, *Coordinator of Disabled Student Services*
University of South Carolina

How is it that we fail so miserably to offer to others what we want so desperately from them: acceptance? You might say that this question has been before me for many years. My own life's journey has led me to the study of human behavior with a goal of improving the human condition. I speak to you not as an expert, because I do not believe in such illusions, but as a human being still very intensely involved in my own journey.

One of my earliest encounters with the special needs of others involved making a new friend. She had no joints in her legs, and ambulation, therefore, was very difficult for her. She had a series of surgical procedures, followed by long periods of convalescence, during which she was confined to her bed. She nevertheless maintained nearly an A average. Eventually, she was able to return to school; after months of standing at the window in her room watching us play, she was able to rejoin us. With great determination, she joined us along the well-trodden path to school, refusing any help.

When she decided to join us in play, one of the first things she did was to come to the lake hoping to learn to swim. Her demonstration of courage when she leaped into the water amazed us all. Her swimming attempts received praise and encouragement, and eventually she became the best swimmer among us. When she graduated from high school, she did so with honors, the first of many other "differently abled" individuals who have taught me many wonderful new definitions of success, and have contributed so significantly to my own growth.

281

This is not a Cinderella story, but rather a story of the ways in which people without disabilities escape their own fears and discomforts about things they don't understand. I later met the parents of this girl, who told me of the painful reality of her college experience at a major university. After three semesters as an A student, the insensitivity of her peers became overwhelming to her, and she dropped out. The jeering at her strained movements became too painful, and the public ridicule taught her that her presence was unacceptable. So she resigned herself to exclusion and returned home. What a tragedy! Again, I ask myself, how is it that we don't give to others the acceptance we so desperately desire from them?

I hope this chapter will enhance your capacity for sensitivity and caring toward your new campus family. Perhaps some of these "lessons" can be a part of your growth, as they have been for me. If so, I would like very much to hear from you.

Disabled student. Stop a moment and picture such a person. Chances are you're thinking of someone in a wheelchair, guiding himself carefully across campus. Or a young blind student, cautiously exploring the path under her feet as she wends her way silently to the next class. Or perhaps it's the short fellow on crutches who's moving as fast as he can to avoid a threatening rainstorm.

And chances are your conceptions of a disabled student (unless you happen to be one yourself) are wrong.

Not all persons with disabilities use wheelchairs. As a matter of fact, I could probably name as many different disabling conditions as there are colors in the rainbow. Some are visible, others invisible. The most obvious conditions, of course, are those involving a person's mobility. In most cases, this person uses a cane, crutches, wheelchair, or an electric cart. But there are many hidden handicaps that don't give a clue to the casual observer. You may have friends who are hemophiliacs, epileptics, diabetics, or who have learning disabilities, and you may not even know it. Others may have more obvious speech or hearing impairments.

A glimpse at the past

Surely you've noticed that more people with disabilities are out and about these days. There are several reasons for this. The first and most obvious reason is the advancement in medical science. Twenty years ago, the severely injured auto accident victim rarely survived. Now this life can be saved. Rehabilitation centers prepare such persons for reentry into society. A second reason is that the 1973 Rehabilitation Act passed by Congress mandates that disabled persons have access to the same educational and employment opportunities as able-bodied persons. A third contributing factor is the response to this law. Today in America, many buildings are ramped and are equipped with brailled elevator buttons, lowered telephones, lever-operated water fountains, special parking, curb cuts, and accessible restroom facilities.

Not only are there more people with physical limitations on college campuses today, but the disabled are gradually being integrated into all aspects of society. You may have a roommate, a dorm director, or a professor who is disabled.

Your expectations of what disabled people are like were given to you. Some of the very earliest writings report that the deaf, the lame, and the blind were thought to be valueless. They were totally excluded from the community. Remember that in biblical times, lepers were not even allowed to enter the city. They were merely permitted to beg for their food just outside the city gates. People who did not hear and could not speak were considered to be not only deaf, but also "dumb," which related the hearing/speech deficiencies to a lack of intelligence.

A physical deformity was often considered to be the result of a "sin" supposedly committed by the individual, or by one of the parents. Believe it or not, some of these negative thoughts about persons with physical limitations are still alive. The modern version implies that handicapped people are helpless, dependent, nonsexual, antisocial individuals who are a "burden" to society. Since these negative perceptions are learned, this chapter will help you unlearn them by dealing with realities instead of myths.

Attitudinal barriers toward disabled students

The important thing for those of us who are not disabled to remember is that it may be wrong to assume that the friends you meet at college can do all the things you do in the same way you do them. It's also wrong to treat individuals who are more obviously disabled as if they were a group apart. These actions stem from what psychologists call attitudinal barriers.

What are attitudinal barriers, anyway? They are thoughts and feelings that limit your opportunities for new experiences. For disabled persons, such barriers may also limit their potential to become fully independent members of their new campus community, as well as of society in general.

To clarify this complex issue, let's explore some of the more common attitudinal barriers toward disabled individuals.

Paternalism

Paternalism is characterized by feelings of obligation to care for the disabled person. It is based on the assumption that disabled persons are unable to care for themselves, and that the nonhandicapped person must become their "caretaker." The truth is, disabled persons are not helpless. They can and do take care of themselves and may be put off by those who treat them as helpless.

Stereotyping

In stereotyping, a particular trait of one disabled person is generalized to cover all persons with physical limitations. You've probably heard statements such as, "All men are insensitive" or "All women are frivolous." Such statements are, of course, inaccurate because they attribute one characteristic to all persons in the category. I once marveled at the immensity of a new multistoried physical education center on a college campus, which was furnished with sporting equipment of every kind. When I asked about services available to the handicapped, the director of the facility quickly told me that handicapped people were not interested in athletics.

This attitude prevents disabled students from participating in many areas of college life, so don't assume that your handicapped friends are not athletes. Ask them!

Fear of change

Fear of change is based on the belief that mainstreaming disabled persons into society (or mixing them into the mainstream of students) may somehow disrupt the status quo, causing the rest of us to do things differently than we did before.

Discrimination

Discrimination manifests itself when people treat handicapped persons differently because of a particular disability. Professors, for example, may not expect the same performance from disabled students as they do from able-bodied students, and may make assignments less difficult for the disabled students. Obviously, this approach may create resentment toward the person with special needs. More importantly, most handicapped students resent this sort of preferential treatment as well. They don't want to be treated differently. Again, the message is, don't make assumptions before you ask.

Prejudice

Prejudice differs from discrimination in that it is a belief that disabled persons are inferior to able-bodied persons. Such negative feelings continue to separate disabled persons from others. If you've ever been slighted because you were nursing a temporarily broken arm or leg, you can imagine how a disabled person must feel, knowing, as she does, that the reasons she's ignored are not going to go away.

Turning the tables

For a more thorough understanding of disabilities, let's imagine for a moment that you're handicapped. Let's imagine your spinal cord was severed in an automobile accident, and you've been taken to a rehabilitation hospital to learn all the daily tasks that used to be so simple, but that now seem almost impossible.

What would you need to learn? First, you would need to learn how to feed yourself, to care for your skin in order to avoid tissue breakdown, and to exercise for muscle tone. You would also need to learn to dress yourself with as little assistance as necessary. You would need to learn about paddings for your bed, sleep positions, dressings, and clothing designed to make you feel more comfortable. And you would need to learn to train your bowel and bladder to function properly for you again.

Let's continue. You plan to enter college in the fall, so you muster your courage and agree to enter with the rest of the freshmen. To get around campus and home, you learn to use your weight and balance in a wheelchair, perhaps one of those fancy electric models. Meanwhile, as you're getting your act together, what's happening in your family? Are your parents remodeling your home so that you can get in and out of the shower? What about your friends? Are they encouraging you to join them for their next party? And is your very special guy or girl waiting for you to be released from the rehabilitation center so that you can go to the big dance?

But certainly there are other kinds of disabling conditions. What if you had lost your vision instead of the use of your legs? You'd have to learn how to get around all over again. Your mobility instructor would teach you to be aware of your environment and those around you in ways you had never thought of before. You could use talking textbooks for your courses, learn braille for note taking, or employ an assistant to read aloud to you. You wouldn't need to think about ramps and curb cuts, but you would need to know which intersections allow traffic to turn right on a red light. You would eventually learn many ways to become a totally self-sufficient person.

Yes, your life would be different. Your friends might cease their relationships with you. Your love life might be on hold for the time being. You might even receive a "Dear John" note from your most significant other person. Nonetheless, despite your handicaps, you would be essentially the same person you'd always been. You'd still enjoy all the same things, from river rafting to walking on the beach at night. You would still want to meet people on campus and be a part of all that college has to offer, from football games to parties—and you'd still be intent on pursuing the career of your dreams.

Sensitivity training

Perhaps you're thinking your lucky stars that you don't have disabilities like those just mentioned. Or, maybe you're relating more deeply to these words because of disabilities you've learned to live with, or close friends who are disabled in some way. If you've never been in the company of a disabled person, there's a good chance you'll encounter several of them during your college years. As a means of relating to them, read the following questions and answers. Some of the questions will sound familiar, but I hope the responses will bring you to a clearer understanding of disabilities and disabled persons.

First, there's the one about the blind person who asks to go to a basketball game. Why, you ask, should he want to go if he can't see? The answer is that he can hear the plays as they're called. He can experience the excitement of the crowd and feel he's a part of it. And as the commentary is spoken, he can keep up with the plays and score.

Then there's the question about handicapped parking spaces. If a student isn't confined to a wheelchair, why does she have this special privilege? The answer is that many persons are not able to walk long distances because of an invisible handicap. Just because the limitation isn't visible, don't make assumptions.

Do handicapped persons participate in intramural events? Many think not, but the fact is that people with disabilities may be excellent athletes.

The list goes on and on—a list of generalized assumptions and unsubstantiated opinions. When you look at the facts, you find that people with disabilities aren't very different from you and me. People in wheelchairs can be politicians, artists, athletes—the capacity to walk has absolutely no effect on leadership ability! People who can't walk can drive. Hand controls on specially equipped vehicles make it as safe for the driver paralyzed from the waist down as a normally equipped car is for an able-bodied driver. Don't be anxious about riding with a disabled person.

People with hearing losses are disabled also, and may ask you to repeat something. Don't become annoyed and, worse yet, don't assume the person is stupid!

The real handicap

Believe it or not, the roughest handicap among people is attitude. This is a barrier that cannot be resolved by the construction of ramps, the breaking of curbs, or the braille signs on classroom doors. It's easy to create bad feelings, even when they're unintentional. Consider the following innocent yet prevalent behaviors.

- *Avoiding Eye Contact.* You're walking on campus and see a student in a wheelchair. Because you feel awkward, you glance down or in another direction until you've passed him. Don't want to make him feel like I'm staring, you tell yourself. Quite often, the discomfort you feel when you see a disabled person is very evident to that person. Next time, you might try saying "Hi."

- *Staring.* Can you ever recall a time when someone or a group of people stared at you until you wondered whether your coat was on backwards, or your face was broken out in red bumps, or your trousers were unzipped? Well, imagine how it feels to a disabled person when others stare without making any other contact. Often this behavior is very innocent, too. People are curious about the equipment the person uses, and how it operates. If that's the case, speak up. Say, "I know I'm staring, but I'm really amazed by your electric wheelchair. Can you show me how it works?" This approach clears the air, promotes friendly conversation, and discounts no one.

- *Making Decisions for the Disabled Person.* This is one of the most subtle ways in which persons with disabilities are excluded. Rather than inviting a student to join an activity, others decide for them that, surely they would not or could not attend or participate. After all, why would a person in a wheelchair want to go jogging with you? Yet such a shared experience can be one of great beauty. You can jog, she can roll alongside, and you both get exercise and convivial conversation. Most importantly, you get to know each other. Don't decide for others—ask. It feels good to be included. If the person doesn't want to join you, she'll tell you. When each individual is in charge of his own decision making, personal dignity is preserved and enhanced.

Finally, some helpful hints

Here are some general suggestions designed to help you relate to persons who are different from you. Just remember that every person is unique, and some are more so than others. Use these suggestions as guidelines, and then use your own good common sense. You'll do just fine.

When you meet a person in a wheelchair

Speak to the person, not to her equipment or companion. Never push a person's chair, unless it's her request. Often people prefer to push themselves. Do not lean on or against a person's "chair" for any reason. This is a very personal vehicle that can be easily damaged. It's okay to use phrases like "Let's walk over here." Avoid any assumptions that a person in a wheelchair has other limitations. Each person is unique, right? So allow persons with handicaps their own individuality, just as you would able-bodied persons. When talking to someone in a wheelchair for longer than a few minutes, consider sitting or crouching so that you'll be at eye level, rather than belt-buckle level, with that person.

When you meet a deaf person

Speak clearly and distinctly, but don't exaggerate. Use normal speed unless asked to slow down. Provide a clear view of your mouth. Waving your hands or holding something in front of your lips makes lip reading impossible. Speak directly to the person instead of from the side or back. Speak expressively, because deaf persons cannot hear changes in tone. Those who read lips best get only about 30 to 50 percent of what you're saying, so expression is very important.

If you have trouble understanding a deaf person's speech, feel free to ask him to repeat. If that doesn't work, use paper and a pencil. If a deaf person is standing with an interpreter, speak directly to the deaf person. Don't speak to the interpreter, or seek permission from the hearing companion. If you know any sign language, try using it. If the deaf person you are communicating with finds it a problem, the person will let you know and will appreciate your effort. Use a normal tone of voice when talking. Shouting will be of no use and may only cause embarrassment.*

When you meet a blind person

When you walk with a blind person, let him take your arm. Don't push him! The motion of your body will tell him what to do. When you eat with him, read the menu and prices to him. If he wants help, cut his meat, fix his coffee, and so on. Tell him the position of his food on the plate. Using the face of a clock and position of numbers is a simple descriptive way to describe the food's location. (Your steak is at 6 o'clock and your potato is at 3 o'clock.)

If he has a dog, remember that the dog is a working dog, not a pet. Don't distract the animal. His master's life depends on his alertness.

If the person is alone, always identify yourself when entering the room in which he's sitting. Don't play "guess who" games. If you live or work with a blind person, never leave a door ajar (this could cause serious injury). Keep corridors clear of clutter. Tell him if furniture has been moved.

---

*Beyond the Sound Barrier, Regional Rehabilitation and Research Institute on Attitudinal, Legal and Leisure Barriers, 1828 L St., N.W., Suite 704, Washington, D.C. 20036.

Remember that a blind person can hear as well as you can, sometimes even better. Always talk directly to her, not through her companion. It's okay to use words such as "see." Blind people use these words themselves. For example: "See you later."

When introducing her to others, give the blind individual some indication of location so that she'll know in what direction to turn her head and extend her hand.

When attending a public gathering, mention briefly those factors that will help her orient herself: size of room, position of rostrum, persons at speaker's table, and so on. In group conversation, address the blind person by name. Otherwise, she may not know the remark is being directed to her.

When you're showing a blind person to a chair, put his hand on the chair's back. He will then be able to seat himself easily. When directing a person who is blind, give directions as clearly as possible. Say left or right, according to the way he's facing. Mention unusual obstacles one may encounter, such as revolving doors. Pause at curbs, doorways, and so on to indicate that you're approaching something that differs from unimpeded walking.*

Use common sense whenever you meet a blind person. He'll let you know what he needs.

More like you than different from you

You cannot experience what it's like to be handicapped, even if you spend a day in a wheelchair or wear specially designed earplugs to simulate deafness. What you can learn, however, is that people with handicaps are people like you. Their bodies may differ from yours, but they're more similar to you than you might think. You should be thankful that our capacity for giving and sharing is not dependent on any single physical function, for most of us will experience some kind of handicap during our lifetimes.

So as you make friends in college, don't exclude someone simply because he uses a chair, a leg brace, or a hearing aid. Choose your friends because you like them, because of what and who they are, and if your circle of special people includes one or more students with disabilities, you'll probably find that life is somewhat richer for you—and for them.

Helpful Suggestions for Families and Friends of Blind Persons. S.C. Commission for the Blind, 1430 Confederate Avenue, Columbia, SC 29201.

Suggested activities

1. Contact the disabled students office on your campus and ask for a presentation on how your college or university helps such people.
2. Ask the same source if they would be willing to furnish you with names and phone numbers of disabled students, and contact them to see whether they will meet with your class.
3. Organize a debate in your class. The issue should focus on whether handicapped students should be mainstreamed into campus life. Discuss pros and cons, both for the handicapped student and the able-bodied student.
4. Write an essay from the point of view of a disabled student. After you have gathered information regarding blindness, deafness, paralysis, and other debilitating conditions, write as if you had this handicap, and relate to others what you're feeling and thinking, and what you must do in order to earn your college diploma.

Suggested readings

Books

Baker, L. *Out on a Limb*. New York: McGraw-Hill, 1946.

Brancato, R. F. *Winning*. New York: Alfred A. Knopf, 1977. (Concerns spinal cord injury.)

Bruckner, L. S. *Triumph of Love*. New York: Simon and Schuster, 1954.

Buck, P. S. *The Child Who Never Grew*. New York: John Day, 1950.

Campanello, R. *It's Good to be Alive*. Boston: Little, Brown and Co., 1959. (Concerns quadriplegia.)

Cheviny, H. *My Eyes Have a Cold Nose*. New Haven: Yale University Press, 1946.

Criddle, R. *Love Is Not Blind*. New York: W. W. Norton and Company, 1953.

Cooper, D. S. *It's Hard to Leave While the Music's Playing*. New York: W. W. Norton and Company, 1977.

Earekson, J. *Joni*. Grand Rapids, Mich.: Zondervan, 1976. (Concerns spinal cord injury.)

Epstein, J. *Mermaid on Wheels*. New York: Taplinger, 1969.

Goldman, R. L. *Even the Night*. New York: Macmillan, 1947. (Concerns polio.)

Greenberg, J. A. *In This Sign*. New York: Holt, Rinehart and Winston, 1970.

Hockern, S. *Emma and I*. New York: Thomas Conglon Books, 1977. (Concerns blindness.)

Killilea, M. *Karen*. Englewood-Cliffs, N.J.: Prentice-Hall, 1952.

Kovic, R. *Born on the Fourth of July*. New York: McGraw-Hill, 1976. (Concerns spinal cord injury.)

Linduska, N. *My Polio Past*. Chicago: Pellegrim and Cadahy, 1947.

Lowenfeld, B. *Our Blind Children*. Springfield: Charles C. Thomas, 1956.

Massie, R. K. *Journey*. New York: Alfred A. Knopf, 1975. (Concerns hemophilia.)

Meyers, R. *Like Normal People*. New York: McGraw-Hill, 1978.

Mullins, J., and S. Wolfe. *Special People Behind the Eight Ball*. An annotated bibliography classified by handicapping conditions.

Ohnstad, K. *The Word at My Fingertips*. New York: Bobbs-Merrill, 1942.

Russell, H., and V. Rose. *Victory in My Hands*. New York: Farrar, Straus, and Cudahy, 1949. (Concerns amputation.)

Viscardi, H. *A Man's Stature*. New York: John Day, 1952.

Warfield, F. *Cotton in My Ears*. New York: Viking, 1948.

Articles

Babbitt, C. E., and M. A. Thompson. "Reactions of Nonhandicapped Undergraduates to Legislation, Their Physically Handicapped Counterparts," *Journal of College Student Personnel* (July 1981):306–314.

Babbitt, C. E., J. J. Burbach, and M. Sutcovich. "Physically Handicapped College Students: An Exploratory Study of Stigma." *Journal of College Student Personnel* 20 (1979):403–407.

Donaldson, J. "Modifying Attitudes Toward Physically Disabled Persons." *Exceptional Children* (March 1977):337–341.

Fix, C., and J. Rohrbacher. "What Is a Handicap? The Impact of Attitudes." *Personnel and Guidance Journal* 56 (1977):1976–1978.

Gentile, Eric A., and J. K. Taylor. "Images, Words and Identity." Michigan State University Handicapped Programs. W402 Library Building, MSU, East Lansing, MI 48824.

The Invisible Battle: Attitudes Toward Disability. Order from: George Washington University, Barrier Awareness Project, RRRI-AIB, 1828 L Street, N.W., Suite 704, Washington, DC 20036.

Johns, Jane E. *Common Sense Notions on Assisting the Handicapped: A Secretary's Perspective. Disability: The College's Challenge*. Order from: Teacher's College, Columbia University, New York, NY 10027.

Rusalem, H. "Engineering Changes in Public Attitudes Toward a Severely Disabled Group." *Journal of Rehabilitation* 33 (1967):26–27.

Rustin, J., and K. Nathanson. "Integrating Disabled Students into a College Population." *Social Casework* 56 (1975): 538–542.

Weinberg, N., and J. Williams. "How the Physically Disabled Perceive Their Disabilities." *Journal of Rehabilitation* 44 (1978): 31–33.

Information exchange centers and organizations

American Coalition of Citizens with Disabilities, Inc.
275 Avenue of the Americas, Room 2203
New York, NY 10001

Association of Handicapped Student Services Programs in Post-Secondary Education
(AHSSPPE)
P.O. Box 886
Ames, IA 50010

Disability Information Center
University of Southern Maine
246 Deering Avenue
Portland, ME 04102

Health/Closer Look Resource Center
Box 1492
Washington, DC 20013

Mainstream, Inc.
1200 15th Street, N.W.
Washington, DC 20005

National Association for Students with Handicaps (NASH)
1430 G Street, S.E.
Washington, DC 20003

National Rehabilitation Information Exchange Center
Catholic University of America
308 Mullen Library
Washington, DC 20064

People to People Committee for the Handicapped
1025 Connecticut Avenue, N.W.
Washington, DC 20036

Regional Rehabilitation Research Institute on Attitudinal, Legal and Leisure
   Barriers
George Washington University
Barrier Awareness Project
Suite 704, 1828 L Street, N.W.
Washington, DC 20036

When You Are the Oldest Student in the Class: The Returning Student

Dorothy S. Fidler, *Coordinator of Special Programs*
University of South Carolina

After fourteen years as a housewife, I returned to college to continue my own education, so I feel a certain kinship with those of you who are also returning to an academic setting after a long absence. On the night of my first college class, I can remember sitting in the classroom and waiting for the professor. I turned to a stranger seated next to me and said in a loud voice: "What in the world am I doing here? I have a baby at home in diapers. She probably needs to be changed right now. I should be at home this minute taking care of my baby." I vividly recall the rush of anxiety, the feeling of being out of place, the confusion of not knowing where I should be or what my proper role was at that moment. Besides, I was afraid I could never learn statistics. I literally had to hang onto the desk to stay seated until the professor entered the room and greeted the class. That was only the first of many anxiety attacks. Many other times during the years it took to earn my degrees, I gritted my teeth and concentrated on channeling the energy generated by anxiety into productive work. Finally, I earned a Ph.D. in psychology.

These feelings of anxiety, inadequacy, and confusion engulf all of us at one time or another, regardless of age. However, they may be more typical of adult students. Because I've experienced them firsthand, I can identify with those of you who feel sheer panic as you begin college. I hope this chapter offers you the encouragement to continue the intellectual growth and personality development that is really an integral part of going to college, regardless of age.

Older students on campus

As you look around the classroom, you may realize that you're the oldest student in the class. If so, you're a member of the fastest growing age group on American campuses! All over the country, mature students (usually defined as those over 25 years old) are enrolling in college courses in record-breaking numbers. Some statisticians predict that by the end of this decade, one out of every three college students will be over 25 years old; other experts predict one out of every two will be an older student. So you see that this is a trend that educators are watching with great interest.

On campus, younger and older students can learn from each other. Each sees the other as a reflection of himself or herself at a different stage of life. Yet at the beginning of college, younger students often feel threatened by older classmates, and older students fear they can't compete with bright young teenagers fresh from college preparatory classes. After several weeks, older students find that their high motivation enables them to compete for good grades, and younger students learn to appreciate the multiple roles of spouse, parent, or employee that many adults play in addition to their role as student.

Assets of adult students

Most educators and younger students heartily welcome older students to college campuses, for you bring many assets to the classroom. One of the assets characteristic of mature students is a high level of motivation to learn and perform well in college. As a mature student, you probably feel greatly motivated to succeed in your college course work. Because professors enjoy teaching students who really want to learn, you will surely be appreciated. Most faculty feel that your motivation to learn is a definite asset in the classroom, with residual benefits for other students as well.

Another asset that you as an adult bring to college is your real-life experience: your personal experiences in working in the community, holding a job, raising children, managing a household. These day-to-day practical experiences enrich the theoretical concepts presented in the classroom. You can learn to relate the different theories (which deal with generalities) to specific examples in your own life. Therefore, your own life experiences become a vast resource of relevant material for written assignments and classroom discussions.

Recent research suggests a third asset for older students: a definite increase in verbal skills. In recent longitudinal studies, hundreds of individuals took tests of learning ability at 10-year intervals. Results of these tests showed that, contrary to popular belief, learning ability does not decline with age. In fact, these studies found that verbal ability actually increases, rather than decreases, with age.

So in some ways, you're smarter now that you're older, for you have better verbal skills, heightened motivation to learn, and a vast wealth of life experiences. As lifelong learning becomes a social reality in our own culture, we can point with pride to these assets that older students bring to the college classroom.

Who, me worried?

In spite of these assets, you may feel a great deal of anxiety as you begin your college career. This is a venture that literally can change your life! You will learn new skills that can open the door to new opportunities, new goals, and new directions for yourself. You may experience spurts of intellectual growth and personality development. You may begin to reevaluate long-held beliefs and values. Any apprehension that you feel at the beginning of such a challenge is real and genuine. One of your tasks in the days ahead is to learn how to manage your apprehension so it acts as a positive, rather than a negative, force in this new venture.

Apprehension is merely a name, a label used to describe a feeling. The feeling itself is caused by heightened levels of adrenaline in the body. When you wish to perform well, adrenaline levels in your body rise to meet the challenge. Increased adrenaline generally improves performance. However, some researchers suggest that too much adrenaline might "blow the circuits" and be detrimental to performance.

You usually select different labels to describe the feelings associated with different levels of adrenaline in your system. For example, if your adrenaline level is only slightly raised, you may label this physiological fact as feeling excited. If the adrenaline level becomes moderately high, you may say you're a little worried or apprehensive. If your adrenaline level is very high, you'll probably label this feeling as intense fear or dread. You can alter the level of adrenaline and the label you use to describe your feeling.

A variety of stress-reduction techniques will reduce the amount of adrenaline to a manageable level. One such technique is to relabel the feeling itself. Relabeling "apprehension" as "challenging excitement" improves your outlook and your ability to cope. It may even reduce the actual amount of adrenaline in your bloodstream! You may want to practice this technique of relabeling as you face the challenge of beginning college.

The remainder of this chapter provides additional ways to help you reduce stress and successfully meet the exciting challenges in your new college environment. Some of these hints may not apply to your particular situation, but they represent bits of wisdom passed on by others who are old hands at being "older students."

Helpful hints from adult learners

1. *Enroll part-time.*

   At the beginning, consider enrolling as a part-time student. As in any new venture, getting started is the hardest part! Returning to an academic setting is a time of great change for you. Small colleges and large universities alike have subcultures: a new language (semester, quarter, grade point ratio, and so on), new regulations, new expectations. In learning the lingo and becoming part of the college culture, you may undergo a bit of culture shock. Some researchers argue that any change (even good change) is stressful. Learning to gauge the optimal amount of change for you is part of learning stress management. Too much change can lead to physical and psychological stress which, in turn, can lead to physical illness. Enrolling as a part-time student and taking only one, two, or three classes reduces some of the stress. A reduced course load allows you the extra time to relax and enjoy the challenge of learning. After adjusting to the new culture, you may want to increase your course load and become a full-time student.

2. *Take a course in how to study.*

   Many colleges offer credit or noncredit courses in study skills. Most adults have not studied since high school and have very rusty study habits. Studying isn't merely reading for pleasure; studying involves organizing, storing, and retrieving great chunks of information. How to organize material meaningfully to aid memory retention, how to study for different kinds of exams, how to read textbooks and take notes in class—these are processes you can learn. You'll develop a few study skills on your own, but a course in study skills helps you become a more efficient student more quickly. With increased efficiency, you can become a more productive student with less effort.

3. *Look for review courses to help you brush up on knowledge mastered years ago.*

   If you learned French or algebra years ago, but have had no need to keep in practice, you probably forgot much of what you once knew. You may need to review basic math, language, or writing skills before beginning upper level courses. The good news is that relearning material you once knew is much easier than learning new material for the first time. There are several ways to review basic skills. You may try studying on your own or attending adult education courses through the local public schools. Many colleges now offer credit or noncredit courses to review math, grammar, and writing skills. So take your time to brush up on the basics before enrolling in upper level courses.

4. *Learn good time-management techniques.*

   Like most students, but especially because you're an adult, time allocation is the single most critical problem you will face. A college education requires a serious time commitment regardless of age; but for a mature student with prior commitments, time pressures are relentless. Because demands from family, job, friends, and school often occur simultaneously, you may well experience serious role conflicts. Such conflicts require you to set priorities and carefully allocate your time. The following excerpt from a mature student's English paper highlights role conflict and her resulting time-management decisions.

My greatest difficulty in going back to college has been scheduling my time. One has to schedule so many activities in a limited time period and the following is on my schedule: time for my son, time for studying, time for housework and cooking, and time to relax. There never seems to be enough time to do everything, so I have to do things that I think are most important first.

I always take time to help my son with his homework, read to him, and play with him because I think he should be first in my list of priorities. Studying comes next on my time schedule. I have discovered if I get behind in my studies, it is nearly impossible to catch up, and I study every day. Although I should cook more and prepare better meals, we have been eating out a lot. A woman and a small child can eat out almost as cheaply as she can cook. We also have more soup and sandwiches than we did before. My house is a disaster area and I hate to live in a messy house, but I avoid looking at messy bedrooms by simply closing the bedroom doors. Washing the dishes is my hardest task, so I buy paper plates and paper cups. Having time to relax has been my most difficult task. This is something I have not been able to do. The only time I relax is when my son goes to sleep, but sometimes I use this quiet time to study.

I will continue taking up time with my son because he is young only once, and I know he needs me. Studying is still very important to me, so I will continue to put study time before housework and cooking because I believe I can make up for that by cooking good meals when I have more time, by getting help with the housework, and by thoroughly cleaning my house on the weekend.

Going back to school has been a wonderful experience, and I hope I can learn to manage my time more effectively.

It's clear that this mature student has already learned a great deal about effective time management. Her priorities are set: first her young son; second, schoolwork; third, housework. She lacks the time to excel in all three categories simultaneously, so she contents herself with doing well in the first two. For her, housework can wait. Setting priorities and sticking by them requires enormous self-knowledge and self-discipline, but these skills can be learned and fine-tuned. Chapter 5 of this book discusses specific time-management suggestions. As you learn to allocate time effectively, you may find that some tasks just have to wait. Striving for perfection in every facet of your life every day can create enough stress to produce illness. Deciding what's important enough to do well is a necessary ingredient of good time management. While setting priorities for what's essential in your own life, your values may shift. Things that were important before college may fade into the background as new priorities emerge. Having a peer group of mature students experiencing this challenge together can be an invaluable aid as you reaffirm some values and discard others.

5. *Be realistic about expectations.*

You don't have to be a super hero to enroll in college, but you do need realistic expectations. Some students expect to make all A's by simply attending class, so the following rule of thumb may help you set realistic goals and allot adequate time for study.

On an average, students spend two or three hours of outside preparation for every hour in the classroom to obtain a grade of C.

Using this rule of thumb, a class that meets three 50-minute sessions a week requires six to nine hours of preparation per week. Depending on your own special abilities and past experiences, you may need to spend more or less preparation time per week to maintain a grade of C. And, of course, if you expect A's in every class, you may need to spend even more time reading assignments, outlining notes, studying for exams, and writing papers. Many adults push themselves to make all A's in every course. Such high expectations may create severe sacrifices in other important areas of life.

A grade of C indicates average college-level work. You may decide that hanging in there with a C is an acceptable goal. After all, at college you're competing with the best and the brightest, and a C means you're holding your own. Whatever you decide, the rule of thumb quoted above provides a ball-park figure for later refinement in allocating appropriate amounts of study time. But remember, it's only a rule of thumb.

Support systems on campus

Support and encouragement to pursue goals can come from several sources: from your peers (that is, other older students), from faculty, and from administrators. You should be able to find encouragement from all three of these sources on your campus.

Peer support groups

Educational research has shown that developing friendships in a peer group helps students stay in school. If you become friends with at least one other student you can confide in, study with, and call in emergencies, you'll be more likely to enroll in college classes again next year. For example, you can exchange lecture notes if you miss a class or entrust your friend with your cassette recorder to tape a lecture if you know ahead of time that you're going to miss it. By simply sharing thoughts over coffee together, you can monitor your own reactions to the college environment.

To help in the development of peer support groups among older students, some colleges offer special orientation programs designed to meet the needs of adult learners. Such orientation programs represent the first chance for older students to meet on campus and begin developing the rudiments of peer support groups. These orientations also deliver information such as availability of special courses, services, facilities, and organizations for adult students as well as the availability of on-campus child-care facilities.

Several large universities reserve sections of courses for mature students only. At some universities these mature students' classes feature a unique curriculum adapted to the needs and interests of adult learners. At other universities, special sections of courses that maintain the regular curriculum are set aside for mature students.

Classes, orientation programs, and student organizations designed specifically for adult learners provide opportunities for you to meet other older students who share your interests and concerns. If no such services exist in the college where you are presently enrolled, you might place an announcement in the college newspaper and form your own group. After all, younger students have many ways of forming mutual support groups: fraternities, sororities, student organizations, dances, and roommates. If your college doesn't provide opportunities for older students to gather and develop friendships among peers, you may need to find a way on your own to build this into your college experience. There's no doubt that peer support is important to staying in school.

Faculty/academic advisors

Finding a good advisor is another critical factor in your college education. At the very least, academic advisors provide information on degree requirements and courses needed in your major. Some universities now designate special academic advisors for mature students. Such advisors must be attuned to the conflicting demands of job, home, and school as well as to the course scheduling problems of adults who work full-time. Knowledge of weekend and evening courses, assistance with registration, and recognition of mature students' time constraints are hallmarks of an excellent adult advisor. If no special advisor on your campus is identified for mature students, ask your favorite faculty member to help you select courses, schedule classes, and plan your college career.

Administrator/ombudsman

The "royal runaround" in administrative procedures probably exists in some fashion on every college campus. Bureaucratic red tape is a major hurdle to older students with limited amounts of time, and lack of experience in dealing with such challenges. Campus procedures were originally established to serve faculty, administrators, and younger students. In order to adapt procedures to serve adult learners as well, many campuses now have an administrator designated as advocate or ombudsman for mature students. In large universities adult advocates are often found in the division of student affairs or in continuing education programs, which schedule evening or weekend classes. The larger the campus, the more likely it is that you'll need help from an administrator who understands procedures, knows how to get things done, and is sympathetic to the special needs of the adult learner.

As you can see, then, some colleges and universities are beginning to change to meet the needs of mature students. These days, you should be able to find support and encouragement on your campus from students, faculty, and administrators. If you encounter obstacles rather than encouragement, remember that a college education requires persistence as well as intelligence!

Student services

In an effort to retain students with high potential, most colleges have established counseling centers, writing labs, centers for academic skills development, career and life planning, academic advisement, and a host of other student support services. These services exist in addition to regular credit courses. Research on student retention shows that the more support services a student uses, the more likely it is that he or she will reenroll for subsequent course work. Thus, you should seek out and use the student services on your own campus. If you need help in selecting a major, ask for the career planning or academic advisement center. If you have a personal problem that interferes with your studies, seek help from the counseling center. If you need help with study skills, look for an academic skills development center. Active use of such student services will improve your own chances of survival in this new subculture of academia.

On many campuses, student services may not be available to adults. Such support services may not exist at all, or they may not be available to part-time students or to adults who must work full-time and need access to services on nights and weekends. If, for any reason, a vital support service is not available to adult students on your campus, consider requesting that it be made available. Some colleges are still adjusting to adults as a new clientele and will welcome formal petitions to extend support services to older students.

Spouse support

If you're currently married and living with your spouse, his or her support for your educational goals is crucial. A nonsupportive spouse who interferes with study time will greatly reduce your chances of success in the classroom. In contrast, an actively supportive spouse will willingly adjust household routines and family responsibilities to accommodate exam schedules. The degree of support from your husband or wife is probably the most important factor in your pursuit of a college education. Enrolling in classes and accepting the challenge to assimilate new ideas and develop new skills may threaten a spouse, and he or she may attempt to sabotage your college career. If this occurs, you'll be forced to make a difficult decision: to enroll in classes and deal openly with the sabotage; to forfeit your education; or to leave your spouse. These are tough choices, but you're poised at the beginning of a period of great intellectual and personal development. Adjustments in relationships between spouses often go hand in hand with any period of enormous growth. The pursuit of a college education is no exception.

Financial aid for mature students

Like much else about higher education, financial aid eligibility and procedures were designed for younger students who are dependent on their parents. Older students often do not meet the eligibility criteria established for younger students. And yet, an adult with adequate income to support a family may not also be able to pay tuition for college courses. On campuses across the nation, administrators of financial aid programs recognize the unique circumstances of mature students. But cutbacks in state and federal student aid have delayed progress in meeting the needs of adult learners.

In spite of this gloomy outlook for financial aid, you'll want to check out all resources on your own campus. For example, some states allow free or reduced tuition to retirees over 60 years old enrolled in state-supported schools. If you're working, your own company may pay college tuition to encourage its employees to upgrade job skills or complete a degree. You may qualify for a loan or scholarship from a local or national civic club or women's organization. The student financial aid office on your campus is a clearinghouse for information on federal and state aid programs as well as on local and national scholarships from business, industry, and civic clubs. If rising costs threaten your continuing education, investigate all possibilities for financial aid. Lack of financial resources is one of the biggest hurdles of adult students. See Chapter 9 on financial aid.

Adult development

You may be feeling guilty about the money you're spending on your own education. This guilt is particularly sharp among wives who are using family resources to pay tuition costs. Perhaps a close look at the reasons older students enroll in college courses can help alleviate those guilt feelings. For both men and women, whether married or single, any one of the following reasons is legitimate for making this financial investment in yourself.

Self-fulfillment

The ultimate reason you choose to attend college is self-fulfillment. This is the single most legitimate reason for you to make this investment in yourself. To take courses for the pure pleasure of learning needs no other justification. Expanding your horizons through the study of genetics or political science, anthropology, literature, art history, or psychology for the pure pleasure of learning is the epitome of self-fulfillment and personal development.

Job advancement skills

In addition some adults take a few specific courses to acquire skills for job advancement and promotion in their present careers. Others enroll in degree programs to obtain credentials in the marketplace. Older women, for example, often seek a college degree as a way to enter the job market for the first time.

Many working women and men seek a degree to implement a career change into an entirely new field. Of course, reasons that lead directly to financial gain are simple to justify. But the reasons that fill deep human needs are just as legitimate as financial gain.

The need to grow to full potential

Some adults seek a college education to fill a vacuum in a stage of adult development. For example, some women and men feel a loss of identity, a sense of stagnation or isolation during certain stages of adulthood. At such times, adult development is somewhat out of kilter, as familiar roles erode. For example, a mother whose children have grown and left home may experience the "empty nest syndrome." Her role as full-time caretaker has evaporated and she may no longer feel needed as a person. Another example is the man who has recently retired or lost his role as breadwinner.

Such major changes in one's life can produce feelings of disequilibrium, an uncomfortable sense of being psychologically off-balance. Some psychologists, however, suggest that stages of disequilibrium are necessary for further development. From the discomfort, a new stage of personality development can emerge. To assist emergence into a new stage, some adults find that the goal of a college education fills a void and reduces isolation or stagnation.

If you have never experienced serious bouts of isolation or stagnation, and your development has been rather smooth and uneventful, you can still expand your horizons and implement growth through a college education. In fact, you may find that learning new concepts or new philosophical systems of thought can trigger a period during which you may begin to question long-held beliefs. Long-cherished values may begin to erode in the face of new information. If so, be assured that you may be on the brink of a new and more advanced stage of adult development.

Of course, a college education is not a panacea for everyone; it offers no guarantees that you'll reach your goals. But, for whatever reasons you decide to continue your education—to fill a void, to expand horizons, to enter the job market, or to advance in the marketplace—those reasons are valid because they're your reasons. You can get rid of any guilt about using time, energy, and money to pursue your goal. You're making an investment in yourself during a critical stage of your development. This investment also benefits those around you as you strive to attain your fullest potential.

The adult learner's impact on higher education

Because you're making an investment in yourself and the stakes are high, approach a college education as a good consumer. You have a real interest in the quality of classroom instruction and the availability of student support services suitable for adult learners. You are here because you want to be. You are probably paying your own way, and you want your money's worth.

This consumer approach is typical of adult students and has the potential of altering institutions of higher education for the better. Already, the structures of colleges and universities are changing (although at uneven rates) to meet the demands of adult learners. By their sheer numbers older students are changing programs and procedures, and depending on how prevalent and how vocal adult students become, they may make a lasting positive impact on the quality of higher education.

If you're one of these pioneers reshaping the structure of American colleges and universities, be proud of your accomplishments! Along with your own growth and personality development, you and many others like you offer to institutions of higher education across the nation the promise of a period of renewed growth and revitalization. It's a worthy challenge!

Suggested activities

1. Invite an outside speaker to your class to discuss the nature of stress and techniques for reducing stress such as biofeedback or self-hypnosis (see Chapter 13). Practice these techniques yourself.

2. Discuss your strengths and weaknesses in basic skills such as reading, writing, and math. Determine what kind of help you need, and find out where you can obtain that help on your campus. Follow through on this, either individually or as a class. Other class members with strengths in your weakest areas may also be willing to provide you with training and support, just as you might do for others.

3. Prepare an oral or written report on several theories of adult development.

4. On sheets of poster-sized paper, draw your lifeline depicting important milestones throughout your life. Describe your lifeline aloud to the group.

Suggested readings

Beal, Philip E., and Lee Noel. *What Works in Student Retention.* Iowa City, Iowa, and Boulder, Col.: American College Testing Program (ACT) and

National Center for Higher Education Management Systems (NCHEMS), 1980.

Erikson, Erik. *Childhood and Society.* New York: W. W. Norton, 1964.

———. *Identity: Youth and Crisis.* New York: W. W. Norton, 1968.

Friedan, Betty. *The Feminine Mystique.* New York: Dell, 1962.

Lenning, Oscar T., Philip E. Beal, and Ken Sauer. *Attrition and Retention: Evidence for Action and Research.* Boulder, Col.: National Center for Higher Education Management Systems, 1980.

Sheehy, Gail. *Passages: Predictable Crises of Adult Life.* New York: Dutton, 1974.

Part Five

A FINAL LOOK

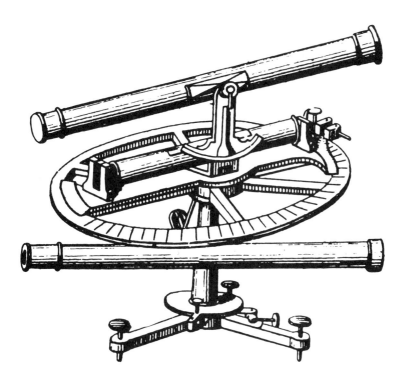

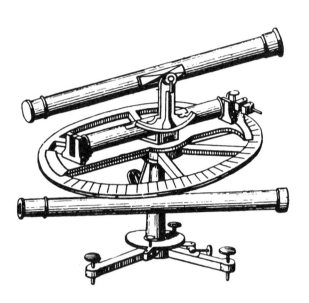

The College Experience: What Difference Can It Make?

Hilda F. Owens, *Educational Consultant*
Educational Consultant Services
Columbia, South Carolina

I can vividly recall my feelings of excitement, anticipation, uncertainty, and fear of the unknown during those first few weeks of my freshman year at East Carolina University in my native state of North Carolina. My school experiences up to that time had been pleasant and successful, but there was still a sense of concern that measuring up to a new level of academic expectation and competition might be more difficult than I had expected.

New friends, competent professors, a developing comfortableness with the next environment, and satisfactory academic performance soon reassured me that I could still meet the challenges of an academic environment and that college would be a challenging and pleasant experience. Time passed quickly, and graduation arrived all too soon. Little did I realize on that graduation day that college was only the beginning of a life filled with new learning experiences, new friends and associates, new and meaningful professional work, and a somewhat changed and emerging personality.

I found challenge, reward, and satisfaction in my years as a student. Each experience added something to the whole of who I am and what I am. I hope you will work to make your college experience as rewarding as mine was.

So you've decided to go to college! Few decisions in your life will have as great an impact on the quality and direction of your life. In addition to increased knowledge and personal self-understanding, college attendance will help you make intelligent decisions regarding career choices, job opportunities, lifestyle, and philosophies of life regarding family matters, social issues, community service, political concerns, health care priorities, recreation and leisure activities, and economic and consumer priorities.

The former president of a well-known midwestern college used to begin his message to freshmen each year by saying, "Now that you have come to college, you can never go home again." His adaptation of the title of Thomas Wolfe's famous novel *You Can't Go Home Again* was not to say that students forsake friends and family when they enter college, but to underscore that the "lenses" through which the past and the future are viewed will now be ground by a significantly new set of experiences, acquaintances, and demands and expectations. Yes, with the decision to go to college, you've begun a course that *will* change your life. This position is not just an assumption; there is now adequate evidence that college students generally differ in some rather significant ways from people who don't go to college and that individuals also change considerably while in college. Those differences and the impact of college will be discussed later in this chapter.

Changing philosophies about college attendance

As you look around at your fellow students, you will most likely note considerable diversity. It hasn't always been this way in American higher education. From the founding of Harvard College in 1636 until about 1862, American higher education had an *aristocratic* philosophy, and college students were primarily white males from the richer families. They studied the classics and prepared for the "professions" of law, medicine, and theology as they existed at that time; they further prepared for positions of leadership in a developing democracy.

With the passage of the Morrill Act of 1862 and other conditions of that and later periods of history, the country began to develop a *meritocratic* stance with regard to college attendance. (The Morrill Act, by establishing the first land grant colleges in America, brought higher education within the reach of the masses.) This meritocratic period, which lasted through the 1950s, expressed the view that any person who had academic ability and who had demonstrated a commitment to collegiate study by performing successfully at the high school level should be given the opportunity to attend college and to contribute to the increasing demand for an educated citizenry and a trained manpower pool. The curricula were expanded to include new options, and new kinds of colleges emerged. Although a more diversified student body enrolled, and the number of veterans, women, and blacks increased, their roles were still very much restricted by the expectations of society during that period.

Since the mid-sixties, an *egalitarian* approach to higher education has enabled many individuals and even whole segments of society who would not have been accommodated earlier by colleges and universities to become a part of the collegiate scene. An egalitarian emphasis encouraged a different type of student to continue her education in order to develop personal and work-related knowledge and skills in accord with her own abilities. This brought many *Nontraditional* and *New Students* to college campuses. Cross (1980) defines New Students as those who need help with basic skills, motivation, and guidance concerning how to make it in the educational system. They may be white or black, rich or poor, but they share the common experience of poor past performance in school, and without special admissions programs they would not generally be considered "college material." Nontraditional Students, as Cross describes them, are adult part-time learners who carry full-time adult responsibilities in addition to their studies. These students generally have been successful in high school and/or college in the past, but other responsibilities plus their experience and maturity mandate special consideration with regard to schedules, curricula, and instruction if their needs are to be met. Perhaps you're a member of one of these new categories of college students who now join traditional students on campus.

Major questions about going to college

The historical development of higher education, then, has brought us from a time when few students were served by a limited number of institutions for highly selective purposes to a time when higher education has over 3000 colleges and universities serving approximately 12 million credit-earning students at a cost of billions of dollars per year to its students and supporters. At the beginning of the twentieth century, fewer than 2 percent of people of college age attended college; today over 42 percent of people of college age formally continue their education beyond high school. You've chosen to be in the college-bound group—whether from a sense of real desire to go to college, or as a matter of necessity just to compete or keep up. You have answered yes to the major question: Should I go to college?

Where should I go to college?

Once the decision to go to college was made, other very important questions emerged. *Where* to go to college? Whether to attend a large or small college, public or private institution, single sex or coeducational college, or a comprehensive university, four-year liberal arts college, or one of the over 1200 community colleges? Although it will make less difference where you attend college than many people think (because of the tremendous similarities among colleges) where you attend *will* make a difference in the impact college may have on your development and on related options available to you. Institutions differ in their goals and purposes, their predominant campus environment, the areas of student development that they are most likely to emphasize, and in other available educational options.

How shall I go to college?

The question of *how* to go to college is also important. Will you be a full-time or part-time student? Will you be an on-campus resident student, live in campus-provided facilities but not on the actual campus, continue to reside with your family, or secure an apartment of your own? Will you work part-time in addition to your studies, or will you finance college by savings, loans, scholarships, or other means? Will you have family and work responsibilities in addition to school? Will you have time to engage in extracurricular activities, or will you stay with course work and required activities as your primary—if not sole—interaction with the college environment?

Decisions in this area are important because studies indicate that development occurs in varying degrees and in different areas depending on these factors. Generally speaking, resident students tend to develop in more areas and to a greater extent than commuters; students who are full-time tend to change more than those who attend part-time. Research indicates that students who become involved in the nonacademic areas of college and those who work part-time (especially on campus) are more likely to persist in college, to be satisfied with college, and to be affected to a greater degree by the college experience.

What shall I study?

What to study is also a basic question. This decision should be made after a careful and honest appraisal of your knowledge and skill level in related areas and/or your ability and willingness to acquire prerequisite knowledge and skills. You should also consider your personality, interests, and values. The decision of what to study is too important to merely major in what your parents want you to choose or what your closest friends have chosen. (See Chapter 7.)

Your decision to major in business administration, education, religion, nursing, philosophy, science, agriculture, journalism, data processing, music, engineering, prelaw, medicine, or any one of hundreds of other choices will make a difference in your future lifestyle, personal happiness, job satisfaction, and so on. Don't be afraid to examine options or reexamine previously stated choices; don't be afraid to admit that you are undecided as to major and/or career option. In fact, an acknowledged undecided student can probably be advised and counseled more effectively regarding choice of major and other areas of goal achievement than an undecided student who "fakes" a choice. (See Chapter 8.)

Your decisions regarding major and field of study will help open some doors and close others. They will help you find challenge and satisfaction in your life and work or possible frustration, and perhaps failure, in these areas. What you choose to study and to do will be a partial expression of who you are and what you value. Your work will consume a major portion of your life; therefore, you should choose carefully and wisely. But do keep in mind that, although this decision is a very important one, it can be changed or modified later, should circumstances necessitate it or should you find it desirable to do so.

Impact of college on individuals

By now you're probably asking, "Just how will college affect me? How will my fellow students and I change in ways that are different from persons who decided to accept employment, join the military service, or assume some other primary responsibility rather than going to college?" Of course, to some extent certain changes in knowledge, attitude, behavior, and skill will occur simply because of increased maturation and experience. In addition to those developmental changes, however, there is evidence that you will also encounter some rather significant changes as you interact with others in the collegiate environment and participate in the college experience.

Many wonderful, challenging, and satisfying experiences will be yours during this educational venture. On the other hand, going to college can also be a stressful and frustrating experience in many ways. You should be consoled that "cognitive dissonance," (resistance to ideas that are foreign to you), "creative tension," and the facing of "crises" are essential if further learning and development are to occur. If you believe that going to college is going to be all fun and games, you should know that, for a full-time student, the college experience should be as demanding as a full-time job—maybe more so.

One of the most important legacies of the sixties was the recognition of the American college student as a subject of needed study. Sanford (1956, 1962, 1966) and Katz (1968, 1976) were early and forceful figures in this area. Feldman and Newcomb's *The Impact of College on Students* (1969), Bowen's *Investment in Learning: The Individual and Social Value of American Higher Education* (1977), Pace's *Measuring Outcomes of College* (1980), and Chickering's *Education and Identity* (1971) have greatly expanded our knowledge of the impact of college on students and of how students change during college, and our awareness of their characteristics and concerns. Levine's recent book *When Dreams and Heroes Died: A Portrait of Today's College Student* (1980) has given us a portrait of the characteristics, concerns, and habits of college students.

Professional journals have published numerous studies regarding the impact of particular experiences, services, and environments on student populations of various sizes and with various characteristics, interests, and concerns. Numerous theorists now have provided some much needed philosophical bases regarding student development.

What follows is a summary of the research findings regarding the effects of college on students.

Major areas of change

On the basis of his own extensive clinical studies as a psychologist and his assessment of the available literature related to the personal development of students in college, Katz (1976) identified the following as major areas of change for students: (1) authoritarianism declines; (2) autonomy grows; (3) self-esteem increases; (4) the capacity for relatedness becomes enlarged; (5) greater political sophistication is shown; (6) asthetic capacity grows; and (7) students have a broader grasp of theoretical issues. Katz also notes that many investigators have found an increase in political and social liberalism and a decrease in formal religious identification and religious activities. A recent trend toward more conservative positions with regard to political and social issues and religious identification in society at large may become reflected in the campus profile. We can expect, however, that college students and gradutes will still differ from society at large in these areas.

Bowen (1977) and Astin (1977) stress, among other things, (1) the importance of the impact of college on increased knowledge and cognitive development; (2) increased correlation between educational attainment, career development, and income; (3) increased personal self-discovery and changes in attitudes, beliefs, self-concept, values, and behavior; and (4) increased practical competence of students, especially in the area of family life. I'll note the major findings in these areas, with special emphasis on the findings of Bowen and Astin.

Increased knowledge and cognitive development

Virtually all the evidence to date suggests that college generally has a strong positive impact on cognitive learning (content and thought process), as measured by comparing freshmen with seniors, college students with comparable persons not attending college, or alumni with comparable noncollege people. Higher education significantly raises the level of substantive knowledge, intellectual disposition, and cognitive powers of its students. Increased verbal skills, aesthetic sensibilities, intellectual tolerance, and an interest in lifelong learning seem to be very recognizable qualities of the typical college graduate. Colleges seem to do a good job at what they claim to do best—increase the knowledge and development of their students.

Correlation between educational attainment, career development, and income

Academic achievement is the most heavily researched topic in higher education. The relationship between educational attainment and income level, however, has been researched for the longest period of time. Findings in this area provide evidence that educational achievement and attainment, career opportunities, and income level are all positively related. Even in a day when critics are pointing out the number of people with college degrees who are unemployed or underemployed, you have only to look at the employment figures of high school graduates, high school attenders who did not graduate, and people with less than a high school education to see that the competitive edge in job opportunity and income level still generally favors the person with the highest educational level. In a day when you may question the desirability of investing time and money in a college education, evidence still supports it as a good investment. As one well-known educator has expressed it, "If you think education is expensive, try ignorance."

Increased personal self-discovery and changes in affective areas

Colleges claim to help total student development, that is, to educate the whole person. They often claim to affect an individual's ability for personal self-discovery and for personalizing and humanizing many attitudes, beliefs, and values. Colleges further contend that the collegiate experience gives students the opportunity to clarify and improve their self-concept (that is, their own view of their aptitudes, interests, values, commitments, and aspirations), to realize a sense of personal identity and awareness of how their identity and role relate to those of others, and to positively affect certain skills, competencies, and behaviors. Evidence exists that colleges do in fact affect students in these areas and that, generally speaking, these changes are in positive directions.

Students tend to leave college not only more competent but more confident; they tend to have a better sense of who they are, where they fit in the scheme of things, and how they might make a difference in the world about them. The only changes that some might regard as negative seem to be the decline of traditional religious values and an increase in hedonistic behavior (drinking, gambling, and so on). The former change may be due to the breaking away, at least temporarily, from certain family-held values, and there is some evidence that the latter may be a result of the maturing process. At any rate, you can expect to experience changes in your attitudes, values, behaviors, and self-concepts as a result of college attendance—most, but not all, in positive directions. Note also that many of these changes are highly affected by your personal characteristics, the environment at the college selected, and your interaction with that college environment.

Increased practical competence

A major goal of higher education is to prepare people for competence and performance in the practical affairs of life. This goal is often stated in college catalogs, but educators and political leaders haven't fully defined how the college experience actually achieves this goal.

Research supports the fact that college graduates tend to be more adaptable and more future-oriented, that they adopt more liberal views and nonideological thinking, develop greater interest in political and public affairs, are more likely to vote and to be more active than others in community affairs, and are less prone to ordinary criminal activity. Regrettably, ethical behavior and integrity have not been shown to be so positively affected by the college experience.

From an economic standpoint, college tends to provide a labor force that has a certain knowledge and skill and tends to reduce unemployment. College further helps people develop the flexibility, mobility, and knowledge needed to adapt to the changing demands of work and life. It also seems to contribute to increased productivity and job satisfaction, and to provide a reasonable financial return on the time and money invested in a college education.

Further, college is an important influence on family life. The stereotypical images of the appropriate roles of men and women in the family seem to change with increased education. As women earn more of the family income (over 60 percent of women in America work outside the home), matters of child care and household responsibilities are more likely to be shared or shifted by marriage partners. College-educated people tend to delay the age of marriage, to reduce the number of children, and to plan the timing of their children's births. They also tend to allocate more thought, time, energy, and money to child rearing. The divorce rate among college-educated people is slightly less than that among others, and the children of college-educated parents seem to have greater abilities and enjoy greater achievements of their own than other children.

College-educated people are characteristically more efficient consumers, with higher financial returns from different levels of income. As consumers, they tend to save more of their money, take greater—but wiser—investment risks, and spend money in ways that reflect their personal values and tastes, including a high priority on home, intellectual and cultural interests, and the nurturing of children. As consumers and citizens, they are also more able to deal with the complexities of bureaucracies at all levels, the legal system, tax laws and requirements, and false or misleading advertising.

They also tend to exhibit a practical competence with regard to leisure time activities. They spend less time and money on television and movies and more time on intellectual and cultural pursuits, including adult education, hobbies, community and civic affairs, and vacations. There is a difference not only in the amount of time spent in these areas, but also in the quality of the activities.

In the health care area, college graduates are likely to be more concerned with prevention rather than just treatment of physical and mental health matters. Diet, exercise, stress management, and other factors result in longer life spans and fewer disabilities. Attention to preventive health maintenance, which is generally a priority for college-educated people, is probably related to their increased self-concept and sense of personal worth.

A college education, then, has a positive impact in the areas of citizenship, economic productivity, health priorities and status, consumer behavior, and leisure time activities. The largest impact, however, occurs in the area of family life; there's an increased emphasis on family life among college graduates and an increase in the quality of their family life.

On the value of college

As I mentioned earlier you'll derive many benefits from a college education. Unfortunately, too many people—including students, parents, educators, and public officials—tend to think of college primarily in terms of its relationship to employment and its effect on income. Bird (1975), one of the most articulate spokespersons against a college education for large numbers of people, argues that a college education is not a good investment. Freeman and Hollomon (1975) discuss the supply and demand issues related to a college education and note that the value of college is declining.

Such critics see college in terms of its monetary value. Others, however, see that, while employment and income are important factors in life and in a college education, these aren't the best, or only, reasons for going to college, and they aren't the greatest benefits to be gained from the college experience. College can and should be much more than a place just to "process" someone into a higher wage bracket. College should help add meaning and purpose to life.

Frankel (1969) noted that there are three ways individuals find meaning and purpose in their lives: (1) by what they give to the world in terms of their creations, (2) by what they take from the world through encounters and experiences, and (3) by the stand they take with regard to their human predicaments. College-educated people, according to research and the observations of many people, usually gain skills, attitudes, and behaviors during the college experience that help them develop meaning and purpose in life—not always, but certainly frequently enough to conclude that college is an important experience in the fuller development of human potential. Such people would argue that economic benefits are not the central purpose of college.

Kingman Brewster, a former president of Yale University, identified the primary goals of a college education as the development of three senses: a sense of place, a sense of self, and a sense of judgment. Brewster clearly argued for the broader and more liberating view of education when he concluded:

The most fundamental value of education is that it makes life more interesting. This is true whether you are fetched up on a desert island or adrift in the impersonal loneliness of the urban hurly-burly. It allows you to see things which the uneducated do not see. It allows you to understand things which do not occur to the less learned. In short, it makes it less likely that you will be bored with life. It also makes it less likely that you will be a crashing bore to those whose company you keep. By analogy, it makes the difference between the traveler who understands the local language and the traveler to whom the local language is a jumble of nonsense words. (Cited by Davis, 1977, p. xv.)

Eddy (1977) concluded that the real task of an educated person is to be able to articulate to himself and others what he is willing to bet his life on. These writers join Astin, Bowen, Feldman and Newcomb, Katz, Sanford, and many others who feel that the real value of education greatly exceeds its monetary value. Its real value is that it improves the quality of life for students, their families and friends, and their world. Perhaps it's time for educators to explain more effectively to *prospective* and *present students* and to legislators and donors who fund higher education the whole story of the value of college.

The decision to go to college and the related decisions of where to go, how to go, and what to study will have a major impact on your life. Most likely you and other students at your institution will change significantly while in college. In addition to increased knowledge and personal self-discovery and understanding, college attendance will tend to affect your career choices, job opportunities, and lifestyle decisions, as well as your philosophy of life regarding family matters, social issues, community service, political concerns, health care priorities, recreation and leisure activities, and economic and consumer behavior.

The extent of your development and change will be directly affected by your own characteristics, the characteristics of your institution, and the extent and duration of your interaction with your institutional environment. Therefore, you and your friends won't all change in the same areas and to the same extent, but most of you will be changed to some degree by the college experience. Tragically, some of you will graduate very much as you entered, only more so, because of your refusal to accommodate new attitudes and behaviors.

College is and should be, most educators believe, a place to learn how to earn a living. But perhaps even more importantly, it's a place to learn some necessary skills and attitudes for building a meaningful life. You should develop a philosophy that will help see you through future changes, both in you and your world. You are on a great voyage. What difference will it make? That will depend a lot on you. Decide today to make the best of this great adventure in learning and living. Through what you've learned in this book, you should be able to manage those changes to your own advantage.

Suggested activities

1. Read and study your college catalog and student handbook carefully so you'll understand your institution's expectations of you and what you have a right to expect of it. Use the suggestions offered in Chapter 2 of this book.
2. Visit the counseling or career planning office to discuss your career aspirations, personal characteristics, and college major.
3. If you find a "misfit" between you and your selected college and/or major, begin to explore other options. A good place to begin might be with the career counselor on your campus. See Chapter 7.
4. Read further on the general impact of college on students and on the more specific impact of the peer group, the college environment, and selected programs and experiences.
5. Develop a good relationship with at least one faculty member who can help you through the academic maze and be your friend or mentor during this important phase of your life. This might be the academic advisor in your major area, or one of your other professors.
6. How do your aptitudes, interests, and values match your stated major?
7. Is the college or university you've selected likely to maximize your development?
8. Is the "fit" between your characteristics and those of your institution such that you'll be compatible enough to be reasonably satisfied but that you'll have enough "cognitive dissonance" or "creative tension" to require new thought and behavior patterns?
9. Are you engaged in appropriate extracurricular activities to extend learning opportunities beyond the classroom?
10. Are you aware of the likely differences in impact that different types of colleges have on students? What kind of impact is your college likely to make?
11. Are you taking advantage of the various cultural, educational, and recreational opportunities available at your institution and in the local community?
12. Are you working toward clarifying your identity and your philosophy of life?
13. Are you identifying what you want to contribute to life as well as what you want to get from life?

Suggested readings

In addition to the resources used as references (see the following "Notes" section), the following materials may be interesting and beneficial.

Astin, A. W. *The College Environment*. Washington, D.C.: American Council on Education, 1968.

Astin, A. W., and R. J. Panos. *The Educational and Vocational Development of College Students*. Washington, D.C.: American Council on Education, 1969.

Dressell, P. L., and I. J. Lehmann. "The Impact of Higher Education on Student Attitudes, Values, and Critical Thinking Abilities." *Educational Record* 47, no. 4 (1965):248–258.

Freedman, M. *The College Experience*. San Francisco: Jossey-Bass, 1967.

Katz, N., ed. *No Time for Youth: Growth and Constraint in College Students*. San Francisco: Jossey-Bass, 1968.

Owens, H. F., C. H. Witten, and W. R. Bailey. *College Student Personnel Administration: An Anthology*. Springfield, Ill.: Charles C. Thomas, 1982. pp. 121–169.

Sanford, N. "Personality Development During the College Years." *Personnel and Guidance Journal* 35, no. 12 (1956):74–80.

Sanford, N. *Self and Society: Social Change and Individual Development*. New York: Atherton Press, 1966.

Sanford, N., ed. *The American College: A Psychological and Social Interpretation of the Higher Learning*. New York: Wiley, 1962.

Yamamoto, K. *The College Student and His Culture: An Analysis*. Boston: Houghton Mifflin, 1968.

Yankelovich, D., and R. Clark. *The Changing Values of Campus: Political and Personal Attitudes of Today's Students*. New York: Washington Square Press, 1972.

Yankelovich, D., and R. Clark. "College and Non-College Youth Values." *Change*, September 1974, p. 45.

Notes

Astin, A. W. *Four Critical Years: Effects of College on Beliefs, Attitudes, and Knowledge*. San Francisco: Jossey-Bass, 1977.

Barna, A., J. R. Haws, and L. Knefelkamp. "New Students: Challenge to Student Affairs." *New Directions for Student Services*, no. 4 (1978):107–115.

Bird, C. *The Case Against College.* New York: David McKay, 1975, pp. 33–34.

Bowen, H. R. *Investment in Learning: The Individual and Social Value of American Higher Education.* San Francisco: Jossey-Bass, 1977.

Chickering, A. W. *Education and Identity.* San Francisco: Jossey-Bass, 1971.

Cross, K. P. "Our Changing Students and Their Impact on Colleges: Prospects for a True Learning Society." *Phi Delta Kappan* 61 (1980):627–630.

Davis, J. R. *Going to College: The Study of Students and the Student Experience.* Boulder, Col.: Westview Press, 1977.

Eddy, E. D. "What Happened to Student Values?" *Educational Record* 58, no. 1 (1977):7–17.

Feldman, K. A., and T. M. Newcomb. *The Impact of College on Students.* 2 vols. San Francisco: Jossey-Bass, 1969.

Frankel, V. *The Will to Meaning.* New York: Plume, 1969.

Freeman, R. B., and J. H. Holloman. "The Declining Value of College Going." *Change,* September 1975, pp. 24–31.

Katz, J. "Benefits for Personal Development from Going to College." Paper presented at the annual meeting of the Association of Professors of Higher Education. Chicago, March 6–7, 1976.

Levine, A. W. *When Dreams and Heroes Died: A Portrait of Today's College Students.* San Francisco: Jossey-Bass, 1980.

Pace, C. R. *Measuring Outcomes of College.* San Francisco: Jossey-Bass, 1980.

NOW? WHAT

College has only begun for you, but this book, and perhaps your freshman seminar course, are drawing to a close. If you've read the assignments in the book and learned through your instructor and classroom visitors about all the things your college or university offers, you've taken the first step toward getting that college degree.

But this, of course, is only the beginning.

What next? First, if you've established a sound relationship with your freshman professor, stay in touch! When college is behind you, you'll value the close relationships you had with a few, very special, faculty and staff members. If your relationship with the person teaching your freshman seminar course was a positive one, let him or her know it, and don't vanish into the woodwork.

Second, start using those resources we've been talking about. The more you use them, the more you'll be taking advantage of all your college has to offer. Aside from that, our research indicates that students who use such campus resources are much more likely to survive the freshman year and move ahead, ultimately to graduation. You've read about them, talked about them, perhaps visited them. Now use them!

On the other hand, don't rush out and see how many services you can use, or how many of the other ideas in this book you can employ, until you feel it's time for you to do so. The longer you're in college, the more you'll realize the value of the information in this book. So, let the right moments suggest themselves. And don't worry. They will.

Finally and most importantly, be kind to yourself as you reach the end of this semester. Don't be overly critical if you're not yet making the grades you want to make or believe you can make. For many of you, college will be a difficult adjustment. What's important is to make the best effort possible, to be persistent, and to apply the principles, ideas, and suggestions in this book. After all, you proved you were college material when you were accepted for admission. The skills and knowledge you learned in your freshman seminar should help you put forth your best efforts, and sometimes that doesn't begin to happen during the first or second semesters.

The editors and contributors put a lot of work into this book because we felt the need to provide college freshmen with the information we believe is so vital to student success. Did we tell you what you needed to know? How can we improve the book when we sit down to prepare the next edition? What topics should be dropped, and which should be added? Please write us, and we promise to respond by letter. Write Professor John N. Gardner and/or Professor A. Jerome Jewler, c/o University 101, University of South Carolina, Columbia, SC 29208. *We want to hear from you.*

We're delighted that you've begun college with our book and hope that *College Is Only the Beginning* has helped you with the beginning of the rest of your life.

Good luck, sophomore.

324

GLOSSARY

From GPR to SAT: A glossary of college jargon

Ed Ewing, *Advisor*
Center for Undeclared Majors
University of South Carolina

One way in which college is different from other institutions is in the vocabulary used by its residents and employees. Many of the terms you'll find in your admission materials, orientation information, handbooks, and catalogs were taken from the literature of the first colleges and universities in Europe, and are used today more out of custom and tradition than for any practical reasons. This appendix takes you on a tour of the unusual language you may encounter from faculty, deans, and your college administration, and will help you understand what it means.

To show you how difficult college jargon can be, look back at the paragraph you've just read, particularly at the terms higher education, orientation, college, university, faculty, *and* dean. *What do you think these mean? Think of a definition for each of them and compare your definitions to those you'll learn here. I'll begin by helping you with the two most difficult words,* college *and* university.

A professor told me, "A college is an institution of higher learning that emphasizes teaching, while a university is one that emphasizes teaching and research." After looking both words up in the dictionary, I became even more confused, because the words don't mean the same thing today as they did when the first university was founded in Europe.

To me, a university is a group of colleges, and the degree programs (majors) are within the various colleges. The college is the degree-granting component of a university, but different types of colleges exist. Some offer only undergraduate degrees. Some offer both undergraduate and graduate degrees, and others may offer only graduate degrees. A college of law or a law school is a primary example of this last. In the following glossary, I've tried to define some common words or terms you may encounter during your college years. I hope it will help you better understand your college life.

ACADEMIC ADVISOR   Colleges have many people who carry the title of advisor or counselor. Your academic advisor may be a faculty member in the academic field you've chosen or a full-time administrative employee of the school who works in a counseling office. You'll be assigned an advisor once you begin college, and this person will serve as your resource to all academic and nonacademic services. While an academic advisor will help you plan your college schedule or choose a major, they can also offer much more. Ask about anything that puzzles you, and you may save both time and money.

ACCREDITATION   Colleges and universities are judged, or accredited, either by an organization of other colleges and universities, or by professional organizations. Accrediting teams visit on a regu-

325

lar basis and judge schools on faculty, degrees offered, library facilities, laboratories, other facilities, and finances. Southern schools are accredited by the Southern Association of Colleges and Schools. A law school must be accredited by the American Bar Association. A college of business must be accredited by the American Association of Collegiate Schools of Business, and colleges of communications or journalism may be accredited by the Association for Education in Journalism. You should seek accredited schools and programs since these are typically the best of their kind, and are recognized as such by many future employers.

ADMISSIONS The first contact you may have with a college or university may be with its admissions office. The people who work there are trying to "sell" their school and its programs to you, and they'll send you many forms. Read these forms carefully and note all deadlines. Send your application to them early, because some schools may assign dormitory space on the basis of the date you're accepted for admission. Some schools offer more than one type of admission status. You may be permitted entrance to one college or major program, but denied entrance to another. Acceptance to a university does not always guarantee acceptance into all of its programs. *See* Major; Associate degree; Bachelor's degree.

ALUMNUS A graduate of a college or university. Schools have alumni offices, which may ask you for money or other support after you graduate.

ASSISTANT PROFESSOR *See* Professor.

ASSOCIATE DEGREE May be an associate degree in arts or an associate degree in science (AA or AS). Although many terms used by American universities were taken from European schools, this term is apparently an exception. An associate degree is a two-year degree. Many associate degree programs are

offered at community and junior colleges and at technical schools, but many large universities also offer such programs. Just because you earn an associate degree does not mean you're halfway toward a bachelor's degree. Some states have agreements that require state colleges and universities to accept all classes satisfactorily completed toward an associate degree, and to count those credits toward a bachelor's degree. This is not true in all states, however.

ASSOCIATE PROFESSOR *See* Professor.

BACHELOR'S DEGREE The formal name for a four-year college degree. Two major types are the Bachelor of Arts (BA) and Bachelor of Science (BS). Requirements for these degrees vary, depending on the standards of the school or college.

BOOKSTORE More than a place that sells textbooks, a college bookstore may also sell running shorts, pens and pencils, greeting cards, and a host of other items. Be certain you purchase the proper edition of required texts, and see if used copies are available at a reduced price. Always keep your book receipt, and do not mark in the book until you're sure you'll keep it, or you may have trouble obtaining a refund. Bookstores are usually located in student centers or college/university unions.

CAFETERIA OR DINING HALL These terms mean the same thing on some campuses but different things on others. The dining hall may be part of a dormitory, and your food may be prepaid if you purchased a meal card or board plan. A cafeteria is a place where you pay for each item you select; it may be located in the student center.

CAREER COUNSELING/PLANNING Most campuses began offering this service in the 1970s because students saw a direct relationship between what they were studying in college and the job market. Students wanted to know where the jobs were, and what they needed to achieve to be eligible for them. Career planning services include but are not limited to: self-assessment and interest tests, job search workshops, decision-making workshops, and resumé workshops. These services are usually located in counseling centers, student affairs offices, or placement offices.

CARREL   A study room or numbered desk and chair in the college library, which can be assigned to students. Not everyone is eligible for one, and you must request a carrel from the college librarian.

CHANCELLOR   Title given to a high academic officer at some colleges and universities. The chancellor is usually just below the president in importance.

CLASS CARD OR COURSE CARD   Usually required for registration unless you register by computer. At registration, you pick up one card for each class approved for you by your advisor. The card usually lists the name and number of the class, number of credits, days, times, and name of the professor. If more than one section of the same course is offered, a section number will appear. *Always check your course cards carefully.* Once these cards are fed into the computer, you are assigned a seat in the class, and your name will appear on the class roll for the card that you submit. See Section.

CLASS STANDING   Most colleges link your standing to the number of hours you've earned, not the number of years you've attended school. A freshman is enrolled in the first quarter of college work. A sophomore is in the second quarter. A junior has passed the halfway point, and a senior has three-fourths of his or her requirements completed. This rule applies to students on the quarter and semester systems in four-year undergraduate programs. See Quarter system and Semester system.

CLEP   Stands for College Level Examination Program, a series of tests you may take to demonstrate proficiency in various college subjects. If you pass the test, you will earn credit for certain college courses. CLEP subject exams cover individual courses, such as Introductory Psychology. CLEP general exams incorporate several courses, such as the one for social studies. Be aware that some colleges will accept CLEP subject exams, but not CLEP general exams. CLEP tests are usually administered through the college testing office. You can also obtain information about CLEP tests from your admissions office and/or your advisor.

COEDUCATIONAL   A school that admits men and women. Most colleges are coeducational. Some schools even have coeducational residence halls where men and women live in the same building, but not in the same room.

COGNATE   A group of courses related to a student's major and approved by his or her advisor. Such courses are required for graduation at many colleges. Cognates are junior and senior level courses. Colleges that don't require a cognate may require a minor. See Minor.

COMMENCEMENT   A day set aside by colleges to award degrees to graduating students. Some schools hold two or three commencements annually, but the most popular ones are held in May or early June.

COMMUNITY COLLEGE   A two-year college that may also be known as a junior college or technical school. These colleges award associate degrees, and technical colleges may offer other types of degrees or certificates as well. Be certain that the community college you select is accredited, and remember that there's no guarantee that all courses you take at a two-year college will transfer to a four-year college or university.

COMPREHENSIVE EXAMINATION Some schools use this term to describe final exams, which are given during the last days of the term. The word *comprehensive* means that all material covered during the term may be included on the exam. Graduate students may also take comprehensive exams to earn the master's or doctoral degree.

CONTINUING EDUCATION Over the years, the meaning of this term has changed. Some schools may still refer to such programs as "adult education." Continuing education programs enable the nontraditional college student to take classes without having to be admitted as a degree candidate. While continuing education students may take college courses for credit, some colleges have established noncredit learning programs under this name.

CORE COURSES/DISTRIBUTION REQUIRE-MENTS/BASIC REQUIREMENTS/GENERAL EDUCATION These terms all mean the same thing. Colleges require that all students complete specific groups of courses. These courses usually occur at the freshman and sophomore levels and include English, math, science, and history requirements. Since many of these lower numbered courses must be completed before other courses can be taken, it's wise to complete your core courses as early as possible. See Prerequisite.

COUNSELING OFFICE Counseling is provided by trained professionals at your college. Counselors can help you with various adjustment problems and may refer you to other services. There are many types of counselors; you'll find them in the following offices: Admissions, Financial Aid, Residence Halls, Career Planning, Placement, Veterans' Affairs, Study Skills, Academic Advising, and Counseling Centers. Counselors treat in confidence whatever you tell them. Once you determine that you need some type of counseling, seek it out. Your tuition is paying for it.

COURSE NUMBER Different colleges number their courses in different ways. Most undergraduates take courses at the 100 level through at least the 400 level, but this will vary on different campuses. Graduate level courses carry higher numbers. The 100-level courses are usually survey courses which introduce that subject, while upper level courses may spend an entire term covering a narrower topic in more detail. Some 100-level courses must be completed before you may take upper level work in that subject. Check your catalog and ask your advisor for help.

CREDIT HOUR See Quarter hour.

CURRICULUM All courses required for your degree. Some colleges refer to all courses in the catalog as the curriculum, and many schools provide students with curriculum outlines or curriculum sheets in addition to the catalog. These sheets show what courses you must take and may indicate the order in which you must take them. The latter is called "course sequencing."

DEAN A college administrator who may have been a professor. Some deans are academic deans, which means they head colleges. Some colleges and universities have a dean of student affairs, a dean of business affairs, and deans of men and of women. The academic dean is a person who oversees your degree program. He or she can grant exceptions to academic policy. The other types of deans are executives who may or may not work directly with students, although most work in the student services area. Some deans may have associate or assistant deans to help them.

DEAN'S LIST If you make high grades, you'll make the Dean's List at the end of the term. This is an academic honor and looks good on your resumé and on applications for graduate study. See what your school requires for you to make the list, and make it as many times as you can.

DEFICIENCY   Another word that can mean more than one thing. You may be told you have a one-course deficiency that you must make up before graduation or entrance to a particular program. Your grades may be fine, but the deficiency exists as a prerequisite for what you want to do. Deficiency can also mean that your grades are so low that you may not be permitted to return to school.

DEPARTMENT   A college is often organized into academic departments. For example, a group of history faculty will develop a curriculum for students studying history. The history department will offer all history courses for every student at the school, including history majors.

DISMISSAL   At most schools, dismissal means the same thing as suspension, and you will be told to leave the school for academic or disciplinary reasons. College catalogs explain the circumstances for dismissal, and you should learn these rules and obey them. Dismissal or suspension usually is noted on your official record or transcript, and the requirements to reenter college will vary. See Leave of absence and Probation.

DISSERTATION   One of the final requirements for the highest academic degree a student can earn in most fields, the doctorate or Ph.D. In some fields, the dissertation is book length. The graduate student is expected to break new ground in research and must defend her or his dissertation before a faculty committee. See Graduate student.

DOCTORAL DEGREE   Requires additional years of study beyond the bachelor's and/or master's degrees, and is awarded upon successful completion of course work, the dissertation, and orals. Most of your professors probably have a Ph.D. (doctor of philosophy), but other types, including the MD (medical doc-

tor) and JD (doctor of jurisprudence) also require extensive study.

DORMITORY   See Residence hall.

DROP   Most colleges allow students to drop/courses without penalty during specified periods of time. Dropping a course can be dangerous if you don't know the proper procedures, since you'll need to complete certain forms and obtain official signatures. If you're receiving financial aid, your status may change if you drop a course. Finally, dropping courses certainly will affect your graduation date.

ELECTIVES   Students who say, "I think I'll take an elective course," may think that electives differ from other course requirements. This is only partially true, for electives are required for graduation for most college degrees. An elective is a course you may select from an academic area of interest to you. The course will not count in your core, major, or minor/cognate. Each college decides the number of electives you may take, and you may take them at any time. Consult your advisor, and see if he or she recommends that you complete core courses before choosing electives.

EVALUATION OF COURSES   See Validation of credits.

EXTRACURRICULAR (COCURRICULAR)   A word describing activities, clubs, or organizations you may join and participate in, above and beyond your academic courses. Such activities provide fun and friends, and also look good on your resumé, but keep in mind that some are more valuable than others. Ask a counselor for advice, since certain activities may lead you into career choices. Activities include student government, student media, clubs, volunteer work, and faculty/student committees.

FACULTY   All the teachers at your college. The names of faculty positions and the ranks held by individuals will vary. See Professor.

FEES At most colleges, fees are costs that are required in addition to tuition. Fees may be charged for housing, health, labs, parking, and many other things. Most college catalogs give a good idea of what fees you'll have to pay and when you must pay them. See Tuition.

FINAL EXAMS Some schools call them comprehensive exams and hold them during an examination week, a period when your instructors may find out how much you've learned from them. Most finals are written rather than oral. Professors usually tell students about finals near the beginning of the term, and not all professors require them. A final may count as much as one-half of your grade, or it could count much less. Some schools may also schedule midterm exams.

FINANCIAL AID A complicated subject in recent years. See Chapter 9. Most colleges have a financial aid office to provide information to students on scholarships, grants, loans, and so on. Some forms of financial aid are gifts, but others are loans that must be repaid with interest. Some aid is offered only to new freshmen, and you must apply before college begins to be eligible. Many grants and loans are provided through federal government assistance, and government regulations control this money. To determine your eligibility for any sort of aid, see your financial aid counselor as early as you can.

FRATERNITY See Greeks.

FULL-TIME STUDENT Students enrolled for a specified number of hours, such as twelve semester hours or more. At most schools, part-time students receive the same benefits as full-time students. At others, part-time students may receive limited health care and no athletic tickets. Ask your advisor about the advantages

of going full-time, but remember, if you must work, raise a family, or handle other obligations, a part-time program may be the more sensible one to pursue.

GRADE POINT AVERAGE (GPA) Sometimes called the cumulative average or grade point ratio (GPR). Most colleges base grades on a 4-point scale, with points assigned to each grade (A = 4, B = 3, C = 2, D = 1, F = 0). To compute your GPA for one term, you need only complete three simple mathematical steps: multiply, add, divide. *Multiply* the number of points representing the grade you receive for each course times the number of credit hours for the course. *Add* the points for all courses to determine the total number of points you've earned for the term. *Divide* the total points by the number of credit hours you attempted that term. The result will be your GPA. Some colleges complicate this with a 3-point system or by using grades in addition to A through F. College catalogs show you how the system works at individual schools.

GRADES OR GRADING SYSTEM Most schools use the A through F system. A is the highest grade and F means failure. A through D are passing grades for which you will earn points and credits. If you ever transfer colleges, however, the D grades may not transfer. D's and F's are bad because most colleges require a minimum 2.0 GPA or C average for graduation, and you might lose financial aid, housing, and other benefits when your GPA falls below a certain level. Bad grades and low GPAs also lead to dismissal or suspension. Some schools have a pass/fail grade (P/F or S/U) and an incomplete grade (I), the latter representing work not completed during the term it was taken. Learning the grading system of your college is one of your first assignments.

GRADUATE STUDENT A person who has earned at least a bachelor's degree (BA or BS), and is presently enrolled in a program granting a master's degree (MA or MS) and/or a doctorate (Ph.D.). Students in law school, medical school, and other specialized programs beyond the bachelor's level are also classified as graduate students.

GREEKS   Used to describe students who join fraternities or sororities. Discuss the possibility of becoming a Greek with someone whose opinions you value.

HIGHER EDUCATION   Any college courses you take or any degree you earn after completing high school (secondary education). Also called postsecondary education.

HONORS   Most colleges recognize good grades in the form of academic honors. Dean's List is the most common award. Honors are also awarded at graduation to superior students, and the following Latin words are used: *cum laude* (with praise), *magna cum laude* (with great praise), *summa cum laude* (with highest praise).

HOURS   Another word for credits. If you enroll for fifteen hours this term and pass all five of your three-hour courses, you'll earn fifteen credits. There is often a relationship between the number of hours you spend in the classroom each week and the number of credits you can earn from the course. After you accumulate the proper number of credits/hours, you will graduate with an associate or bachelor's degree.

INCOMPLETE   See Grades or grading system.

INDEPENDENT STUDY   Can mean at least two things. An independent study course is one in which you complete course requirements on your own time, under the direction of a professor, and in a non-classroom setting. This term may also describe some work you've done, either by yourself or with others, that is creative and that shows your ability to work with minimal direction.

INSTRUCTOR   See Professor.

INTERNSHIP   An arrangement that permits students to work and receive college credit in their major. Internships are required for graduation in some fields, such as psychology, nursing, and medicine. Prerequisites must be completed before you may take an internship, and you must complete an application and obtain the proper signatures before you will be allowed to intern.

JUNIOR   See Class standing.

JUNIOR COLLEGE   See Community college.

LABORATORIES   Colleges are like high schools in that many science courses come with laboratories. Many large universities call other learning experiences "laboratories." For example, courses in foreign language, computer science, education, psychology, and journalism may have labs. Many courses require labs whether you want to take the lab or not, but in other cases labs may be optional. Check your catalog to see what labs are in store for you.

LEAVE OF ABSENCE   Another way to say you've withdrawn completely from college. Most students take a leave of absence while still in good academic standing, with the intention of seeking readmittance at a later date. Remember to read the rules and regulations in your catalog, since colleges have different ideas about the meaning of a leave of absence.

LECTURER   See Professor.

LOWER DIVISION   Many colleges and universities have divided their academic programs into lower and upper divisions (also called preprofessional and professional). Your standing depends on the number of hours you've accumulated, prerequisites completed, forms completed and signed, and grade point average. Students in the upper division usually enjoy greater privileges and certainly are closer to graduation.

MAJOR Your field of specialization in college. As much as 30 percent of the courses you need for graduation may fall into this category. Major courses usually carry higher course numbers. Your advisor will explain the requirements of your major to you.

MASTER SCHEDULE See Schedule of classes.

MASTER'S DEGREE STUDENTS Students who have chosen to continue their education in either a Master of Arts (MA) or Master of Science (MS) program. Master's students may have entered a different program from the one in which they earned their bachelor's degree. Comprehensive exams, a thesis, and/or practicums and internships may be required. See Thesis.

MATRICULATE An uncommon, admissions office term that means you've applied for a degree program, have been accepted in that program, and have enrolled for classes. At that point, you're considered matriculated.

MINOR A group of courses that may or may not be required for your degree. Not all colleges require a minor. Your advisor may tell you that your minor must be "academically related" to your major, as government is to history. Minors may also consist of courses taken in a professional school, such as business administration.

ORAL An examination during which your professor will ask you questions about your class and you will answer aloud. Undergraduate students usually don't have to undergo orals.

ORIENTATION Most colleges now set aside a single day, several days, or even longer for orientation. During this period, new students and their parents are introduced to academic programs, facilities, and services provided by the college. Orientation may also include academic advisement and preregistration for classes.

PART-TIME STUDENT See Full-time student.

PASS/FAIL OR PASS/NO PASS OR SATISFACTORY/UNSATISFACTORY Many colleges allow you to take certain courses on a pass/fail system. By passing the course, you will earn credits toward graduation, but the grade will not count in your GPA. Pass/fail grades do not have grade points assigned to them. Most schools will not allow you to take core courses, major courses, or minor/cognate courses on this system, but may allow free electives as pass/fail options. To take courses pass/fail, you must fill out the proper forms before the established deadline in the term.

PLACEMENT Several definitions are appropriate here. Placement tests tell academic departments what level of knowledge you've achieved in their subject. A college placement office can help you in resumé writing and interviewing. This office may, with your permission, keep a job file on you and release information to prospective employers upon request. Recruiters from business and industry often recruit graduating seniors through college placement offices.

PRACTICUM Generally, a practicum experience covers a limited amount of material in depth, rather than trying, as an internship does, to provide an overview of an area. The terms may be used interchangeably, however, and refer to practical types of learning experiences, usually for college credit.

PREREGISTRATION Many colleges employ preregistration systems (often computer-assisted) to simplify the process of signing up for courses. Preregistration usually occurs in the middle of the term prior to the one you're registering for. This early registration also tells colleges what courses students want, when they'll want them, and what professors they request. Preregistration gives students a greater chance of receiving the courses and sections asked for.

PREREQUISITE   A prerequisite is a course or courses that must be completed as a condition for taking another course. Catalogs state prerequisites. Often a GPA or class standing may constitute a prerequisite for certain classes.

PRESIDENT   The chief executive officer of the university or college. Presidents report directly to governing boards (trustees). Unless you attend a small school, you won't see this person very often, except at official functions such as commencement.

PROBATION   A warning that you are not making satisfactory academic progress toward your degree. Probation is followed by suspension/dismissal unless the situation is corrected. Probation may also exist for disciplinary reasons.

PROFESSOR   College teachers are ranked as teaching assistant, instructor, lecturer, or professor. Professor is the highest rank and includes three levels: assistant professor, associate professor, and (full) professor. To avoid confusion, note how your teacher introduces himself the first day of class. When in doubt, call her "professor." While most professors have earned a doctorate degree, this is not a rigid rule for holding professorial rank.

PROFICIENCY EXAM   A test used to measure whether or not you've reached a certain level of knowledge. Such exams may allow you to exempt, with or without credit, certain lower level courses. Math and foreign language departments make use of proficiency exams.

QUARTER HOUR   A unit of credit given at colleges whose terms are called quarters, which last approximately ten weeks. See Semester hour.

QUARTER SYSTEM   Colleges operating on this system have four terms, or quarters: fall, winter, spring, and summer. If you attend full-time and plan to finish in four years without attending summer school, you'll take courses for twelve quarters. See Semester system.

REGISTRAR   The college administrator who maintains your transcript, directs the registration process, and performs other academic duties as assigned by the faculty. When faculty submit final grades, the registrar posts them to your transcript, and mails you a copy.

REGISTRATION   The act of scheduling your classes for each term. Whether you preregister (see PREREGISTRATION) or sign up just prior to the term, you should seek academic advisement first to be certain you're taking the proper courses. When in doubt, ask your advisor first!

REINSTATEMENT OR READMISSION   A return to college following suspension or a leave of absence; you must apply for reinstatement or readmission. In some cases you'll be readmitted with no restrictions. If your GPA is low, you may be readmitted on probation. Check the academic regulations at your school.

RESIDENCE HALL   A fancy term for dormitory, a residence hall is operated by the college as student housing. Ask your residence hall or dorm counselor to explain the rules that apply to your place of residence on campus.

RESIDENCY   State-supported colleges and universities charge a higher tuition to students who do not reside (maintain residency) the year around in the same state and who are not considered legal residents of that state. If you live in the same state in which you attend college, you have residency in that state, and are eligible for in-state tuition, provided you meet other specific requirements of your school.

SABBATICAL   A period of paid or semi-paid vacation awarded every six or seven years to professors, who are expected, during this time, to conduct academic research or writing that makes a contribution to their academic discipline.

SCHEDULE OF CLASSES   Also called a master schedule, this is a listing of all classes that will be offered during the coming term, including days and times of class meetings, name of instructor, building and room, and other registration information.

SCHOLARSHIP   A financial award made for academic achievement. Many scholarships are reserved for new freshmen, and may be renewed annually, provided grades are satisfactory. The money is applied to tuition.

SECTION   The different classes offered for a single subject. For example, a large college might offer fifty different sections of freshman English. Depending on the section you register for, you may have a different teacher, different textbook, and different meeting time than your friends who are taking different sections of the same course.

SEMESTER HOUR   The unit of credit you earn for course work that takes a semester to complete. Many college courses carry three credits, or semester hours.

SEMESTER SYSTEM   As opposed to the quarter system, a semester system consists of a fall semester, a spring semester, and summer school. A full-time student can complete a bachelor's degree in eight semesters without attending summer school.

SEMINAR   A class containing fewer students than a lecture class, in which the teacher leads discussions and all students participate. The majority of classes in graduate school are operated this way, although you'll find seminars in undergraduate programs as well.

SENIOR   See Class standing.

SOPHOMORE   See Class standing.

SORORITY   See Greeks.

SPECIAL STUDENT   In most colleges, this is a student who has not matriculated (has not been accepted into a degree program). A special student may have one degree, but may wish to continue his or her education by selecting courses without regard to a degree program. Military personnel are often admitted as special students. Special students may be exempted from certain prerequisites, but they can't receive financial aid or free athletic tickets.

STUDENT TEACHING   An internship that all education majors must complete before graduation.

STUDENT UNION   A building, also called the student center, where you can eat, see a movie, meet friends, and take part in extracurricular activities.

SUMMER SESSION (SUMMER SCHOOL)   For students who wish to make up deficiencies, get ahead, or just can't seem to get enough of school. Classes meet every day for longer periods than during the regular sessions. Since things move quickly, good academic advisement is essential before you consider summer school. You may also take summer courses as a transient student at another school, provided your advisor has given you prior approval. Since many schools will not let you take courses you failed at another school, be careful.

SUSPENSION   See Dismissal.

SYLLABUS   One or more pages of class requirements a professor will give you on the first day. The syllabus acts as a course outline, telling when you must complete assignments, readings, and so on. A professor may also include on the syllabus her or his grading system, attendance policy, and a brief description of the course. Be sure you get one and use it.

TECHNICAL (TEC) SCHOOLS Technical education systems established by many states offer specialized two-year degrees and certificates. While these schools may be accredited, course work may be so technically oriented that it won't transfer to a bachelor's degree program. If you plan to attend a TEC school, be certain to ask about the "college parallel curriculum." See Associate degree.

TERM PAPER Not all college courses require one, but when you're assigned a term paper, you should treat it as a very important portion of the course. The instructor may give you the entire term to research and write a term paper; hence, its name. Be certain you know which style manual your teacher prefers, and footnote accordingly.

THESIS A longer research paper, usually written as partial fulfillment of the requirements for a master's degree. Some schools still require a senior thesis of graduating students.

TRANSCRIPT The official record of your college work, which is maintained and updated each term by the registrar. Your courses, grades, GPA, and graduation information will be included in your transcript.

TRANSFER CREDIT If you should transfer from one college or university to another, the number of courses the new college accepts and counts toward your degree are your transfer credits.

TRANSIENT STUDENT A student who receives permission from his regular college to take courses (usually in the summer) from another college.

TUITION The money you pay for your college courses. See Fees.

UPPER DIVISION The opposite of lower division and much closer to graduation. See Lower division.

VALIDATION OF CREDITS Procedure in which a school determines which credits from another school may be transferred. Despite good grades, not all of your courses may be accepted at your new college. Courses with a grade of D normally will not transfer. If you ever consider transferring from one college to another, it's your responsibility to learn which courses and grades will transfer.

WITHDRAW Although you may withdraw from one course, this term usually denotes the dropping of all courses for one term and leaving school for whatever reasons you may have. Withdrawal requires a form and signatures, and if you don't follow the prescribed procedure, you may receive failing grades on all courses, which could place you on academic suspension. Withdrawal in good academic standing, following established procedures, will allow you to request readmission later. See Reinstatement or readmission and Leave of absence.

So there you have it: a comprehensive glossary of the many unfamiliar terms you'll be hearing during your next four years in college. Now go back to the first paragraph of this appendix and reread it. It should make more sense to you than it did the first time around. In the future, you'll want to begin using these terms in conversations about college. When someone asks, "What did you mean by that word?" you'll be able to explain with confidence!

To the owner of this book:

We hope that you enjoyed *College Is Only the Beginning* and found it helpful. We would like to know as much about your experience as you would care to offer. Only through your comments can we learn how to make this a better book for future readers. Thank you!

Your school: _____

Your instructor: _____

Department of: _____

Course title: _____

What did you like most about *College Is Only the Beginning?* _____

_____

_____

What did you like least about it? _____

_____

_____

Was the entire book assigned for you to read? _____

If not, what parts or chapters were not assigned? _____

If you have any other other comments, we'd like to hear them. Thanks!

John N. Gardner

A. Jerome Jewler

Optional:

Your Name _____ Date _____

May Wadsworth quote you in the promotion for *College Is Only the Beginning?*

Yes ___ No ___

- -

FOLD HERE

CUT PAGE OUT

FOLD HERE

FIRST CLASS
PERMIT NO. 34
BELMONT, CA

BUSINESS REPLY MAIL

No Postage Necessary if Mailed in United States

John N. Gardner/A. Jerome Jewler
Wadsworth Publishing Company
10 Davis Drive
Belmont, CA 94002